West Indies

Atlantic   Ocean

DOMINICAN REPUBLIC

BRITISH VIRGIN ISLANDS

PUERTO RICO

ST CROIX

ANGUILLA

ST MARTIN

BARBUDA

ST KITTS
NEVIS

ANTIGUA

MONTSERRAT

GUADELOUPE

DOMINICA

MARTINIQUE

ST LUCIA

BARBADOS

ST VINCENT
BEQUIA
MUSTIQUE

THE GRENADINES

GRENADA

TOBAGO

TRINIDAD

DEC

A Walk Around the
West Indies

Hunter Davies

A Walk Around the
West Indies

Weidenfeld & Nicolson
LONDON

First published in Great Britain in 2000
by Weidenfeld & Nicolson

© 2000 Hunter Davies
The moral right of Hunter Davies to be identified as the author
of this work has been asserted in accordance with the
Copyright, Designs and Patents Act of 1988.

A CIP catalogue record for this book
is available from the British Library.

ISBN 0 297 84250 1

Typeset by Selwood Systems, Midsomer Norton

Set in ITC Stone Serif

Printed in Great Britain by
Butler & Tanner Ltd, Frome and London

Weidenfeld & Nicolson
The Orion Publishing Group Ltd
Orion House
5 Upper Saint Martin's Lane
London, WC2H 9EA

For my granddaughters Amelia and Ruby
who will be travelling soon.

Contents

Illustrations

General photographs of the West Indies courtesy of the Caribbean Tourism Organisation.

All other photographs by the author.

Maps by John Gilkes.

Foreword

Of course I didn't actually walk around the West Indies. There's all that water for a start. I did some walking on each island, but the title merely echoes travel books I have done before. It's a wander round rather than a walk around the Caribbean islands, and it's mainly about the people who live or who have gone to live there, for various reasons, rather than a book about the landscape.

The Caribbean wanderings I have done over the last ten years or so have taken me to twenty-seven different islands in all, but I have concentrated the main chapters on ten different islands, trying to balance them by size, variety of landscape and culture. Mostly they are English-speaking West Indian islands, but there is one Spanish-speaking island, one and a half that are French islands and one half Dutch.

The twelve main wandering-around chapters are the travel book part, the bulk of the book, the people part. They are meant to be of interest to anyone, not necessarily those contemplating the West Indies: bedside or beachside reading to amuse and entertain, perhaps even stimulate.

After that comes the guidebook bit. In extensive appendices, there are facts, figures, background material and opinions on all the islands of the West Indies. These are meant to help and inform those thinking of visiting the West Indies for the first time – perhaps after having read the main chapters – as well as those who already know them well.

The people in the wandering-around chapters are not quite chosen at random. I set myself the task of finding and talking to two types, both of whom have fascinated me ever since I first visited the West Indies.

First, the expats. They are mainly from the UK, though some are from Germany, France and the USA. The common denominator is an urge to find paradise which comes over many Europeans, usually in the middle of winter, or a bad moment in the middle of their lives. They experience a sudden desire for the sun, for a culture and climate that they think will suit them better, where they can be themselves, find themselves. They are active, working people, not the retired or well off, who have managed somehow to find a job out there. They escaped to fulfil a fantasy, which many of us have had at some time, some stage in our lives, if only fleetingly. They did it. So how was it for them?

Then there are the returnees. Almost every West Indian who set out for Britain over the last fifty years, ever since the *Empire Windrush* took 492 Afro-Caribbeans from the West Indies to the UK in June 1948, has told him- or herself: I will return. Most never did, though they kept warm the fantasy at the back of their minds. But now, after many decades in Britain, more and more are returning, for a variety of reasons. But can they fit in, be accepted, after so long away? How did it turn out for them?

So, those are the two running themes. A travel book about people and a guidebook. Have a good wander.

Introduction

Barbados was the first West Indian island I ever visited. On 7 January 1986 we flew there on Concorde. It was my birthday. For the first eighteen years of my life I always woke up on my birthday to a frosty, freezing morning, on a dull, grey, concrety north of England council estate, in a bedroom which was so cold that putting one foot on the lino meant frostbite. So I promised myself, if and when I ever got to fifty, I'd lash out, treat myself to warm sea, white sands, palm trees, the full works. Which we did, my dear wife and I. Concorde had of course not been invented when I first had that fantasy, lying shivering in my Carlisle bedroom, but with any good fantasy you are allowed to add to it, improve and update.

Thanks to Concorde, we arrived so early at our hotel, Cobblers Cove, that the room wasn't ready and we had to hang around. I couldn't wait to check in, unpack, suss out the room, read the guff, recce the hotel. I wanted to go into the sea at once for a swim, having waited fifty years for my first feel of the Caribbean, my first experience of that smooth, silky water. So I ran straight in from the back of the hotel, and ran straight out again, screaming in agony. I had stepped on a sea urchin. My own fault. Not checking first, not asking, not knowing anything about coral reefs. A waiter in what appeared to be full evening dress came over and helped me out of the sea. He squeezed the juice from a fresh lime on the wound then took a box of matches and a candle from his pocket. He lit the candle and let some hot wax drip on the wound, saying when it cools, it will fall off and bring out the needle of the sea urchin. Which it did. Have I made all that up? Sounds more like 1886 than 1986.

He was dressed up because I had arrived in the middle of the hotel's mid-morning hot consommé on the beach, dished out from large silver tureens by uniformed waiters. Cobblers Cove used to do that in those days, when Richard Williams was the manager, a rather fancy and pretentious ritual, which I scoffed at the first day: how silly, imagine having hot soup on a hot beach, but then I found myself making sure I was there for my helping and, do you know, it was surprisingly refreshing. Richard Williams later moved on to Sandy Lane Hotel, where such affectations were much more in keeping.

We have been back to Cobblers Cove almost every January since for my birthday. Under the management of Hamish Watson it is still as high class, still as efficient, but a bit more casual. We have also stayed at other hotels in Barbados over the years, and there are about ten others down that west coast, equally comfortable, just as desirable, which is remarkable, that such a small island should have so many top-class hotels.

Once you leave Barbados, most islands are less developed because Barbados is about the most developed island in all the West Indies. Parts of the Bahamas are now overdeveloped, as are parts of Puerto Rico, becoming almost like American cities. Barbados has most facilities a tourist or resident might need, phones work, buses run on time, it's prosperous and at ease with itself, no antipathy to visitors, comparatively little crime and violence, and the highest literacy rate of any country in the English-speaking world.

Travel snobs don't recommend Barbados, as it's not the real Caribbean, my dear, far too developed. Other West Indians are hardly fans of Barbados either. Jamaicans and Trinidadians, from their two main rival islands, dismiss Bajans as Little Englanders, well off, well run, well educated, but boring, man, boring. They admit Jamaica and Trinidad might have more crime, but they also have better music, better writers, more cultural depth and generally more excitement. I don't actually want excitement on my holidays. I can get all that at home in London.

On my holidays, I first want good weather, especially my winter holiday, and by good weather I mean the sun being hot enough to be out in all day long, but not too hot that you can't take a step without sweating. I can't stand the humidity of tropical Africa or the Pacific. I also don't like the midday burning heat of the Mediterranean when you have to collapse or skulk indoors. In the

Caribbean, you don't get that glaringly empty, starkly blue sky, stunning though it can be. There are always some clouds hanging around on the horizon, a gentle wind stirring on the beach, sudden downpours of rain inland, if only for forty seconds, long enough to freshen rather than drench the day. Yes, there can also be violent winds, heavy rain, even hurricanes, which can cause appalling devastation, but they happen at certain times of the year only, and not every year, not every island, and the advance warning systems let you know about them well ahead.

Second, I want attractive landscape on my holidays, clean beaches, clear water to swim in, with no pollution, no oil and debris. A coast I can walk along and explore, some tropical rain-forest I can wonder at, the sort of flora and fauna I am never likely to see in Kentish Town.

Third, I want nice people, friendly, affable, not grasping or aggressive, and on the whole, with some exceptions, you will find them all over the Caribbean. As a tourist these days, the whole world is open and available to us in the so-called developed world, even to those on modest incomes, though of course an income is pretty essential. Why then go to places where they might hate or despise us, see tourists as opportunities to be exploited rather than people like themselves who just happen to live elsewhere? West Indians do tend to treat tourists as friends visiting from abroad, which is how it should be.

So that's the three attractions to me about the Caribbean and why I've been back so often. I remember on that first visit in 1986, after I had recovered from my poorly foot, walking down the empty beach next morning, breathing in the pure freshness, the expectations of another perfect day, and finding four words coming into my head: The Med is Ded. I do tend to think in headlines. We'd been the previous year to Portugal, as we had been for twenty years, and dearly loved it, but the sprawl of nasty, concrete developments seemed to be taking over every Algarve village and the tar was getting nastier each year on the beach. Life shouldn't be a competition, between people or places. I know I'll return to Portugal one day, and again to France and Italy, for they have splendours and beauties which the Caribbean will never have; yet since that year we have not been back to Europe for our holidays.

And always, on our annual Caribbean trip, we start with Barbados, as we did that first time. The flights are good and frequent, it's nice to know what to expect, that I can acclimatise myself, de-Londonise myself, flop and relax for a few days before we go on to other, further-afield, harder-to-get-to islands, where I'll also probably just flop and relax.

This time, in Barbados and elsewhere, I am also here to do some work, to meet those people I have in mind, and pick up and pass on some information and opinions which might be of use or interest to all West Indian lovers.

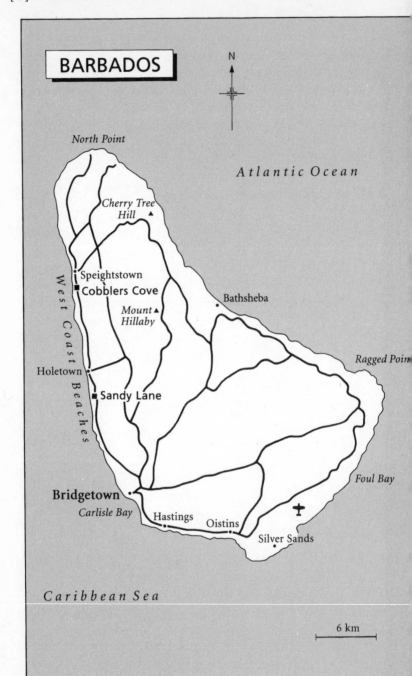

CHAPTER ONE

Barbados

I caught a bus for Bridgetown on the main road outside Cobblers Cove. There was a time when I didn't take buses in the Caribbean, I suppose for snobbish reasons, fearing that they would break down, be unbearably crowded, but I now take them all the time in Barbados, either blue or yellow. I'm not sure of the difference, but one is government and one is private, but they each go like the clappers. There's a set bus fare of 1 dollar 50 cents (about 50p), a real bargain, wherever you pick it up on that main road along the west coast. Despite the simple standard bus fare, they still have a conductor, unlike most London buses where the driver takes the money, and takes for ever. The conductor is usually a youth in a lurid shirt who is mostly busy chatting to the driver, before eventually flinging himself up the aisle, pushing everyone aside, leaving the driver to concentrate on his imitation of a Grand Prix race.

On Sundays it's best, with locals in their Sunday suits and frocks, but during the week it's just as good, observing the schoolkids close up, immaculate in their school uniforms, so bright and shiny in their appearance. The drivers see their bus as their personal space, with their personal slogans and decorations. On the bus I got on I was greeted with a notice which said 'Welcome to De Challenger'. Challenging speed and safety, judging by the way he was throwing his bus around corners. I got a seat near the front and admired his other posters. 'No smoking. No nuts.' 'Don't hoot. Driver asleep.' 'If you see me bubbling, don't come troubling.'

I almost forgot to get off at my stop, and also where I was heading, which was to a part of Bridgetown I'd never been to before. Staying on the west coast as a tourist, amongst the hotels and the beach life, you forget that urban life goes on out there, with people in suits, people in careers.

Bridgetown is in the south of the island, at the bottom of the west coast, which is where most Caribbean capitals seem to be situated. Barbados is in many ways a typical Caribbean island in that it's pear-shaped. The pear doesn't always face the same way, but it's surprising how many are roughly that shape. On the west you have the calm Caribbean coast with stunning beaches, brilliant swimming, while on the east coast it's the Atlantic, much wilder, with huge waves, emptier, rockier beaches. In the case of Barbados, this wild east coast is equally magnificent, especially the Scotland district and Bathsheba Bay.

In the middle it used to be all sugar plantations on the lush rolling hills, but most have gone, though some handsome plantation houses remain, several open to the public. There are also many English-style churches which always strike first-time English visitors as very peculiar, stuck among the palm trees.

The airport, as on so many islands, is also on the south, the more boring part, with busy roads and modern development to get through before you hit the tropical vegetation inland, or reach the white sandy beaches of the west.

And like all Caribbean islands, the locals think it is bigger than it is, considering people in the next parish as foreigners, crossing the island a huge adventure and a trip to the capital as a massive outing. Yet Barbados, a so-called leading West Indian island, one we have mostly all heard about, is only twenty-one miles long by fourteen miles wide, hardly big enough to be a small English county. Its population is 250,000, smaller than Bradford.

I was looking for the Sir Frank Walcott Building. Even traffic islands in Barbados are named after famous cricketers. It appeared to house several government agencies and departments. Outside I could see parking for the chosen few, clearly signposted, such as Solicitor-General, Director of Public Prosecutions, Permanent Secretary. Some joker with white paint had tried to delete the l in Public, but only faintly.

Inside it could have been offices in New York or London's Docklands. Imposing reception area, marble floors, security guards, fussy signing-in procedures, issuing of pointless badges, jobsworths trying to look important, or at least busy.

I was heading for the main office of the Caribbean Tourist Organisation which represents thirty-one countries in and around the Caribbean Sea, from Anguilla to Venezuela. My own definition of the Caribbean, or West Indies, both of which terms I use as if they are the same, refers only to Caribbean islands. For the sake of this book, I have omitted mainland countries such as Guyana.

My appointment was with Arley Sobers, Director of Research. I had decided to start where I don't intend to continue – by talking to an official. We have enough officials back home, but I hoped this one would be an interesting beginning, giving an overall view of what might be to come.

I had to wait in a corridor. While I did so I picked up an American monthly magazine devoted to honeymoons. A whole magazine, on honeymoons. Out of it fell a subscription notice, offering special bargain rates. Second and third marriages are common these days, so perhaps people take out a subscription in anticipation of their next union and pleasures to come.

A phone rang on a desk and a schoolgirl of about thirteen in her sparkling uniform, who had been sitting beside me reading a hairstyle magazine, stood up, went over to the desk, picked up the phone and said, yes, can I help. Cheeky, or what. She dealt swiftly with the call, telling the person to ring back tomorrow, then sat down again beside me with her magazine. Five minutes later the real receptionist appeared. The schoolgirl started moaning about something in a Bajan accent I didn't catch. The receptionist told her just to be patient, she would be finishing soon and driving her home. Obviously her big sister.

Arley Sobers is a Barbadian in his fifties, rather plump, rather serious. He was on the phone to some official in Guyana and having difficulty explaining the finer points of VAT. In front of him on his desk was a hotplate on which was perched a decorated teapot. From time to time he topped up his large cup of British-style tea. The British civil service traditionally ran on tea. How nice to see one legacy of colonial rule continuing.

Arley was born in Barbados and went to Harrison's College, Barbados's number one grammar school for boys. At sixteen he left and went to Holland Park Comprehensive. I was watching the thick tea coming out of his teapot at that moment and so didn't quite catch the name of his new school. Was it in Bridgetown? No, England, he said. Holland Park School, London, England. Quite a jump.

'Well, I'd not been, er, well-behaved at school, so my father thought if he brought me over to London, he could keep an eye on me.'

I asked what 'not well-behaved' meant but he would not elaborate. Just a spot of bother, he said. By a coincidence, I later met someone, Theo Williams, who had been in his class at school and said that Arley was one of three boys who were always in fights. One ended in prison, another was dead, but then there was Arley, today a solid and serious member of the community, sitting supping his tea in front of me.

Arley's dad had gone to London to work for North Thames Gas. When Arley arrived to live with him he found he was ahead in many subjects at Holland Park and had done subjects, such as Latin, none of them had heard of. 'They thought I was crazy, having studied Latin.' He was also an expert on Biggles books and *Just William*, which he had consumed in his Bajan childhood.

He went on to university in Cardiff to study for a degree in statistics and found himself immediately picked for the university cricket team.

'That happened all the time. Being from the West Indies and called Sobers, people thought I must be related to Gary. It is a very common surname in Barbados. Nobody here would ever ask if I am related. I probably am, in fact, but only as a third cousin. I did play a bit of cricket at Cardiff, but not very well.'

On graduation, he worked in London as a social worker in Ladbroke Grove, before returning to Barbados to a job in the civil service.

'I enjoyed my ten years in London, though I didn't always think so at the time. It was hard at first understanding the cockney accents. And they couldn't understand me. When you are part of a minority, living in a foreign country, you do develop a garrison mentality. West Indians do stick together, from whichever island they're from. But England did have its charms.'

Charms? Seemed a strange word to use. 'I mean that England, by comparison, seemed charming when I returned here. While I'd been away for those ten years, American influences had infiltrated our culture. You just have to watch BBC TV and then CNN to see what I mean. North Americans do tend to be self-righteous. They assume that North America is the whole world.

'I go swimming every evening after work, to keep my weight down, to a local beach, and I often sit afterwards with the old fishermen and play dominoes. Quite a lot have lived overseas, in Britain or in the USA. Last night they were discussing the fact that Bajan Brits are nicer than Bajan Americans. The consensus was that Bajan Brits are not as loud or complaining.'

His job at the CTO is to provide research and statistics on tourism for all the member countries in order to help them with marketing and promoting themselves. 'A lot of the small countries have no statistics and their records are in an appalling condition. They also find it hard to understand things like the difference between hotel tax, which some countries impose, and VAT. They all of course want to raise more taxes, especially from tourists.' He has a small team, and a small reference library at his disposal. They produce assorted facts and figures which can be bought by interested bodies. 'Which we try to sell for vast amounts of money.'

The director-general of the CTO is from Barbados, as is Arley, which could become a bit embarrassing now that the most dynamic parts of Caribbean tourism are Cuba and the Dominican Republic. Both are Spanish-speaking, with no old British colonial connections, and very little in common with Barbados. They might not be so keen on having their tourism co-ordinated from Barbados in future.

'Over 90 per cent of the tourists who actually go to Cuba are Spanish-speaking, because of course there were virtually no Americans or British going to Cuba for so many years.' In the Dominican Republic, however, the tourists are mainly Europeans. The Germans started the modern mass market, with low-budget holidays, followed by the Brits.

Tourism as a whole in the Caribbean is booming, with Europeans providing the fastest-growing market. Traditionally it has been easier, cheaper and quicker for North Americans to get to the Caribbean, but long-haul flights from Europe have come down in price, and are often cheaper than Mediterranean holidays. 'The majority do still come from America, but over the last decade, Europeans have increased by roughly 15 per cent while the North American increase has been only 3 per cent.'

In 1998 the total number of annual tourists to the Caribbean – not counting people on cruise ships – came to 15 million. Around half, 7.2 million, came from North America, 3.5 million from Europe and 2.7 from the rest of the world. The figures also included 1 million intra-Caribbean tourists, people going between islands.

Puerto Rico had most tourists: 3.4 million; followed by the Dominican Republic: 2.3 million; Bahamas: 1.5 million; Cuba: 1.4 million; Jamaica: 1.2 million.

Tourism is now the main source of income in the Caribbean, providing about 20 per cent of the GDP, having overtaken agriculture. Sugar has almost gone and bananas have only survived because of preferential treatment, and now that is in danger. Industry is still a long way behind and mainly means oil, sugar-refining and bauxite.

'With tourism, we have arrived at the world table with no artificial supports. We just have to offer a good product.'

The worry now is keeping up the good work, now that long-haul flights from Europe to the Far East and Australia are so much cheaper. 'Tourism gets more competitive all the time. There are more and more new destinations. At the same time, you have a trend in North America at present for more and more Americans to holiday in their own country.

'When I went to the World Travel Market in London last year I realised how small we are in the Caribbean, just specks on the world map.

'When tourists choose a place to go to, it is often a matter of fashion and taste, which you can do little about. I was in a travel conference in Nassau in the Bahamas last year and all the British delegates hated the hotels we were staying in. They thought them too American. I've noticed that when Americans come here, they don't care for our west coast hotels, finding them too small, and lacking things like TV in the bedrooms. Now in each case, these were upmarket people, staying in upmarket hotels, yet they had such different tastes.'

Barbados itself is doing very well. It attracted 512,000 visitors in 1998 compared with 447,083 in 1996. Unlike the rest of the Caribbean, where Americans are still in the majority, the UK has taken over in the last decade as the major tourist market for Barbados. In 1998, 186,690 came from the UK compared with 108,000 from the USA.

I said that Brits loved Barbados because it was rather British, with people who liked us, and it was well developed.

'I'm not sure you can say Barbados is more developed than other islands. It depends how you measure it. Martinique and Guadeloupe have for example some very good highways, but there again, they don't have the autonomy that we have in Barbados.'

He did agree that Barbados has traditionally been seen as a developed, advanced West Indian island. I wondered what he thought of the theory that this was to do with Barbados getting the best of the slaves, the first pick when the slave ships arrived from Africa. No, he didn't think so.

'I think it's more to do with Barbados being relatively flat, hence all the plantations and hence the slaves were easier to manage. We became the administration centre for the British in the eastern Caribbean, so that gave us a head start when it came to infrastructure. Under the British colonial system, we were always allowed a certain independence, able to create internally our own micro-systems. The French islands were never allowed to do that.'

I asked him about Barbados's traditional rivalry with the two other big ex-Brit islands, Jamaica and Trinidad.

'I have to admit Trinidad has the richer cultural base, thanks to their mixture of races – Spanish, Chinese and Indian. They do rather look down on our cultural offerings. They consider us very conservative. The "Little England" perception has turned out to be a help for us, once tourism became so important. British people like to come here. In Barbados we are all very proud that this is the only place, outside New York, which Concorde regularly flies to.'

I had noticed during the 1999 election that the Prime Minister, Owen Arthur, in taking a whole page in the *Advocate* to list his achievements, started off with 'Concorde services from both sides of the Atlantic to Barbados'. Tourism, so this advert said, 'pays for wages and salaries, pays for bread on the table'. He did get re-elected.

In talking to Arley I had noticed that now and again he had used the term West Indies, but mainly he referred to the Caribbean. I have found myself using both terms as if they were inter-changeable, yet these days 'West Indies' appears less and less. Apart from the West Indies cricket team, which is best not to talk about at present anyway, you hardly see it used. I checked by looking in the local Yellow Pages, and Caribbean is a common prefix, in business and commerce, but not West Indies or West Indian. In his own mind, did he see a difference?

'I suppose when I am thinking or referring to the "West Indies", I have in my head brackets which say "(British) West Indies". That's to differentiate, show I'm not thinking of the French West Indies.'

Thanks, Arley. I think he has put his finger on the distinction. West Indies is history. It refers in some way to past or long-standing British West Indian connections, such as the cricket team. Caribbean is geography. We use it to refer to a present-day geographical area, with no reference to its historic, cultural or linguistic past.

One of the reasons I'm interested in expats is that I did it once, in a half-hearted, temporary sort of way. Many years ago, we had a year in the sun. We went first to Gozo, for reasons I now can't quite remember, but English speaking was one of the attractions, and then to Portugal. We had two young children at the time, so it was difficult amusing them, finding kids of their age to play with. We got a lot of writing done, but it was also hard finding folks to amuse us. Getting to know locals properly, when you're a foreigner, being accepted by them, is always hard, so we were thrown up against other expats for any social life. At first glance, most of them appeared to be pigs, right-wing hangers and floggers, who had fled from Africa when it went all liberal, the sort we'd run a mile from in England. When we got to know them, some were quite decent, usually very kind. But in that year abroad we did run out of people. In fact we ran out of stimulation of any sort.

As for the weather, after six weeks abroad I was waking up and saying, 'Oh no, not another perfect day.' After six months, I felt I'd turned into a cabbage, if a nicely tanned, awfully healthy cabbage.

Perhaps we chose the wrong places, at the wrong time of our lives. But I'm glad, looking back, we got it out of our system, did it when we did. I've come across too many people who have carried this fantasy through life and regret never having had the chance to try it out.

To some, of course, it happens by chance. Events take them abroad, then they just stay there, preferring that sort of life.

Jimmy and Jill Walker were about the longest-serving expats I came across in the West Indies, having lived and worked abroad for almost forty-five years. They are the founders of Best of Barbados, a chain of gift shops selling local arts and crafts.

I saw them at their stately home in the middle of the island. Stately is not quite the right word, but the nearest. It's a tropical version of living in state in what was once a colonial plantation house, formerly owned by Sir Frank Worrell, very artistic and gracious, the centre of their operations, and also where they live.

Jimmy, now in his seventies, was born in Aberdeenshire, the son of a doctor. He still has a trace of a Scottish accent, plus the sort of old-world Scottish bedside-doctor manner which charmed them in Morningside but often concealed a tough, determined brain.

He trained in Edinburgh as an architect, went for a spell to Washington on a Fulbright scholarship, then joined the British Colonial Office as an architect. I said I didn't know the Colonial Office ever employed architects. Oh yes, he said, they liked to have a range of professional experts when they had colonies to run, to give help or advice. In 1954 he was sent out to help on some building project in British Guyana. Which was where he met Jill.

Jill is very English, home counties accent, pale complexion, quiet and dignified, probably very shy, preferring to let Jimmy take command and be front of house. She was born in Devon; her father was also a doctor. She trained in fine art in London at the Royal Academy Schools then worked in theatre for a while, painting costumes for the Old Vic. One day a friend from college, who had married a Guyanese, said come out for a holiday, Jill. She did – and straight off the boat she met Jim.

'Yes, the very first night,' says Jim. 'I'd heard this young lady was coming from England. I was invited to meet her, along with another young bachelor. And that was it.'

A year later, Jim was moved to Barbados to help with rebuilding work after Hurricane Janet. Jill followed and they got married in St James's Church, Barbados in 1956. 'At seven o'clock in the morning. That's the best time in the tropics. We only knew five people on the whole island, but the governor sent two bottles of champagne.'

Later that year, they spent three months sailing round the West Indies on tramp ships and schooners. 'There were very few planes in those days. I think only St Lucia and Barbados had any sort of airport. We didn't book anywhere. We just took whatever boat was available and went round the islands. We were often sailing in immigrant ships, with West Indians on their way to Britain or Italians on the way to Venezuela.'

For most of the next twenty years, Jim was a partner in a leading firm of architects, working all over the world, till he got fed up with the travelling, hardly seeing his wife and three daughters. He gave up, not knowing what to do next.

'We had a friend called Budge O'Hara who owned Coral Reef Hotel. He was thinking of opening a shop in his sandpiper hotel and he said to us, why don't we run it. Neither of us had any family experience of the retail trade. All our friends said it was madness, but we decided to give it a go.

'At the time you couldn't get local arts and craft work, apart from raffia mats. Most souvenirs came from Hong Kong. I could see there was a demand for modest presents from the new people who were starting to come on holiday to Barbados, the sort of present you might want to buy to take back for your secretary.'

Jill had been painting all these years while Jim had been architecting. For her own amusement, she'd been doing watercolours of chattel houses – the local wooden houses in Barbados. When slaves moved, they took their goods and chattels with them – hence the name.

They decided to make prints of her chattel houses, which no one had done before. They moved on to designing and producing tea towels and trays, mostly using Jill's designs. The whole family helped to fold and package T-shirts in the evenings on the dining room table. They were soon opening more shops, ending up with fourteen shops and 100 staff. At one time they even had cafés attached to the shops, serving light refreshments.

They make it sound all very easy, which it wasn't quite, needing a lot of time, energy and organisation. Today, not just in Barbados but in every West Indian island where two or three tourists are gathered together, somebody will be trying to sell them the sort of Caribbean souvenirs that Jill created, all those years ago.

They did at one time think of overseas expansion, opening shops round the Caribbean, but decided they would stick to Barbados. It had all started as an amusement, then, to earn a living, developing without any business plans. Expansion in Barbados had created enough headaches. The caffs went because they were not worth the effort. Today, they still keep an eye on their workshops, which are in the grounds and outhouses of their home, but they are slowly handing over the running of the business to one of their daughters and husband.

All three daughters were sent to boarding school in Britain, to St Leonard's in St Andrews. One became an accountant, one went into art and design, and the other into hotel management. Only one now lives in Barbados – the others are in Australia and England.

Jill and Jimmy have thought of moving back to Britain, but probably won't, though they usually spend a couple of months there each year. They still see Barbados as their paradise island, despite all the enormous changes in forty-five years.

'When we arrived, people travelled by donkey cart and you saw no lights round here at night. There has been a massive upsurge in the economy – mainly for the good. Education and health care are better. The arts and music are doing well and there are now a hell of a lot of local bands who are very popular. People go out and enjoy themselves more. They spend a lot of their money on cars and clothes – not so much on their houses.'

Jill has watched those chattel houses slowly disappearing. 'And so has the way of life that went with them. In the beginning, I was really setting out to record them, where they were, what they looked like, not to sell copies of them.'

Jim admits they were lucky, hitting on an area no one had done before, but also in that there were few restrictions. 'Today, you just can't arrive and open a business. All governments protect their own. You have to have the right permits and so forth. All the same, there are still opportunities. Barbados is booming.'

After forty-five years, what do they like and not like about West Indian life?

'West Indian unpunctuality,' said Jim at once. 'I still seethe when I have to sit in a meeting for forty minutes before it starts.'

They both love the people, that's the best thing, and think they have not basically changed in all the years. 'They do remind me of people from my boyhood in the north of Scotland, many years ago. You still get a cheery hello every morning and everyone talks to you here. I wouldn't quite say the same about Britain today.'

And what about things they miss from Blighty?

'The radio,' said Jill after a lot of thought. 'National newspapers. And the seasons. You are not aware of them here. Leaves do fall for about three weeks each year on our mahogany trees, but that's all.'

The weather of course is still a huge attraction. Before I left they took me out into their garden to look at a huge date palm tree in front of their house.

'I grew that myself,' said Jim. 'Twenty-five years ago, I put two date stones in my pocket after a dinner party in London. I then took them out with me to the West Indies – and planted them here. Fortunately, one turned out to be male and one female. Now look at it. You wouldn't achieve that in a London garden, now would you?'

I went to have a pizza with my first returnees, Theo and Margaret Williams. Margaret isn't technically a returnee, as she had never actually lived in the West Indies till she 'returned' to the land of her fathers; nor was it the first time I had met her. By an amazing coincidence, it turned out we had met before, back in 1976 when I was doing a book about a year in a comprehensive, Creighton School in Muswell Hill, north London.

She was then called Margaret Burnett and I remember walking down the corridor one day and hearing this great booming laughter from the music room, a hearty Joyce Grenfell type of voice, teasing someone called Jeremy. I opened the door to see a West Indian woman and a couple of sixth-formers, working on *The Magic Flute* for A-level Music.

She was then Head of Music and making a fantastic job of it: not just getting pupils into music colleges, but organising the lower years into a prize-winning steel band which went on British and even European tours.

She was born in Birmingham, daughter of a doctor, and went

to a very select independent school, Edgbaston High School for Girls, and then to Dartington College of Art. A middle-class background, but black middle class, as both her father and mother had been born in the West Indies.

She was twenty-nine at the time, unmarried, very sociable, in lots of groups and organisations. After I'd finished the book, I never heard what happened to her, so in the pizza parlour I had quite a lot of catching up to do. Not just any old pizza parlour. A rather swish one called Pizzaz in Holetown – owned by her husband Theo Williams and his brother. Quite a jump, from music teaching to pizzas. So what happened?

First she insisted on ordering a Bajan Pizza for me. She chose one of their specialities with sweet peppers, plantain and smoked flying fish. 'Right, well, let me see. I met Theo in London in 1975. I was in a Caribbean Teachers Association and he came to one of our parties, brought by a cousin who was a head teacher in Nottingham.'

Theo was born and bred in Barbados, but was working in London at the Waldorf Hotel. He'd gone from school in Bridgetown into the hotel industry as a trainee manager, starting at Sandy Lane. They got married, had their honeymoon at the Belsfield Hotel in Windermere in the Lake District, then moved to Barbados where Theo eventually became manager of one of the smart hotels on the west coast, Tamarind Cove, the first black Bajan to manage a top Barbados hotel.

It was returning home for Theo, but for Margaret it was completely new. I said her father must have been pleased, that she was going to live in his home island, Barbados.

'Not quite. He wasn't keen on me leaving England. He and my mother were still living in Birmingham – and I'm an only child.

'My father never wanted to go back to Barbados, even when he retired. He was born in 1900 and left Barbados when he was sixteen. In those days, in parts of Bridgetown, a black man could be arrested by the police, just for walking round the streets at night. This had upset him so much he never ever wanted to return. He went to Glasgow University, where he qualified as a doctor, then set up in practice in Birmingham. He loved it there, and they loved him.

'It was only in 1994 that he finally decided to return to Barbados.

He was ninety-four, so it was his first visit to his homeland for almost eighty years. He was in poor health and died in ten weeks...'

Margaret and Theo have two children, Alex, now sixteen, and Zahra, twelve. After they were settled at school in Barbados, Margaret went back to work part time, teaching and training choirs.

In 1996 Theo decided to give up hotel work. After thirty years, he wanted to work for himself. He didn't have the capital to buy his own hotel, certainly not in Barbados, but he teamed up with his brother, a chef, to open a pizza parlour. They now have two, one in Holetown and one in Bridgetown with a total staff of thirty-four.

Theo arrived at that moment, and joined us for lunch. He said things were going well, they were ahead of their business plan in the way of customers and income, but costs had turned out higher than they had anticipated. It was still going to need a lot of hard work to make it succeed.

Since independence in Barbados, professions like the law, which used to be dominated by white Brits doing the colonies a favour, are now largely filled by black Bajans, but in commerce and business the old white-style plantocracy, families who have been in Barbados for generations, are still dominant as they own much of the wealth. Black Bajans, starting from scratch, still find it hard to build up a new business.

Theo went off to chat to some customers, so I asked Margaret what the culture shock had been like, arriving as a black Brit in Barbados.

'The worst part was that everyone saw me as English. They still do. I spent my whole life in England seeing myself as Caribbean – and in the Caribbean they see me as English. I suppose with my voice it can't be helped...'

Apart from her voice, did she feel English in other ways?

'Well, attitudes are very different. They're very conservative.

'One surprise was that I expected all the schools here to have steel bands. We had introduced them so successfully to English schools, originally to retain some cultural identity for the West Indian children, though in the end many of the bands were made up of English players. I did find some good ones here, but not in schools.

'I also couldn't get over the slow pace of life. I worked in a government office for a while and everyone thought I was putting in extra effort to impress. They eventually realised this was my normal pace of work.

'I wanted to have 300 children for a choir, from different schools all over the island. They thought I was crazy. It couldn't be done. How could I rehearse, when the children were from schools all over the island? It was a problem of course, but problems are there to be solved. It was done, by endlessly travelling.'

Apart from those minor things, she feels perfectly at ease in Barbados. She loves the people and the climate and can see no reason ever to return to England. Their son is at Harrison College, the one Theo used to go to (and Arley Sobers) and she thinks it's as good an education as he could get anywhere. She has even come round to compulsory uniform, which of course went out in England several decades ago. Creighton, her old school in London, never had it.

'I have no problem with uniform. It's a good leveller. You can't tell the social class of each child. I know that in some poorer homes they have to struggle to save for the school shoes and school shirts, but they still manage to have their children looking immaculate.

'And the old-fashioned discipline, that's fine by me as well. We still have corporal punishment here. I think it's better that children should be a bit scared of teachers than teachers being scared of the children, which is what now happens in England. I keep hearing these horror stories of teachers in England being physically assaulted. Glad I'm out of that...'

One thing she has noticed is how West Indians are scared of a little rain. 'In England we are so used to rain, but here, the slightest shower makes everyone rush for cover. When I was running my choir, I used to drill into them what to do if it rained. "You do not move one inch. You stand there. You keep singing." Oh I could be very tough.'

Like the Walkers, and most expats brought up in Britain or Europe, she misses the changing seasons. 'The first Christmas I was here I cried. It just didn't seem like a real Christmas in 80-degree sunshine.

'And I do miss the radio. When I was a little girl, in bed with a cold or whatever, I used to love lying listening to the radio plays, or *Desert Island Discs*, or *Just a Minute*, those silly radio games. We don't have anything like that.

'You have to live with fewer shopping options, which can be a bore, but you get used to it. In the West Indies you need less, and you wear fewer clothes. But what I don't miss is London traffic or London dirt. Ugh.'

Expats come in all ages, stages, conditions, from all backgrounds, classes, cultures. Many of them are unusual people, who didn't quite fit in elsewhere. Some of course are downright eccentric. I wouldn't quite say that about Dr Colin Hudson. At one time he might have been considered as such, but now most of his obsessions are the world's obsessions.

However, in Barbados he is still seen as a character, someone they don't quite understand, though they marvel at what he is doing.

What he has done is create something called Barbados's Future Centre Trust. After several hours with him, I still wasn't quite sure what it all meant, but I was convinced it was dynamic and exciting.

He has set it up in a run-down plantation house in the middle of the island. When I arrived, I noticed a scruffy bloke in an outside yard, wearing a tatty T-shirt and working an ancient cement mixer. But not very well. The mixer was backfiring, sending cement spray all over him. I presumed at first this must be some passing volunteer, an amateur lending a hand.

He stopped the machine, wiped his brow, cleaned most of the cement from his face, and I noticed the bright gleam in his eyes, the thin ascetic body. When I heard the well-modulated, half-apologetic, English middle-class tones, I thought, hmm, this must be the man himself, Dr Hudson, a legend in Barbados for his almost single-handed battle for the environment.

Ecological warriors are well known today in the UK, and in the USA and most of Europe, running pressure groups, action campaigns, working for good causes, fighting pollution, trying to save the whale, the forest, the planet or mainly to save us from ourselves. You don't think of such warriors fighting away on Caribbean islands, supposedly natural paradises, supposedly not suffering yet from the ailments of the nasty developed world. But then Colin Hudson is a pioneer, in every sense.

He is aged sixty, English enough, though he spent his early years in New Zealand where his father happened to be living. He went to Corpus Christi College, Cambridge, read natural sciences, did a diploma in agriculture. In 1961 he came out to Barbados to help with their crop production. While here he did a PhD at the University of the West Indies – and became fascinated by the history of Barbados.

'The slaves were rugged and independent, but there was a respect between masters and slaves which created a very successful economy. Three hundred years ago, Barbados was the most densely populated country in the world. Because of that, living so tightly together, people showed respect for each other. During wars and blockades, Barbados ran a sustainable economy, growing everything it needed.

'When I arrived, some people were encouraging Barbados to do this again, as it had done during the last war. As an agronomist, I set to work on this project. The leading light was Sir John Saint. He'd just retired from government work, but was still interested in making Barbados self-sufficient, which meant of course keeping agriculture alive. I was put in charge of a unit to slow down the changes.

'By the 1970s, people were leaving the plantations in droves, moving to the tourist trade. The remaining plantations had to survive on smaller returns and a smaller labour force. We invented a cane cutter for the sugar plantations. We got twenty-three different world patents on it, but of course it didn't stop the rot. The sugar industry continued to recede.

'In 1962, when I first arrived, there were 23,000 people in the sugar industry in Barbados and about 3,000 in the civil service. Now the figures are roughly the other way round.'

Dr Hudson talks at a mile a minute, going off at tangents, but I stopped him to ask about those patents. What happened to them?

'Oh, people were very interested. We did create prototype models, fully working, which I demonstrated and we got orders from India. We exported several, but each time we made the same mistake. We built them, sent them off – then no orders came in.

The machines worked, but the sugar plantations usually went bust and never paid us. So we lost a lot of money.

'But a few years later, out of the blue, a technology company in Nebraska, USA, happened to see copies of our patents. They realised we had solved some problem they had. We got $150,000 from them, just for the patents, so that helped me continue our work for quite a few years.'

By this time, Dr Hudson was no longer an employee. Independence came in 1966, life moved on, agriculture grew even less important. So a research unit was set up, financed by donations, from people or groups who liked what he was doing.

One of his triumphs, which first made people in Barbados aware of him and his work, was in 1994 when the UN Global Conference on Sustainable Developments in Small Islands was held in Barbados. He helped organise something called the Village of Hope, to which the then governor-general of Barbados, the late Dame Nita Barrow, gave her personal support. 'Over 45,000 people came to see it in seventeen days. That's a huge number for a small island. No, we didn't make any money. Three more days, then we would actually have made a small profit.'

Out of this came the Future Centre Trust. He is now not so thrilled by its name, admitting people don't know what it means. The Village of Hope was a much more glamorous title. People didn't know what it meant either – but it sounded good.

For the last three years he has managed to survive, somehow, on donations and grants, plus his own savings, such as they are.

So what does he do?

'Well basically we have a research unit, working on sustainability.'

Yes, one of today's buzz words, but what does it really mean?

'The object is to use resources today which will not compromise the needs of future generations. We don't inherit the earth from our fathers. We borrow it from our children.

'Most things that make people happy are free, yet the consumer society makes us feel we won't be happy unless we have a bigger car or two holidays a year in the Caribbean.'

So what does make people happy?

'Feeling secure and safe, well housed, having a job, self-esteem, a sense of being part of creation. I don't necessarily mean having a religious belief. Religion can be manipulation, very cynical. I mean part of nature, part of the ecosystem. *Eco* is Greek for house and the word economy originally means managing the household. Ecology means the planet as the home for all species...'

I was getting a bit lost, so I asked what he thought about tourism, something I can understand, although arguments about it, for and against, its uses and abuses, are just as complicated and confusing.

'That's a hard one. There is little option now. We have to live with tourism, but what we can do is look back at the wisdoms of the past. In the past, Barbados was considered the healthiest island in the world. There are references from 1782 to invalids being sent here to recover from their maladies. That could be the future, as opposed to damaging the environment with all the present-day tourist developments.

'In Barbados we are awash with new golf courses at the moment, taking over prime land, which used to be sugar plantations. Why do they need such prime land? If you look at the word "link" as in golf links, which is what they were called in Scotland when golf first began, link meant a sand dune, a stretch of unusable beach. That's where golf was first played. We have such land in Barbados. Why not use that, instead of the best? It's because golf today is not a sport – golf is landscaping.

'Ultimately, of course, it's property development. That's why they build expensive villas with views of the golf course. The new marina is the same: property development, not sailing. All very cynical, and divisive. Only the wealthy can afford these golf clubs or marinas, while we are losing prime land for ever, selling off the family silver.'

What would you do then?

'I'd try to integrate Barbados into a different economy. I mentioned the invalids who used to come here. Well, why not create convalescent homes? That would mean people would come here for longer. It would provide a lot of work, as convalescence homes need a large staff and good medical care.'

Yes, but it would still be divisive. Only rich people could afford to come here and be ill.

'Hmm, you're right. I don't pretend to have pat answers. All I'm trying to do is create a centre where these questions are being asked, to have a focal point for discussions.'

He then took me on a tour of his centre, starting with all the posters and leaflets and displays they have produced to make people more aware of things like recycling, conservation, saving coral reefs from dying, beaches from being eroded. He has audio-visual rooms where schools and groups can be given displays and lectures. He also goes out and about, leading island hikes, clean-up campaigns and anti-litter walks. His fantasy is to attract 100,000 a year to the centre.

Getting funds is a constant struggle. The building itself is quite extensive, but somehow seems home-made, bashed together, with lots of rooms empty or unused. That day he appeared to have only one full-time paid helper, though several volunteers popped in while I was there, to see if they could help.

Just when he thinks that's it, he'll have to pack up completely, some organisation or person steps in with money, or he manages some sort of sponsorship.

He asked me if on arrival at the airport I'd been given a book-mark. I hadn't. He sighed and went to get one. Coca-Cola had sponsored the printing of 150,000 bookmarks advertising the Future Centre Trust, which were supposed to be given out to every person arriving. 'They can't say they don't have them, because I took them there myself. I suppose sometimes they forget to give them out.'

He is anyway a bit ambivalent about seeking funds. 'I wonder all the time if we should be professional or amateur. If we were to get a lot of money, many of our volunteers would stop coming, thinking we don't need help any more. I'd rather have donations of 10 dollars per person than one person giving us 100,000 dollars. We don't know really what we want to do, that's the problem. Oh dear. I hope that doesn't imply that we're totally incompetent.'

We ended up in his garden which was a sea of tyres – old rubber tyres, as dumped after use by lorries and motor cars. He uses them as growing containers. 'They create an interesting sort of mulch in which things like spinach grow wonderfully. They're also useful for handicapped people. You don't need to bend down as much. And of course we are recycling.'

In one corner, he had just started a new tyre garden which he called his medical garden. There were about fifty tyres, all neatly labelled, in which he was growing herbs that have medicinal properties. The tyres were laid out alphabetically, like the index of a medical book. In fact he's based it on an index from a real medical book by Penny Honeychurch in which the maladies are listed, from A to Z.

I started my walk through the medical garden at a sign saying A for Abortion. Were there really many herbs and plants good for abortions?

'Oh, there are. In Barbados alone we have nine abortives, plants which are known in Indian and African cultures. A lot haven't really grown yet, as I've only recently started. Come back in a few years, then you'll really see them.'

I moved on through his old tyres filled with little herbs and plants, passing C for Constipation, F for Fainting, L for Labour, P for Poultices, S for Skin Diseases.

By the end I was shaking my head in wonder and also amusement. Not just at his medical garden, but at the wonderful Dr Hudson. Now, back home in England, when I think of Barbados, I not only imagine myself back swimming at Cobblers Cove, but walking with Dr Hudson, through the index of his medical garden.

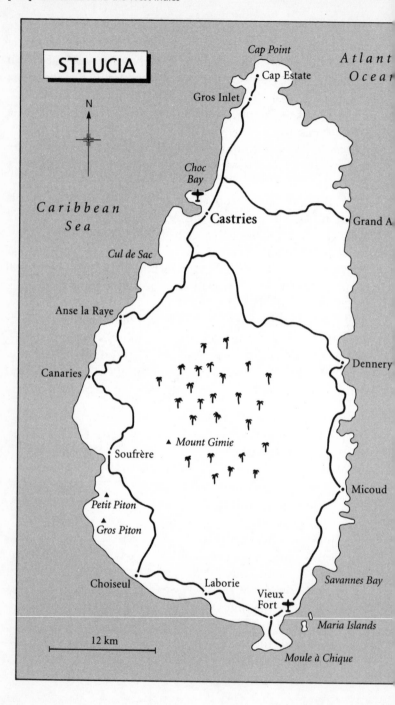

CHAPTER TWO

St Lucia

St Lucia is also pear-shaped, but its capital, Castries, and main airport is up in the north, so that's one difference, ruining my generalisations. It's about the same size as Barbados, but with only half the population, the reason being that St Lucia is volcanic, with mountains in the southern half rising to 3,000 feet, making Barbados appear flat and tame and overcrowded by comparison. The two best-known and most majestic mountains are the Pitons, cone-shaped peaks whose outlines are national symbols and considered natural wonders throughout the Caribbean.

There is a French colonial connection to St Lucia which Barbados never had. It was the French who first began the plantations and they controlled the island for much of the seventeenth and eighteenth centuries, till the British grabbed it after the Napoleonic Wars. The French influence remains, in most place names, such as Castries, Vieux Fort. The locals still speak a French patois, though the official language is English, and about 80 per cent of the population is Catholic. Some French influence can also still be seen in the architecture, but not much, now that modern stuff looks the same everywhere. But St Lucia does appear more exotic, more Caribbean in a way than Barbados. You would never mistake it for Little England.

There is one other thing which is most surprising about St Lucia. In fact it is unique. It must make those highly educated Bajans quite jealous, not to mention the public schools of the UK and the preppy colleges of the USA. St Lucia has a little secondary school which is the only school I know on the planet that has produced two Nobel prize winners.

I went to visit the school, on my first trip to St Lucia, a couple of years ago now, and then on my return I rang Eton, Westminster and Manchester Grammar School and said, come on, bring out your Nobel laureates. None of them could beat little St Mary's College, Castries, a school of just 500 pupils in a town of just 40,000 on a rugged island of only 150,000.

Their first Nobel prize winner was Sir Arthur Lewis who won it in 1979 for Economics. Then came Derek Walcott in 1992 who got it for Literature. How did they manage it? Breeding, tradition, education, pure chance or what? That was what I was hoping to discover when I went round the school.

The main building, just on the outside of Castries, looked most forbidding, grey and grim, more like military barracks than a school, which they were, till 1952 when the school moved here from its original site in the middle of the town. The classrooms looked just as forbidding with tin roofs, wooden walls. The playing field, such as it was, needed to be re-laid, the school hall had a bare concrete floor and they didn't even have a properly equipped gym. Could that be the secret? Deprivation.

Looking out from the school, the views are excellent, over the town and towards the Caribbean. Might that be it? Give the pupils an inspirational view and they'll aspire? I doubt it. In my experience, teenage boys are rarely turned on by scenery.

It's a Roman Catholic school, opened in 1890 with twenty-seven boys, and the first head was an Englishman, Mr Bundy, first name not recorded. It was thought in those days that all education in the British colonies had to be controlled by a real Brit or, failing that, an Irishman, which was the case till Michael Mondesir was appointed head in 1981: the first black head, the first St Lucian and the first old boy of the school to become head.

I went to see him in his little, overcrowded office where he was sitting looking strict and solemn, aged in his mid fifties, his spectacles glinting, his cream safari suit gleaming. Piled up around him were books, trophies, medals, a large brass bell and bits of a microphone stand. It had the feeling of a store cupboard rather than the centre of a dynamic educational enterprise. A bit like Liverpool FC in its heyday, winning everything in Europe, yet being run from a boot room.

Mr Mondesir spoke seriously, solemnly, then, for very little reason, he would burst into giggles, holding his mouth, usually at his own schoolmastery-type jokes.

When I asked him why there was a large photo of the Pope

surrounded by two Union Jack flags, he didn't appear at first to be aware of the juxtaposition.

'It is because the two shelves of books below were donated by the British government,' he replied, after some thought. 'It doesn't mean the Pope is an Anglican!' He was so convulsed by this I thought I might have to pick him up from the floor.

The school doesn't have a sixth form today. You have to go on to a sixth-form college for A-levels. It did in his day, and he did his A-levels in geography, French and Latin, then joined the staff as an untrained teacher. After four years he won a scholarship to university in Puerto Rico and got a degree in economics. Then he returned to St Mary's.

Despite its Catholic background, it's not technically a religious school. Religion is not compulsory, around half the boys are not Catholics and there are today no priests on the staff. Around 60 per cent of the boys have middle-class backgrounds. As in most countries, those with the most favoured backgrounds tend to do best at exams, and you have to do well in the Common Entrance to get in.

Each boy has to wear strict uniform which includes a shirt emblazoned with the school badge and motto: *Summum Attingitur Nitendo*. This does not mean, as some boys allege, that 'We All Play Nintendo' but 'The Top is Reached by Striving.' Tuition is free, as it's a government school, but as in all schools in the West Indies, the uniform can prove expensive for poor parents. All pupils have to provide their own books, most of which are published abroad and are very expensive. Mr Mondesir estimated that the parents of each boy have to fork out the equivalent of £400 a year – about half what a labourer in St Lucia might earn in a year. Hence the middle-class kids. Is this one reason why St Mary's has turned out to be a world-beater?

Not really, said Mr Mondesir. In fact at present they are not even the best school in Castries. Their sister school, St Joseph's, which is for girls, now gets better exam results.

'This is a recent phenomenon,' said Mr Mondesir. 'In Derek's time [Derek Walcott] we did much better, but today boys are much more distracted than they used to be. They watch more TV, play more games. When you visit St Joseph's, you'll see that in recess time the girls are sitting reading. Here they are all out playing.

Girls are more mature at this age, easier to control and discipline.'

Discipline, that is one of Mr Mondesir's crosses in life, feeling that standards are slipping. You should come to Britain, sir, if you want to see lack of discipline in schools.

'No, it is my biggest problem. We live in torrid times. There are so many pressures on young people today – to keep up with parties, clothes, TV shows, new lifestyles. The boys are not avid readers any more and don't like homework.'

In order to keep discipline, Mr Mondesir uses a cane about four feet long. It has a silver knob at one end, covered in masking tape, just in case it should do real damage to any bottom. 'It's quite an ordinary cane, really – just the sort a police sergeant uses. When boys are to be caned, they often wear two or three pairs of trousers, but they can't fool me. I can tell by the muffled sound what they have done.'

What awful crimes result in the cane?

'Rudeness,' he said. Oh no, that is shocking.

'Boys often make sarcastic remarks under their breath or mutter "Get off" to teachers.'

Caning's too good, I said. How about shooting? It's the only language they understand. But he didn't think this was funny. His other worry is the low status of teachers. 'A pop singer in Castries has more attraction than a teacher. Our status has gone right down.'

None the less, St Mary's College still manages to produce St Lucia's top barristers, doctors and diplomats. Mr Mondesir gave me a list of present old boys in top jobs which included Dr Winston Parris, professor of medicine at the University of Tennessee in the USA.

I then went on a tour of the school, encouraged to walk around, ask any questions, go into any classrooms. Quite noisy in the corridors, but dead hush from every classroom. The head had gone on about boys these days being influenced by fashion, but I counted just two skinheads. Only ten boys in the school that day were white, and there was only one white teacher out of the thirty-two staff. They have a tuck shop, called the Tuck Shop, in best Brit style, a cadet corps and their houses were named after such Brit worthies as Rodney and Abercrombie.

I went into one class, of fourteen-year-olds, and asked the class why they thought their school had done so well, producing two Nobel winners.

'We are good at cultural things, which helped Derek,' said one boy. 'We have a rich tradition of plays and arts festivals. In Jamaica, they are good at producing athletes and musicians.'

Good point, but of course Sir Arthur Lewis was an economist.

'We are a very small country,' said one boy. 'You can't find us on the world globe, however much you spin it round. We have to try harder at whatever we do to put us on the map.'

'Every human being is like a torch,' said another boy. 'But we need a battery to light us . . .'

The whole class stared at him, wondering what was coming.

'Our school provides that battery!'

Loud cheers. Plus a few laughs. Was that original? I asked the boy, Peter Lewis. Of course, he said, insulted that I should doubt him.

I finished by going into the staffroom. First surprise: no one smoking. In a British staffroom, you can still be flattened by the fug. Second surprise was to see them sitting at desks, as if in their own classroom, marking books.

In a corner I found two women teachers having coffee. About half the teachers now are female. One of them said she preferred teaching boys. 'Girls are more withdrawn and ladylike. Boys are more upbeat and outspoken, far more restless.'

I asked if they thought St Lucians were particularly clever, compared with other islands. They said you can make certain generalisations, the usual ones, that Jamaicans are aggressive, Bajans boring, but they didn't see any evidence that St Lucians were intellectually gifted.

'If you look at our two laureates,' said one teacher, 'you'll see that in both cases their backgrounds were not pure St Lucian. Derek Walcott's parents came originally from Antigua and Lewis's family had connections with Barbados. Their triumph was in fact a triumph for the Caribbean, not just St Lucia.'

I went to see one of their more recent Old Boys, who also happens to be a returnee, who went to England for many years to complete his education, before returning to Castries.

I arranged to meet him at his office, first thing in the morning, so I booked a taxi to take me into Castries from the hotel where I was staying, East Winds. I just couldn't believe the traffic. It was nose to tail for four miles. The driver said it was like this every morning, from eight to nine o'clock, and then again in the evening. They were clearly locals, going to work, not tourists. Next time a Caribbean expat tells me he left London to escape the traffic I'll take him to Castries in the rush hour.

Luckily, I had allowed enough time and the legal chambers I was looking for were still locked and bolted when I got there. I wondered if I had the right address as Jeremie Street looked fairly tatty. The chambers appeared to be upstairs, over a rather scruffy video shop, with the entrance down an alley and up an open staircase. I checked with a woman aged about thirty who was also waiting outside. Yes, this was Peter Foster's office. Everyone in Castries had heard of him. His family were all lawyers.

Peter Foster himself arrived just a few minutes after nine, parking his rather smart car in a private section of Barclays Bank, just opposite. He led me up to his chambers, which were incredibly classy, just as distinguished and legal-like as anything in the Inner Temple where my dear son works, but a lot more spacious. Peter's own room was oak-panelled with some tastefully framed legal cartoons on the walls. I could see a selection of his legal collars hanging up on his coat peg. He was wearing a sparkling white shirt with cufflinks, sensible tie, dark suit trousers, sensible black shoes, well polished, just as a good lawyer should. His jacket was off, however. Well, it was the tropics.

The English atmosphere goes back to his time in London where he arrived from school, aged eighteen, to take A-levels, then study for a law degree at North London Poly.

'When I first arrived, on 6 June 1977, I found a bedsit for £6 a week in Finsbury Park. My landlord was a chap from Trinidad. On my first evening he took me down Stroud Green Road and pointed out where I could buy vegetables and groceries and paraffin. I didn't know what paraffin was. He said it was for my heater. He then took me back and gave me a lecture, saying how lucky I was that my father was paying for me to be here. "This country will make you or break you," he said. "Your dad has given you this opportunity. It is up to you take it." I then went to my room and cried my eyes out.

'The first time I used the heater I practically set fire to the whole house. For the first nine months, I found it very hard, with no friends. At college, my friends were mainly foreigners, from other foreign countries. The English kept to themselves. It wasn't prejudice. They just had their own friends.

'My father is a lawyer, but he did it all himself, with no help from anyone, or his family. He worked on an oil refinery in Curaçao and did his LLB by correspondence. It took him a long time to qualify and become a lawyer. So that was another burning pressure, which of course he often reminded all his children...'

Peter got his law degree then became a barrister, which meant another year of exams. 'And dinners. The first time I dined at Lincoln's Inn I thought it was very funny, all the suits and gowns, bowing every time a judge or master came along. Then you do it without thinking, all part of the tradition. Now I would frown if other people mock it.'

After six years in London – two for his A-levels, three for his degree, one to become a barrister – he was in love with England and wasn't really all that keen about returning. He even had an English wife – an air hostess he had first met in St Lucia then met again in London.

'I was called to the bar on 20 October 1983, then returned to St Lucia and organised my first case three days later. I was defending a man who was accused of assaulting three policemen with a cutlass. I won – and the three policemen were disciplined.'

He had joined his father's legal firm. In the West Indies there is no separation between a solicitor and barrister: they are all lawyers, able to appear in court. But he also became a Notary Royal at the University of the West Indies, to give himself a local qualification as well.

After five years with his father's firm, he decided to go it alone. 'No, we didn't have rows. I still have a close relationship with my dad, but I felt he never treated me as an equal business partner. We had different ideas on administration. Anyway I wanted to be independent. I have a brother a lawyer, and he is on his own in Castries as well. And a sister who is a barrister in England.

'I set up on my own in 1988, which was pretty bold as I didn't have much idea or much work. It was just myself, plus secretary and a clerk, but it gave me confidence, being on my own.'

He now has two other lawyers in partnership, plus a staff of five. The two other lawyers are both women, both St Lucian. I met them later in their respective offices, looking very young, but most high-powered in their crisp white blouses and legal suits. The majority of people entering the law in the West Indies today are women – the same trend as in Britain.

He calls his office his chambers, but runs it like a solicitor's. He and his two other lawyers are partners, sharing the proceeds, as opposed to being self-employed and freelance like English barristers. His firm does everything, but mainly works on the civil side: negligence, contracts, defamation. The procedure is much the same as in the UK, with magistrates courts, then a high court. They have one high court judge, a St Lucian woman, and six QCs, one of whom is his own father. Peter was recently in the high court in London in a case which had a West Indian connection, acting as junior barrister to a British QC.

So approaching the age of forty, with his firm established, he might have been expected to be taking things a bit easier, but he had recently taken on a position which he was already finding a bit harder than he had expected – chairman of the St Lucia Tourist Board.

'We got a new government here and out of the blue I got a call on my cellphone. I had never been active in politics, but they said that was what they wanted, someone who would be an independent figurehead. It would mean travelling abroad about three times a year, chairing the odd meeting. All I had to do was liaise on policy with the minister. I thought about it for two days, and said yes. Well, I've been abroad five times in the last month alone.

'I went to the Travel Trade show in London – just to see the competition. I had never realised what we are up against. It's all a new language, which I'll have to learn.'

So are you enjoying it?

'Er, well, it's a responsibility, let us say. And more controversial than I thought...'

One of the recent controversies was about possible development around the Pitons, which had drawn world publicity when Derek Walcott, and others, said it would be a tragedy for their natural inheritance if anything touched the Pitons.

'My goal is to develop tourism, but in a controlled manner. I don't want to see St Lucia like Aruba – all manicured, with nothing natural.'

The other running argument is about the present trend for all-inclusive resorts which are particularly strong in St Lucia.

'Yes, we do have a lot, about 50 per cent now, which means the local communities don't gain much. We do want more community-based tourism. The public perception is that all the tourist money goes abroad, which of course it doesn't. We have to explain it better. If only certain people are thought to benefit, the rest of the people won't care.

'We also have to improve the litter situation in St Lucia. That is also a matter of perception. Driving in today I noticed that a cemetery wall was still down and did look unsightly; yet I've passed it every day and it didn't strike me till the local paper started a campaign to get it rebuilt.'

He usually visits London several times a year, for business or pleasure, and there are things he still misses. 'General efficiency, that's one. If a business tells you something will be ready in two days, then it is. I miss the feeling of exposure to world matters. You feel London is a seat of learning and culture and business, things that we only read about here. I like just walking about London, going down Chancery Lane, looking at the bookshops. I find that rejuvenating. And I miss English comedy. I loved *Only Fools and Horses*.

'But I have no desire to go back. I just need the injection a couple of times a year. That's enough. Here I do feel truly independent. I'm able to handle a wide range of legal matters, and I feel my work is appreciated. I'd be a fool to think I could make as good a living in London as I can here.'

So does a top St Lucian lawyer earn the sort of sums they are supposed to do in London?

'Er, nothing like London, but we do quite well...'

I was wandering round the hotel grounds, East Winds, when a rainstorm started, the sort that usually lasts only two minutes, so I told myself, being an expert, but two hours later it was still pelting down. Perfectly pleasant rain, being warm and soft, but in the end, walking around in wet clothes, even in the Caribbean, does become annoying. The rain takes away the colour from the landscape, the brightness from the day, turns the sea to soup. It's only on a bad day you realise how much the Caribbean needs its sun. Things that look lovely and artistic under a clear blue sky look flimsy and shoddy on a bad day, especially anything made of concrete. I was once stuck for five days during a storm at Biras Creek, a stunning resort on the British Virgin Islands. The lawns turned to mud, the beach became a dump, paths and many rooms flooded and the guests, my God the guests, they were going mad, feeling they'd been misled, cheated, demanding their money back.

While standing at the reception area, wondering if the rain would stop, I heard an English voice shouting my name. It was a rep, in uniform, making one of those quick visits, sometimes so quick they are in and out of your hotel like a gas man, saying sorry you were out, but we did call. Then you never see them again.

I had come, as ever, with Elegant Resorts of Chester, who had done my bookings. I knew they didn't have their own staff rep on St Lucia, which they do in Barbados and elsewhere. I hadn't realised they had a local firm to look after their guests.

She was called Margaret, a St Lucian, I presumed, aged about forty, but with a real English accent, so I asked where she'd got it from. England, she said. I asked if I could chat to her, as I wanted to interview returnees, if that's what she was. She said not now, she was in such a hurry, so many places still to visit.

I looked up at the heavens. Still dark, still raining, set in for the rest of the day, so I found myself saying to her, can I come with you? She looked surprised, and rather hesitant. Probably never had such a request from a guest before, though some do ask for unusual things. I said I wouldn't keep her back. I'd just watch her working. That's all. Okay then, she said, but she wouldn't be able to bring me back. Don't worry, I said, I'll get a taxi back, or hitch-hike.

We ran out of the hotel together, trying to keep dry, across to the car park where a minibus with black windows was waiting. Its engine was running and I could hear the noise of loud pop music from about a hundred yards away. Inside were five other reps, all in the same uniform as Margaret. I had presumed she would be in her own car, not part of a team. No wonder she'd been a bit hesitant.

I clambered in, apologising for my wet clothes, but they budged up, making room for me. The five reps were all young men, much younger than Margaret. I could see them catching each other's eyes, wondering who is this bloke, how come he's here? I felt an intruder, bursting into a private staffroom, behind the scenes where outsiders were not allowed, but they were polite enough, saying no problem, man, no problem.

The driver set off at a frantic speed, throwing the minibus round corners, ploughing through potholes. He'd obviously been kept waiting and I'd lost him valuable minutes, persuading Margaret to let me come. The loud music was his, and he certainly wasn't going to turn it down because of some interloper. I was beginning to regret what I'd done. How could I have any conversation with Margaret in such a cramped situation with that noise blaring? But as we went round the hotels, the other reps got out and I managed in the end to talk to her, after a fashion.

'I left Jamaica when I was thirteen, on 31 August 1965. I went with my mother and six other children. My father had gone ahead some years earlier and was working in Birmingham in a factory. When I arrived, I could remember the name of his factory, but I couldn't actually remember my father. When I first met him, I didn't know him.

'My first impression of Birmingham was looking out and thinking what a lot of factories, they're everywhere. I could see the smoking chimneys and the brick buildings, so I thought they must all be factories. I didn't realise they were just terrace houses. In Jamaica, only factories are made of bricks and have chimneys.

'We got a taxi to West Bromwich where my father had rented two rooms. My brothers were older and they went to work right away. I think in about a year we had bought our place, our own home.

'I went to school at George Salter Secondary Modern. I was the only black girl in the school. I couldn't understand their Black Country accents and they couldn't understand mine.

'They weren't unkind or horrible to me, but I was just so homesick. I cried for weeks till my father said that's it, you've got to stop crying, so I did.

'I did have a problem with one girl at school. She came up to me in the playground, in about the first week, and said she was cock of the school. Yes, really, that was the phrase she used. She was cock of the school, and she'd like to see me at four o'clock, after school. So I met her at four o'clock. I punched her before she could punch me and knocked her down. I beat her. And that was it. She didn't bother me again.'

But you are so small and slender, even now.

'Yes, I was even smaller then, and the girl was much taller. But I had all these older brothers, you see. They had taught me to box. I was able to look after myself. I became quite good friends with that girl, in the end.

'I was good at maths and English. I got four O-levels then I left at sixteen to become a cadet nurse. I lived in a nurses' home for two years then I went into the RAF, as a nurse. I spent four years in Cyprus which is where I met my husband Paul. He was originally from St Lucia. He'd gone to England aged nine.

'We got married in 1975 and lived in Watford. I went out to Saudi Arabia for two years as nurse – on my own. I earned very good money. Paul worked as a driving instructor with BSM.

'In 1991 we decided to come to St Lucia. I hadn't thought about it, and probably wouldn't have done, as it's not my home, but every winter Paul used to say, "This is my last winter here, I'm going home." People teased him, saying he'd never do it, not till he retired. In the end I could see that he did want it so much, so I said yes, we'll go then.

'Most West Indians do say they'll return one day, but of course most never do it. I suppose I wouldn't have returned, but for my husband.

'Paul went ahead for six months to look for a job and got one with the local version of Yellow Pages. I came on hols with our daughter Talila, who's now ten. She loved it, all the sea and sand. She said yes, she'd love to live here.

'We rented a house at first and I got a job as a nurse, in a hotel, quite well paid, but pretty humdrum. I left after a couple of years.

'We'd had a big house in England – four bedrooms in Nuneaton. In fact we had a few houses, because we moved around a bit. We'd done well and sold it for a lot of money.'

How much?

There were three of the young reps on the minibus at the time and their ears pricked up, though they were pretending to read their notes. Margaret declined to give the house price.

'But it meant we were able to build our own house here. It's nice, a lovely house, but I do miss England. I miss the shops most of all. The availability of things, just ordinary things like curtains and rugs. It's so hard to get decent ones here, or any choice.

'And the upkeep here is so expensive, which I hadn't realised. Because of the strong sun, we have to paint our house almost every year. Then we do get strong winds, heavy rains, even when there's no hurricanes. You are repairing all the time, because the houses are not as well built as in England. In England, if you have a new house, as we have here, you get a ten-year warranty on everything. Here there's no guarantee on anything.

'I got this job about a year ago. I was used to dealing with people as a nurse, so I thought I could do this. The pay is better but the hours are longer. I work from eight in the morning till seven and I cover eleven hotels. So it's non-stop. I mainly deal with the British guests, like yourself, because of my English background.

'No, we don't get a lot of problems. People are okay, on the whole. They get upset if they've paid for something, like air-conditioning, which turns out not to be in their room. I have to sort it out. I can understand that. They've come a long way, saved for a long time. It is expensive to come here on holiday.

'The other reps call me the E and J girl. J because I'm from Jamaica and E because I'm English. I lived in England all those years, so they look upon me as English.

'I walk quicker than the other reps, so they are always taking me off. "Here comes Margaret," they say, putting on a quick walk. I hadn't realised I walked quickly till I arrived here. Perhaps it's because it's hot here people walk slowly. In England people walk quickly to keep warm. I suppose my general attitude is different as well. I want things done now.

'I don't miss British TV. I didn't watch much, but I do miss Marks and Spencer. You can't get the quality here or the variety. You can't beat English clothes for quality.'

So would you go back to England?

'Not now. This is my home, for now. My husband loves it. He

says he is never leaving this island. He won't even go to the airport.

'Our daughter misses the cinema, but we have satellite TV. We vet it, to make sure she doesn't watch rubbish. We are pleased with the school she's at. She is more certain of a good education that she would be in the UK. If she gets her A-levels, I hope she'll go to university. And if she goes to university, we'll send her back to the UK. Oh yes, we have made financial plans. We have an insurance to cover it. So she has to do well! But I think she will. She's a good student. In England there's no discipline. You learn only if you want to learn, which is hard, with all the distractions.

'We're Catholics and she goes to a Catholic school. It's mixed, but that doesn't worry us, though there could be distractions as she gets older. My pretty girl. My beautiful girl. But I would think that, wouldn't I? She does work. She's an A student. So I do think she should be okay...'

The minibus was now nearing the end of its calls. Margaret herself has got out a couple of times. I tried to talk to the other reps while she was out, but they were a bit wary.

What about the future? I asked her after her last call.

'I don't think I'll be doing this job next year. It's a young person's job. I'm twice the age of most of them. It's well enough paid, but you do get burned out quickly. I think I'll probably go back to nursing.'

The boys at St Mary's College had boasted about St Lucia's traditions in the arts. Derek Walcott was not on the island, though his address is in the phone book. He was in the USA where he spends a great deal of his time. So I went to see a local artist instead, Llewellyn Xavier, a friend of Walcott's.

He lives in the far north of St Lucia in an area called Cap Estate, high up on a hill, with panoramic views all around. I arrived just as the sun had set, so missing the best of the situation, but I admired his garden, his path, his garage, the walls of his house. Almost everything was stark white, as if the builders had not quite finished, so I asked him if he'd just moved in. Oh, no, he said. He'd been here for some years. Blank white walls were deliberate. That was the design.

He showed me round inside, opening a glass partition to reveal a little rainforest in a sort of indoor conservatory, filled with palms and lush trees. In another conservatory the foliage was all cacti, to represent a desert. All very artistic.

Llewellyn is aged fifty-three with the smoothest, fruitiest of upper-class English accents and manners. I naturally presumed he'd gone to some posh English public school, but no. He is pure St Lucian, born and bred, and left school at fourteen. His father gave all his children rather fancy names: his brothers are called Gilchrist, Hogarth, Elius and Aiden, and his sisters Carmelita and Cleticia.

After leaving school he worked as a shop assistant and then a gardener. He then moved to Barbados, still working as a gardener. When he was aged about twenty-one, he met someone in Barbados who worked in the theatre who saw a drawing he'd done and said he should have an exhibition.

'One had never thought of art before,' he said languidly. 'Never. But I sold all the work in my exhibition and "fired my job", as we say in St Lucia.

'In 1968 I went off to London. I'd met a man who was a director of Barclays Bank who had said if I ever came to London to look him up. He became my patron, in a sense. I stayed in his apartment in Westminster, just behind Marsham Street; perhaps you know it. I was astounded by the grandness of London, and of course the art. I went to places like the Tate all the time. I saturated myself in art.'

His first London exhibition was at the DM Gallery in Fulham, mainly consisting of twenty-five prints on the life of George Jackson, one of the Soledad Brothers, imprisoned in the USA in the 1970s for his political writings.

Llewellyn became known for his creation of Mail Art – art that went through the mail. He sent cardboard tubes, with his drawings on, to various celebrities, such as John Lennon, Yoko Ono, Jean Genet, Peter Hain, James Baldwin, asking them to add their own drawings and comments, and post them back, which they did.

After about ten years in London, he went off round the world, giving exhibitions in various countries. During that spell abroad, he studied art for a while in Boston, as a mature student, but basically, he says, he is self-taught.

In 1985 he disposed of all his worldly goods and decided to become a monk. Quite a jump.

'You see, I'd stayed in Trappist monasteries in various countries while travelling the world. One day in Boston a shaft of light seemed to envelop me. A benevolent glow just seemed to come down beside me and hit the ground. I decided there and then to go into a Benedictine monastery in Montreal.

'I'd always read the scriptures and had visions. It could have been to do with the fact I'd been searching spiritually. Or it might just have been a reaction to the wild hedonistic life I'd been living for so long as an artist.'

After a year, he decided to come out. The monkish life was not for him after all. He then fell very ill. While recuperating, he was visited by an English girl called Christina, whom he had met a few years earlier in St Lucia. 'She was very kind and caring and helped me to recover. We got married ten years ago.'

I hadn't realised he was married, nor that there was someone else in the house, as it had seemed empty. Where did you get married – here or in England?

'Darling,' he shouted, 'where did we get married?'

Christina then appeared, carrying a basket of what looked like flowers and sat down at the glass-topped table with us. She said it was sorrel. She was picking the flowers to make sorrel tea.

'We got married in London at St Gabriel's, Cricklewood,' she said, carefully taking the flowers to pieces. The secret of good sorrel tea, she said, was to add cloves to it.

She was brought up in Brondesbury, north London, and went to Brondesbury High School. She first came to St Lucia working for a British travel firm, Pegasus. It collapsed, but she stayed on. Her mother was Italian and her father Polish so she never felt completely British.

'I feel I was born here. I feel West Indian. I love their joie de vivre, their sense of humour. Yes, I do miss some things. I miss Soho, the London parks, but all the views here are beautiful.

'The trouble is the people don't all appreciate what they've got. The authorities haven't much vision. People don't look after the place. They drop litter and leave mangoes to rot.

'It's also becoming more Americanised with US TV and boogie boxes, drugs and violence.'

They both get very upset about litter and carry on their own anti-litter campaign. 'It's typical of the West Indies,' said Llewellyn. 'People have nice cars, dress up in nice clothes, go to nice restaurants – then they throw horrible litter out of their cars as they drive along. To me, that is a ten-headed dragon. I don't understand why they do it. They are human beings, with presumably a soul, yet they still do it.

'This morning I saw someone throw some litter from a car so I gave chase, ran after them. "Excuse me," I said, "I think something fell out of your car, sir." The person had no idea what I was talking about. He was totally unaware that he had thrown anything out.'

Did he then thump you or verbally abuse you?

'No, not quite. I'd been perfectly polite. When I tell children off, I am much stronger. With adults, I am always very polite.'

He has of course got a very polite, not to say extremely pukka accent. Where did it come from?

'When I moved from St Lucia to Barbados I was quite young, so I lost my original St Lucian accent. But it was going to England that did it, I suppose. I picked up the accent of my patrons. It was the company one kept. A writer in the *Guardian* described it as a cross between the BBC and a Kensington drawing room.'

In recent years, since his return to St Lucia, he has been working on a series of environmental paintings, using recycled material, old postcards and stamps showing extinct animals and plants. One message is that contemporary art need not use new materials. The idea is, he says, to make people conscious of the destruction of the environment.

He has included in the paintings the seals of well-known international environment groups, such as the World Wide Fund for Nature, and also the signatures of well-known campaigners, such as David Bellamy, Chris Bonington, Derek Walcott.

When he returned to St Lucia, he had been horrified to hear that some business people were hoping to have a cable car up the Pitons, build hotels, knock down rainforests, flatten hills. He and Derek Walcott and others got involved in a campaign against such developments. They managed to stop the more extreme plans, such as the cable car, but didn't manage to stop a new hotel, the Jalousie, being built just below the Pitons.

He is still very worried about tourist developments on the island, especially the all-inclusive hotels and resorts. 'Locals need passes to get in and visitors never go out. They don't visit our street markets, villages, shops, museums or other attractions. The senior management tend to be expats and the travel and hotel companies who make money are foreign-owned.'

He does of course depend on people or bodies with money, many of whom live overseas, to buy his art, which is not exactly cheap. The paintings in his gallery, which is inside his house, now sell for between $10,000 and $20,000. His work is in the permanent collections of the Museum of Modern Art in New York, Oxford University and Sussex University in England and in many other countries.

So, he's done pretty well for an ex-gardening boy. I went round his gallery with him, and admired his environmental paintings, confirming that yes, I recognised Chris Bonington's autograph was genuine. He smiled and insisted on opening some sparkling wine in my honour, which naturally I accepted. His wife had a glass of wine, but he didn't. I asked if perhaps he preferred Piton beer, the local brew.

'No, it's because I gave up drinking two years ago.'

Too much over-indulgence?

'No, no. For spiritual reasons.'

The man behind the development of the new hotel under the Pitons was Lord Glenconner, formerly the Hon. Colin Tennant, friend of Princess Margaret and a legend in the Caribbean, and the British gossip columns, for having created Mustique. And also well known, alas, for the tragedies that befell his three sons: one dying of Aids, one a heroin addict, one crippled in a motorcycle accident.

On my first visit to St Lucia, I hadn't been aware that he had now moved to St Lucia, but I eventually did manage to see him, flying down for a few days to the south of the island where he kindly said he would meet me at the airport. He happened to be going there to pick up something, then he would take me to Jalousie.

This was not long after the Jalousie hotel had opened – it has since changed hands and become the Jalousie Hilton – and everything was very exciting and hopeful. I'd booked into the hotel itself, just completed at a cost of $50 million, with 115 bedrooms and 375 staff. The situation was incredible, on a virgin hillside, just under the Pitons, though the actual beach was a bit disappointing, being small, with dark sand and rather scrubby.

I had expected that he would be staying there as well, as he had done so much to create the new hotel, but he said no, not quite, he had his own little place next door.

Mr Tennants, as his driver and the locals called him, is in a way the ultimate Caribbean expat, part of the Caribbean fantasy image he has helped to create. At sixty-six, he looked tanned and healthy, rather exotic in a sort of flowing Indian shirt, piercing blue eyes, not a wrinkle. Little hair, that's true, but then he usually wears an amusing straw hat so you don't often see his head.

He doesn't smoke, take coffee or tea and rarely ever drinks alcohol. A perfect gentleman, charming and at ease with all classes, all races, as I could see. He is still a close friend of Princess Margaret and she had recently been out to stay at the Jalousie Hotel, thereby helping to get it some publicity on its opening.

'She is one of the friends who has always stood by me,' he said. Whatever could that mean?

Even more puzzling was when he took me to see where he lived. He led me through a hole in the fence from the hotel grounds to a simple wooden shack where he was living alone. Quite attractive, in a simple Caribbean style, but still without any water. He was sleeping on a foam-rubber mattress on the floor. In the mornings, to clean his teeth and face, he was sneaking next door, into the hotel, to use their lavatories.

How could someone born with so much, who has created so much, who inherited wealth and a title, be living like this?

We'll go back 200 years, to the founding of the family fortunes in Scotland. It was based on bleach, not beer, as many people assume – that's Tennent, not Tennant. 'My great-great-great-grandfather brought the Industrial Revolution to Scotland.'

By 1925, they had sold out the messy, manufacturing side of things, helping to form ICI, by which time the family were landed aristocrats, connected with the Asquiths, Wyndhams, Lytteltons. The first Baron Glenconner had been created in 1911.

Colin was born in 1926, went to Eton and Oxford. In 1953, partly to get away from his family, he moved to the West Indies for a year to look at some Tennant land in Trinidad, 15,000 acres, which the Tennants had ignored for about a hundred years. His own father had not visited since 1921. 'It was like a graveyard, run-down and badly managed. The West Indies was very mouldy in those days. No tourism, no airports. For a hundred years these British-owned plantations had been run by people who were drunk or mad, mountebanks or refugees from justice.'

He came back to England, got married to Lady Anne Coke, daughter of the Earl of Leicester, then returned to the West Indies, honeymooning in Cuba, though his wife never liked the Caribbean, finding it horribly sweaty. The Trinidad land was sold and in 1958 Colin bought the island of Mustique for £45,000. Sounds a bargain. 'Not quite. It was 1,400 acres of nothing. Not like buying 1,400 acres of Gloucestershire. I bought it for its beaches. I thought if everyone in the rest of the world goes on strike, I'll have this island, a place I can retire to – at the age I now am. If only my life had not changed...'

He returned to London, settled down to work in the family's offices in the City, when in 1963 his father decided to sell up completely. Colin was deprived of the firm he expected he would spend his life running – but it turned out to be in his name. He ended up with £1 million.

'Every man-jack today is a millionaire, but in 1963 a million was worth something. I was frightfully rich. My father was never interested in money, but I always have been. Such a shame I have not been terribly successful at handling it. If I had done nothing with that £1 million, I would be very rich today.'

With the money, he decided to develop his empty island of Mustique, moving out there with his wife and children, building his own house, then building others for the rich and famous: fantasy houses, in exotic styles, costing fortunes. Mick Jagger had one in the Japanese style. Bowie's was Balinese. He gave a plot for nothing to Princess Margaret.

There always seemed to be money coming in, from selling new sites and homes, which he ploughed back into the island. He was virtually King of Mustique, responsible for health, roads, administration. The locals wanted schools for their children. The wealthy foreign home-owners wanted a proper airport. Pop stars wanted modern telephones. All of which he had to install.

'It was frightfully successful, almost from the beginning, but then in 1975 everything started to go wrong. There was a high dollar premium, a crisis in secondary banking, wages, water and fuel rocketed. When I sold the houses, I had not built in an agreement for service charges. That was my mistake. People refused to pay and it all became very tiresome. I had to borrow money and sell my paintings.'

In the end, he was forced out, selling his stake for £1 million, which he says was equal to the total amount he'd put in. 'Now I should think it's worth about £200 million. I took no income in all the years I was there. It was very cruel.' Yes, but whose fault? 'My own. You should never sell to the rich. They always make sure they get the best value. The owners and bankers made all the money, not me. I got a lot of publicity, but it got me nowhere. Even my barman ended up a millionaire.

'I am capable of making money. I have good ideas. But I need a real brute to help me, keep an eye on me, someone hard and horrible. I didn't keep track of what I was spending till it was too late. I did have an axeman for a time who restrained me but he died. There was no tax to pay in those days, so I got into the habit of not keeping accounts.'

In 1979 he left Mustique and came to St Lucia. He bought a plantation, inland, planning to grow fruit and vegetables for export, but this did badly and he sold it. Then one day his son Henry (who later died of Aids), while out visiting him, went walking in the south of the island and 'discovered' the Jalousie estate, virgin land between the Pitons. Colin bought the land, paying £200,000 for 488 acres.

Then began a struggle on two fronts: to get planning permission and get development money. This lasted eight years, during which time he lived in a local fishing village in rented accommodation, often in some squalor. Several times he had all his possessions stolen, including his clothes. 'I took to wearing Indian clothes, so no one would steal them.'

The campaign against any development around the Pitons, the one involving Derek Walcott, maintained it should all be kept as a national park. But planning permission was eventually granted, as long as the rainforest slopes were preserved.

Next came the problem of getting development money. After

endless meetings round the world with possible investors, the money came from an Iranian family. He sold them half the land, plus the planning permission, for a sum he won't reveal. 'I made no profit. I spent about $100,000 a year for those eight years, setting up the project. Since 1966 I've had no income.'

He ended up owning no part of the Jalousie resort, despite what most people in St Lucia believed, nor with any position with it. He was clearly not on the best of terms with the Iranians, though the American company which managed the hotel appeared friendlier, appreciating the PR job he had done, allowing him the occasional free meal.

'I don't want to talk about the relationship with Lord Glenconner,' said the then general manager when I spoke to him. 'There is a perception that he is still a major player in Jalousie, which is not true, but he has done great service with his family name.'

While I was there, half the hotel's guests were from Britain. When they saw Lord Glenconner, strolling elegantly around, many imagined it was his hotel. The main reception room was called the Lord's Room and contained his family furniture, which came from his Mustique home, plus a modern table, made by Lord Linley, but these were just on loan till he had his own place again.

'The more I look at my life, the more it seems to have been a complete waste of time,' he suddenly said. We'd had dinner in the hotel together and were now walking in the dark to his wooden house. So far, despite his money sagas, he'd been frightfully cheerful. Oh, come on, you've lived well these last thirty years, and in the Caribbean sun, and can take satisfaction from two beautiful creations.

'No, I should really have used my brain more, perhaps become an academic. I did after all get a scholarship to New College. Or I should have followed my interests, such as the arts, and not tried to make money. If I'd kept my paintings, I would have had status and a fortune today. I sold my Constable, *Whitehall Stairs*, for £63,000. Probably worth £25 million today. I had fifteen Lucien Freuds. They'd be giving me dinners at the Royal Academy if I had them today.'

I asked if he believed there was some sort of curse on the

Tennants, thinking of what happened to his three sons. He dismissed the idea. He wouldn't talk about his sons, except to confirm that Charles (the ex-drug addict) was living in Edinburgh, while Christopher was managing well since his accident. He also has twin daughters, born later, when his wife was thirty-nine – a complete surprise, as twins were not expected. One of his daughters was due to visit him in a few days, though he still had not found a place for her to sleep. He himself goes home to London in the summer to join his wife.

'People say to me, "Oh, how ghastly, having a son into drugs," but far worse things can happen. During the First World War, thirteen out of sixteen Tennant first cousins were killed. That was a real disaster for the family. Then think of Bosnia. None of our women has been raped or killed. You just have to bite on the bullet, and somehow survive.'

He doesn't plan to return permanently to Britain ever again. He finds us 'bitter and envious', preferring the West Indies, the climate, their attitude to life. 'I once took six West Indians to Ghana and life there is feudal. Compared with that, I think the slaves were lucky to be taken from Africa, in that their descendants have a better life here, with no civil wars.

'In the West Indies, people are not neurotic, so they don't notice my neuroticism. They have a simple, fatalistic attitude to health and death. Last week there were three deaths by drowning on a beach not far from here, but people accepted it without any fuss. Such a relief when people don't talk continually about their health, or their pills. I agree with what Lady Diana Cooper used to say. There are only three statements you should ever give out about your health: Comfortable; Sinking; and Gone. That's all there is to say.'

Despite his own radiant health, he is going to refuse from now on to be photographed, unless with his wife and daughters. Yet in the old days he was for ever posing. 'I've attracted publicity ever since my christening. Now I'm too old. All old people look pretty much the same. I don't want to draw attention to myself any more.'

He has, however, not completely lost his touch. In his little wooden house I noticed a photograph of some elephants which he has been sent on approval. For ten years he had an elephant called Bupa, who died two months ago. 'People used to say how cruel, keeping a single elephant; she must be very lonely without a mate. People these days think about sex all the time. My elephant was quite happy just to stand there all day eating, and not being interfered with, but I think this time I will get a pair. They'll be flying here soon.'

That's going to cost you.

'I hope not. I'm negotiating with a magazine who will sponsor them.' Very smart.

So also was his next venture. Yes, you can't keep a good developer down. His little wooden house was to be the focal point of a Caribbean settlement he was now building on his half of the Jalousie estate, using original buildings, transported from other parts of the island. He was calling it the House of Flowers, opening soon, with a restaurant, bar and some shops. Then he was going to sell off forty-five plots for holiday homes. This time he was thinking small, compared with Jalousie and Mustique, and doing it by himself, with what's left of his own money.

'I try not to think of the past. It's been a sorry tale. What matters is the future. As a developer, I'm probably a late developer. But I have got staying power.'

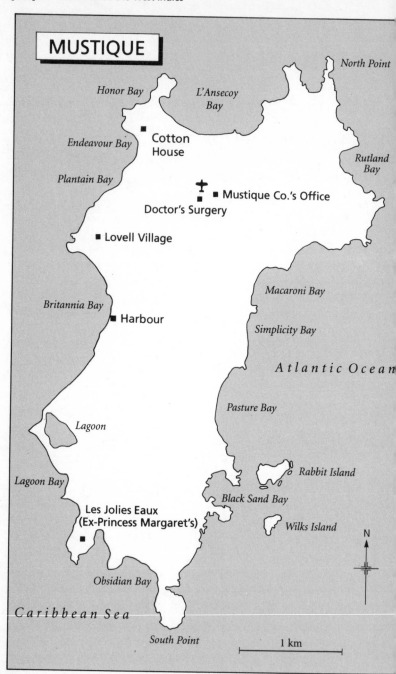

MUSTIQUE

North Point

Honor Bay

L'Ansecoy Bay

Endeavour Bay

Cotton House

Rutland Bay

Plantain Bay

Mustique Co.'s Office

Doctor's Surgery

Lovell Village

Macaroni Bay

Britannia Bay

Simplicity Bay

Harbour

Atlantic Ocean

Pasture Bay

Lagoon

Rabbit Island

Lagoon Bay

Black Sand Bay

Les Jolies Eaux
(Ex-Princess Margaret's)

Wilks Island

N

Obsidian Bay

Caribbean Sea

South Point

1 km

CHAPTER THREE

Mustique

So I felt I had to go to Mustique, find out what happened afterwards. I'd been putting it off for years, convinced it would be like a golf club, manicured, prissy, twee, full of braying aristos. And very very small.

It has retained its glamorous image, despite Lord Glenconner moving on, and Princess Margaret's house, which she subsequently gave to her son Lord Linley, being up for sale when I arrived. The asking price was $4,150,000. Cheap for Mustique. There was another villa, the Terraces, on the market at $22,500,000. Sotheby's International, who were selling both, said they had no doubt both would be snapped up, proving that the rich are still in love with Mustique. But would you want to live there, or even go for a holiday?

Anyone can, of course, either renting a villa or using the island's hotel. It's not an exclusive club. All it takes is money. And it's quite handy to get to, just a forty-five-minute flip from Barbados to their awfully sweet little airport. At present it takes only six-seaters but they are improving it to take slightly bigger planes.

First impression was indeed clipped grass, all about the little airstrip, and nearby a couple of gaily painted little gingerbread houses, neat and orderly, postcard pretty. These turned out to be the island's surgery and the offices of the Mustique Company who own and run the island.

No signs of any flash villas, not on first arrival. They must be hidden away; yet how can you hide away all those plush villas on an island which is only three miles long by one and a half wide?

The island is titchy, a mere dot on the Caribbean map, yet on the ground, in situ, it feels surprisingly big, as if it's grown into a little country, with upland and lowland, urban and rural. Half of it has been left wild, which was the nicest surprise of all. The total coastline, if you had to walk round it all, is about twelve miles, which gives a better impression of its size, and it contains seventeen named bays and beaches. Big enough to get away from any braying voices.

I had also been unaware that there is still a proper local village, where seventy-five Mustiquans live, and have mostly lived, since before the arrival of the white settlers led by Colin Tennant. He hadn't mentioned that. But it was true that there had been no fresh water, no electricity, and it was all fairly scrubby until he set about creating his own fantasy resort.

I soon discovered that on Mustique he is still a hero, their king over the water, who begat them, even though by general agreement the man who has made it all work is the Hon. Brian Alexander, managing director of the Mustique Company since 1979.

He's the son of Field-Marshal Lord Alexander, one of Tennant's old chums, having worked with him in London. I went to see him the morning after we arrived, knowing he keeps a very close eye on everyone coming in and out. He was in his gingerbread office, a relaxed if distant-looking Old Harrovian aged fifty-nine, but his cool blue eyes suggest a keen business brain.

'Mustique was dead in the water when I came in 1979. There were only twenty-one houses, the infrastructure was poor, water and electricity inadequate, everything had to be done on a shoe-string.'

Today, there are eighty-four villas, with a maximum of 105 in their development plan, most of which are for rent through the Mustique Company. The company employs 250 staff, plus another 275 indirectly, who work for the villa owners and other businesses on the island. And there are quite a few, including three shops, a bar and restaurant, a school and a library. The company provides all services and is responsible for the six-man police force, customs, the harbour and the airport.

The resident, working, population is normally 900, but the total was 1,200 when I was there, because of construction work being done on some new villas. One is being built by the fashion designer Tommy Hilfiger at a reported cost of $25 million.

I had a gape from outside. It looked huge and horrible, more like Hampstead's Bishop's Avenue, where the sheiks have their grandiose palaces, than a Caribbean hideaway. Perhaps it will improve with age. Mick Jagger's Japanese-style house, which he still owns, is discreet and tasteful, though I only saw it from the outside.

Mr Alexander has the double problem of keeping the owners and the workers equally happy. 'Some owners and renters expect First World standards in a small, isolated island.'

As for the West Indian workers, most of whom come from St Vincent, there have been grumblings about their accommodation, but that was being improved. 'More skilled workers do expect better housing, which we are now building.'

There is also the problem of providing enough work for the Mustiquans, the seventy or so who live in the village. 'The better-educated ones have to move away, because we don't have those sort of jobs for them.'

I asked him what it was like, personally, living on this island for the last twenty years, which outwardly did appear a little paradise, carefully controlled, but awfully pretty.

'Oh, I don't live here full time,' he said. 'No one could, or they'd go crazy. I try to get a month or so away, in September and October. Otherwise you become institutionalised. I remember reading about people on nuclear submarines who spend weeks under the water. When they come ashore, they are not allowed to drive for forty-eight hours as their sense of depth and perspective has gone. It's a bit like that here, if you stay on the island too long. A sense of perspective does go. I often think being on Mustique is like being on a stationary cruise liner.

'Having the right temperament to live and work here, that's vital. We look for that temperament, but you can't always spot it. We can make mistakes. It's usually people's wives who become bored and feel it's claustrophobic. But the majority do find it very rewarding and satisfying and stay for many years.

'We work seven days a week in the season and it can be exhausting. It might look like a toy-town island, when you're visiting, but it's real to us, with real problems to be solved. It is like running a small town, so you have small-town problems. Plus the problem of everything having to be brought in.

'We do run the company to make money. All the shareholders, which means the villa owners, get a small dividend, but we also run things that don't make money, such as the riding stables.

'There is the danger of overdevelopment, but there is also the danger of stagnation. You can't freeze what we have here. It always has to move on. So we do want new people.'

What he misses from England are sausages and apples – and the English sense of humour. 'There is no substitute for the cultural system you have been brought up with. But I don't feel a stranger when I go back to England. I feel at home. Nor do I feel like an expat when I am here. I don't actually consider myself an expat, but then we do always find it hard to consider ourselves. When I read a report in a newspaper and there's a reference to "a man aged fifty-nine" I think, hmm, quite an old man, forgetting of course that I am now aged fifty-nine.'

Good point. Not feeling like an expat could be explained by the fact that Mustique in some ways doesn't feel like abroad, with all the Brits, the luxury accommodation, all the facilities, things that work, all clean and organised, nothing nasty. Well, not on the surface.

I had my dear wife with me on this trip. I do like to treat her sometimes, and we were staying at the island's hotel, the Cotton House, which has only twenty bedrooms, all exquisite, and the nicest lounge and terrace of any hotel I have seen in the Caribbean. It also had two facilities I have never come across in a hotel anywhere. Neither of which I happened to want. I just mention them. On arrival, you are offered a choice of *six* pillows – soft or firm, and filled with either white goose feathers, cotton or latex. They just confused me, but then I'm easily confused. The other service, at no extra charge, was to have all your clothes pressed on arrival. No thanks, I said. Don't want someone looking at my clothes, not after travelling all these weeks round the Caribbean.

In the main drawing room of the Cotton House I found a privately printed book about the early history of Mustique, with photographs by Lord Lichfield. Even from the early days of Tennant's arrival, when there was no fresh water and they were basically camping, you can clearly see him and his chums drinking champagne, enjoying gourmet food and driving around in a gold-plated buggy bought in the US from Neiman Marcus. The book explains that Tennant wanted only 'nice' people, and to be 'exclusive but not excluding'. Thus he refused Imelda Marcos and the Shah of Persia when they wanted to buy plots, but Basil, of Basil's Bar fame, and still on the island, was accepted into their society, despite being black, because he was handsome and amusing and sexy. Several aristocratic young ladies fell madly in love with him.

During the early 1970s, it appears to have been endless parties and prancing around in fancy costumes. In one party on Macaroni beach, four naked oiled men carried Bianca Jagger on a litter draped with mosquito nets. When she arrived, Tennant slashed the mosquito nets with a machete to reveal Bianca. At another beach party it was arranged for a naked man to dash into the sea and save a naked woman, then bring her back on to the beach and make love to her. The naked man was real, but the naked woman was an inflatable doll. What fun, what larks. Alas, the doll had deflated by the time the naked man had dragged her on to the beach. I was beginning to see why Colin Tennant has always been so fondly remembered on the island. And why Princess Margaret always loved Mustique. Such japes today would have press helicopters hovering on the beach and instant images going round the world by satellite.

I did manage one small glimpse of the island's social life today when we were invited to a cocktail party at the Cotton House. This is a weekly event for villa owners and villa tenants. My wife refused to come. All the way to the Caribbean, just to stand around at a boring cocktail party. No thanks.

There were about a hundred people there, most of whom seemed to know each other. A lot did seem aristo Brit types. I met a woman who said she was Colin Tennant's cousin, but didn't catch her name.

The other weekly social occasion of note is Jump Up night at Basil's Bar and Restaurant. For an island just three miles long, there is quite a choice of eating out: at either the Cotton House, a small but bijou guest house called Firefly, or Basil's. His bar is right on the sea, with wooden terraces, and boasts live music and dancing every Wednesday, the so-called Jump Up night. I persuaded my wife to come this time – what a mistake. The noise was awful, the service slow, no sign of Basil, no languid English aristos or international pop stars. We got stuck on a table right amongst a large party of braying Germans who had come ashore from two huge luxury yachts.

But the island itself was a delight, once we started exploring. The villas, on the whole, are totally hidden away, and very hard to find, or even be aware of, as their drives are long and secluded or fenced off. And the wilder half of the island has been left alone, as nature intended, rocky underfoot or with dense tropical undergrowth. It is possible to get away to remote beaches, either walking to them, as distances are so short, or being taken in little electric buggies with a picnic hamper, then picked up later in the day. All very civilised.

As on all Caribbean islands, the beaches on one side are calm and white and perfect for swimming, but rougher on the other side. Even on the so-called rougher side of Mustique, as on Macaroni Bay, it wasn't really rough; sort of civilised rough, as if Colin Tennant and his artistic friends had knocked them into shape. The winds were refreshing rather than strong, perfect for beach walking, and the waves nice rather than nasty, ideal for swimming, naked or otherwise. I looked for any remnants of the inflatable doll, but found nothing. They do keep the island awfully clean.

Ken Will is one of the people who helps keep Mustique clean, in several senses. He is Head of Security and chief assistant to Brian Alexander. When you think of expats, working abroad, you think of them running bars or restaurants, which doesn't need a lot of previous experience. But there are lots of different sorts of jobs, requiring different experiences.

Ken, now aged fifty-seven, was born in Aberdeenshire. At nineteen he joined the Metropolitan Police in London. In 1966, as a sergeant, he was on duty at Wembley Stadium during the World Cup. 'When Rattin of Argentina was sent off, I escorted him off the pitch.' So I must have seen Ken before, without knowing it, as I was at that match.

He rose to become a chief inspector at Vine Street in the West End and then was moved to Scotland Yard as a member of the Special Patrol Group, looking after VIPs, royalty, government ministers. He was on duty in Brighton during the IRA bomb explosion at the Tory Party conference. He then became commandant of the Police College at Hendon.

'At the age of fifty I was thinking of retiring, but hadn't decided on anything. Then someone happened to ask the commissioner to suggest someone for a job in Mustique. It was all a matter of being in the right place at the right stage in life. We have three daughters, who were then in their early twenties. If the job offer had come up nine months later, when we had our first grandchild, I don't think I would have taken it. My wife certainly would not have wanted to come.'

After eight years, he and his wife – who works on the villa rental side – feel settled and happy on Mustique, though he does miss the rugby. 'Brian and I are about the oldest people working here. The rest are much younger, but we all get on. You have to. Tempers can get overheated when people are living too close together.'

He looks after the airport, personnel and various other things, as well as security. In the Met he had charge of 220 policemen. Now his force consists of six: an inspector, corporal, and four policemen, two of whom are also customs officials. They are officially employed from St Vincent, but their salaries are paid by the Mustique Company.

In any one year there are about fifty reported crimes on the island, half of them taking place in the work camps, amongst the construction workers. 'Someone taking someone else's shoes, or his torch, all very minor.'

A quarter of the offences occur on the actual building sites, with materials or tools being stolen. The remaining quarter take place on the beaches, or from cars or villas. 'If you leave your camera in your unlocked car outside Basil's Bar on a Jump Up night, then it is a bit of a temptation.

'There's little stealing from the villas. There are 200 people working in the villas, so you do get the odd bad egg, but they're always easily identified, like a child stealing from a mother's purse.'

So, crime-wise, all fairly humdrum and routine? After all, it is a fairly small, sleepy place with a total population of only 1,200.

'Oh yes, normally very very quiet. Apart of course from the two deaths...'

He said it, almost in passing. The what?

'The shooting and the murder.'

I knew about the murder, but had been warned that Brian

Alexander did not want people being asked about it. They had already had several journalists, pretending to be travel writers, who had produced scandal-mongering stories. But I hadn't heard about any shooting on Mustique.

'This was in 1994. Sir Rodney and Lady Touche were in their villa one morning, very early, and happened to look out towards the bay. They saw what looked like a fishing boat, behaving rather strangely, so they contacted my security people. As the fishing boat landed, an officer went to investigate. He was told they'd run out of petrol, so the officer said if they got into his vehicle he would take them to get some petrol. When it dawned on them they were being taken for questioning, all of them jumped off the van and ran away.

'There were five of them – four escaped prisoners from St Vincent, plus a fisherman. He gave himself up quickly, saying he had been forced to take them here in his boat. That was his story. Running away to Mustique, of course, was the worst thing they could have done – to an island wholly owned by one company, with its own security system. He said it was a mistake. They thought they had landed on Union Island.

'We soon learned that one of the escapees was a convicted murderer, and was armed. It took us a while to get details on the others. It turned out two had in fact escaped from prison a year earlier, and had gone back to help two others escape. It was all a bit confusing at first, not quite knowing who we were looking for.

'The four of them went to ground. At night, they came out to eat; not stealing from villas, but living off refuse bins. Within three days we'd caught three of them, but the armed one, the murderer, was still on the loose.

'We divided the island into segments, and searched each segment in turn. The company hired a helicopter which flew back and forward over the segment we thought he was hiding in. I organised all the vans and vehicles on patrols to make it look as if we had more vehicles than we had. Armed police from St Vincent had arrived, and they were, how shall I put it, eager for a shoot-out. In the end, that's what happened. The one who was armed, the murderer, let off one shot, which I think he did out of bravado, or drunkenness. We found out later he'd got a bottle of rum and had drunk most of it. Once he fired a shot, the police fired back – and he was dead almost instantly. He was a weedy little bloke. Technically a murderer, but it had happened in some fight he'd had with someone.

'It all lasted eight days. No, there was no panic on the island. It was just a matter of flushing them out, without any shooting, so we hoped, until they gave themselves up.'

The second big drama happened on 26 February 1998. A wealthy Frenchwoman, in her fifties, returned to her villa after a dinner party, at which Ken himself had been present. She wasn't the owner of the villa, but had been a regular on the island over many years and was well known in the community. Next morning, her maid found her stabbed to death.

The maid had heard nothing, as the staff quarters were in a separate building. Nothing had apparently been stolen, nor had there been any sexual assault, though there were signs of some sort of struggle. She had been living in the house alone.

She was a French citizen, so police from Guadeloupe were called in, plus a French pathologist, along with the St Vincent police, who had their own pathologist, all of which didn't help to speed up the investigation. The Mustique Company was naturally keen to have it all solved quickly, aware of the possible bad publicity for its paradise island.

Yet a year later no one had been charged, despite endless rumours and theories. One theory concerned a young Frenchman, a so-called toy boy, who had been befriended by the woman, helping with his education. He'd been staying with her, but had returned to France ten days earlier. So it couldn't have been him. Or could it? He was said to be in debt, and supposedly due to benefit by her death, so could there have been a hit man?

Another possibility was that someone had come ashore that night from a boat, looking to steal from a villa. This theory is supported by some locals remembering that the murdered woman had been spotted making friends with a party from a yacht a few days earlier, one of whom had made advances to her.

A third theory is that it was one of the resident construction workers. A rather worrying theory, this one, as it could suggest the murderer was still on the island, lying low. After the murder, there had been a marked drop in their normal crime rate. But was this because someone was lying low, or had long since the left the island?

There was enough blood found at the scene of the crime to provide evidence for DNA testing. It was eventually done, on a purely voluntary basis, but after a lot of people had left.

So, all very mysterious. Ken says he has no theories himself. 'The white Europeans would like it to have been an outsider, who has now left. The West Indians would like it to have been a white hit man, who has also now gone. The St Vincent police are still working on it.'

According to Brian Alexander, the lurid tales in the British tabloid press have not affected the island. No villa owners have sold up because of the murder, or any guests cancelled.

But they have since brought in even stricter security measures. Detailed information is now kept on every person who comes to the island, by air or sea.

Mustique's resident doctor, Michael Bunbury, also thought he was coming for a quiet, undramatic life, little thinking that he would be involved in matters of international interest.

The sort of things he expected to be treating were blocked-up ears, which of course can be very nasty – and was the reason I went to see him.

I got earache once before in the Caribbean, but then it was clearly an infection. I happened to be in Montserrat at the time, not exactly the best place to be ill. The first stages of the volcano eruption had begun, with people being evacuated and the island's hospital moved from Plymouth to some concrete huts in the far north of the island. It took for ever to get there, on bumpy roads which made my earache worse. I was treated by an Indian doctor, who had just arrived on the island. He gave me some penicillin and in three days it had cleared up.

This time, it was the inconvenience and weirdness of it all that was the problem. I found myself straining when interviewing people, sitting on my good side, yet still finding it hard to hear. It makes you feel stupid and slow, not being able to hear, and your other senses become dumbed as well. The only plus was that it made the air-conditioning bearable. Our room at the Cotton House was excellent, beautifully furnished, lovely terrace, all very quiet – except for the bloody air conditioning. It was either very old or on the blink, but it was like to trying to sleep in the engine room of the *QE2*.

It's about the only thing I ever dread in the Caribbean, or in any hot country: having to live with air-conditioning. If you choose an inland hotel, on a hill, you can usually make do with fans, which are much more bearable, even artistic, but I always want to be near a beach, which usually means the dreaded AC. I hate the sound and look and feel of it, and always drive myself mad trying to regulate or minimise the noise. You put it on full when you go out, and either return to an igloo or a hot house as the maid, under orders, has switched it off.

So I made an appointment with Dr Bunbury at his sweet little wooden surgery beside the company's office. It looked like a toy surgery and his name sounded a made-up toy-town name.

I knocked at the door and a rather fierce-looking nurse told me to wait, surgery hadn't started yet. The waiting room was outside, on the little terrace, in the open air, but well supplied with glossy magazines such as the *New Yorker* and *Country Life*. A construction worker was already waiting, looking very grim, holding his hand, which he'd obviously damaged.

The doctor appeared bang on 8.30. He was wearing a red striped shirt, rather officer class, late thirties, but young, public schoolboy-looking, relaxed and friendly.

'I'll just see this guy first,' he said. 'Looks very fit, so I'm sure I won't be long.'

When it was my turn, I admired all his electronic gadgets and equipment, a surprising amount for a small surgery, then quickly got on to the important topic – my ear. He had a look, confirming that, yes, my left ear was bunged up, but not infected. He could put some oil in it, and in a few days the stuff would ease itself out, or he could syringe it here and now: it was up to me. A year or so ago, the nurse at my London GP's had attempted a syringe job, but had got nothing out and left me in agony.

'It's not a problem. I look at ears twice a day.'

He took his tackle from a drawer and in three minutes out of my ear came a huge wodge of nasty dull-orangey stuff.

'Some dead skin in there as well, but I was right, there's no infection.' I could instantly hear again. Oh, the relief. Dr Bunbury, my hero.

He was born in South Africa, Anglo-Irish family, school in England at Downside, then Cambridge, finishing his medical training at the Westminster Hospital.

'I became an NHS houseman, and never worked so hard in my life. The senior registrar, whose job I hoped to have some day, was ten years older than me, so ten years further down the line, yet he was permanently exhausted and on his third marriage. I thought, this is not for me, waiting to step into dead men's shoes. I decided I'd use medicine for my good, to let me see the world.'

He became an army doctor for the next seven years, some of it in Northern Ireland, then he got a job in Zululand, in a missionary hospital.

'Six years ago, I saw an advert for this job in the *BMJ*. I was lucky with my CV. The fact that I'd been in the Irish Guards appealed to Brian, as his father had been in that regiment. I played rugby, which appealed to Ken. I also sent a photo of my wife with my application, surround by about twenty African children. I think that helped, having a wife. They didn't really want a single man. They do get bored, on islands like this, or start doing things they shouldn't do...'

He and his wife have four young children, all born on Mustique. Three are at the village school. 'Mustique is probably the best place in the world to have small children: it's safe, clean, hassle-free, they get so much freedom and need so few clothes. I don't think they would survive in London. I know I wouldn't, having to drive them everywhere.'

It's the next stage, of course, that causes headaches, when children get to secondary school age, but as their oldest is only six, they have time to think about it, or move.

'I was amazed how friendly the locals were when I arrived. In most countries, in Africa or elsewhere, a white man is either a curiosity or a customer. Here they pay little attention to you.'

There are some problems with his work, being on a remote island. Under the company's rules, a doctor has to be available all day and every day. Getting a locum for a few weeks while he's on holiday is easy, as most urban doctors jump at the chance, but filling in for a few days is hard. 'I had a toothache last year, but I just couldn't leave the island to go to a dentist.'

There is also the problem that many of the villa owners and renters are rather elderly, and also extremely wealthy, more than willing to pay for him to come out several times a day or night.

For workers on the island – construction workers, office or domestic staff – there is a nominal charge of 10 East Caribbean dollars (about £2.50). Villa owners, guests, tourists pay $40.

In his surgery he has an EEG machine, a defibrillator and a small X-ray machine, enabling him to do minor operations.

'I thought the army was well equipped, but this is better. I can do anything a normal GP can do in the UK, but I am obliged to do more, such as ante-natal treatment, or dealing with strokes, because of course I can't get people off to hospital in the middle of the night.'

Even when it's Princess Margaret. He had been called to her the previous January at nine o'clock in the evening after she had collapsed at dinner. He arrived to find her unable to talk or stand up. He didn't know whether the worst was over, or to come, so he brought her back in his ambulance to his surgery and gave her various tests. At the same time, he contacted the royal physician, back in England, for her medical details.

'By this time, I could see she was getting a bit better, so we took her back to her own villa and she slept in her own bed that night.

'Some papers later reported that she had cut her holiday short and was flown out to Barbados in the middle of the night – but this wasn't true. We can't fly at night, and she went out when she was due to go, which happened to be the next day. I flew with her to Barbados, in case she collapsed again, and then left her there for tests.'

The royal drama was on the Tuesday night and Wednesday. On Friday came the murder. He was the first person to see the dead woman, apart from the maid who'd found her. 'The first report said it was suicide. When I got there, I could see it wasn't.

'Yes, it was a dramatic week. And in the middle of it, the Thursday, there was the eclipse of the sun. That was very exciting. During that week, I also had a sequence of urgent calls from a man whose dog was sick. In the middle of all that. I did go and see the dog, after I'd been to the scene of the murder. Well, there wasn't much I could do, hanging around beside a dead body.'

Dr Bunbury was also the island's doctor when the runaway prisoner was shot. His total so far of dead bodies in just six years is three – counting one from natural causes.

I thanked him once again for treating my ear, and as I left I asked where he would go if he was really ill. If, say, he needed urgent hospital treatment, where in the Caribbean would he like to be flown to? Barbados, I presume? He shook his head.

'No, the French West Indies are generally better. I'd say the best island is Martinique. They have a really excellent hospital. I'd have no worries about going there.'

Nice to know. Especially as I would be going that way soon.

Not much chance of meeting many returnees on Mustique. Since it became a white, European enclave some thirty years ago, privately run, how can any native Mustiquans get back, when villas now cost millions of dollars?

Their own village, Lovell Village, is on a steep slope, overlooking Britannia Bay. Colin Tennant moved it when he arrived, as he had better plans for their plot, but the situation is pretty good, with sea views, and the houses are all neat and tidy. They have their own bar, so no need to go to Basil's for a drink, unless it's Jump Up night and they want to watch the action and listen to the live music.

I went to see the leader of the local community, Cardinal Simon, and he did turn out to be a returnee. He was in his garden when I arrived, wearing red football shorts, silky ones, like Liverpool used to wear, sandals and white socks. He took me inside, to the house which he said belonged to the village organisation, but seemed to be where he lived. We sat at a long table, set for some sort of meal, with glasses laid out. On the walls were various notices and posters, most of them done by hand, aimed at members of the village organisation, plus photos of Cardinal in his days as a chef.

Cardinal, aged sixty-eight, was born in Mustique, as were his father and grandfather. In 1960 he decided to move to England. 'I got on a boat that went to many many countries. Curaçao, Barcelona, Genoa, Tenerife, I can't remember them all now. But it took a long time. When we got to England I went on a train, day and night, from Southampton. It was very cold, yes, sir.'

I presumed he meant to London, which shouldn't have taken him a day and a night, even in 1960, but I might have misheard. I was finding his Mustiquan accent a bit hard to follow, but then I am sure he finds the public-school tones of Mr Alexander and Dr Bunbury a bit hard to follow as well.

In London, his first job was in an old folk's home, mainly peeling potatoes. Then he became a chef, working in many places.

'Well-known places, yes, sir. The Gloucester Hotel, the Penta, BOAC Terminal, the City Livery Company Club at Blackfriars. For six years I was at Woolwich Barracks, as a second chef in the officers' mess. In 1974 the Queen made an official visit. I was highly respected in England, yes, sir.'

So why did you leave?

'After nineteen years, I decided it was unfair. I was not reaping what I had sown. I am a single man, sir, with no children, yet I was paying 30 per cent tax. If you make a lot of children, you can live in England on social security, but that is not fair. I like to work for my daily bread, so I came home.'

On his return, he ran a little bar for a while but now in his retirement his main work is for the village organisation, officially known as the Mustiquan Indigenous People's Association.

'When we began, we had 100 members, but many didn't pay their subs, so we are now down to sixty-four, but we are progressing.'

He appears to be endlessly in meetings with the Mustique Company, usually with Ken Will, who looks after island affairs.

'What I don't understand is how one person came to own this island in the first place. Not Colin Tennant, who bought it, but the person he bought it from. I've looked at all the records, and I still don't know how that person came to own it. It was populated with people. There were families that had lived here for years, like the Simms, my family, the Trimminghams, the Lewises, and others. How could someone buy it? It's a mystery.

'But I've nothing against the Mustique Company. They have been good to us. I just want to make all the indigenous Mustiquans get a piece of the cake. We must be allowed a decent enough space here, until the Lord is ready for us.'

One of his current campaigns was for his sister, who lives in

England. 'She works for the Midland Bank. I don't know which one, just the Midland Bank. She's on computers. She wants to retire here and buy a certain piece of land, but they won't let her. She can buy a piece of land in London, but not a piece of land in Mustique, where she was born. I am going to fight it, yes, sir. I am going to the Privy Council in London and if that fails, I'm going to the Court of Justice in The Hague, yes, sir.'

His many years in England, and observation of the officer class, have obviously helped in his work as a negotiator. They all do appear to be on good terms. Later when I asked Ken Will about Cardinal's battle for his sister he gave a smile, then a small groan. It wasn't as straightforward as Cardinal had led me to believe. Cardinal was always finding relations who always seemed to be after prime plots, but something would be settled.

Amongst the Mustiquans, Cardinal is known as the 'English Man', which I presumed must be due to his years in England, and knowledge of how to handle the English, rather than his accent.

'No, nothing to do with either,' he said. 'I'm called "English Man" because I wear white socks. I am the only person on this island who wears white socks, yes, sir.'

I asked if I could take a snap of him, but he was worried about the clothes he was wearing. I assumed he must mean his sandals and white socks, but no, it was his red shorts. He didn't want to be seen in shorts. I said I was wearing shorts, as I always did in a hot country, and even in Lakeland summers. Mature gentlemen are allowed shorts these days.

'Yes, but you fat. I thin.'

Cheeky sod, was my first thought. Not that I'm fat. Certainly not. Then I realised it wasn't being fat or thin he was worried about – but his legs. They were a bit spindly. I said the photo was to jog my memory of what he looked like, and if I used it, I wouldn't show his legs...

One of the many multi-millionaires with a house on Mustique is Felix Dennis. Not as world-famous as Mick Jagger, or as well bred as Princess Margaret, but a great deal more entertaining.

He was first famous in 1971, for all of fifteen minutes, when he bobbed into public consciousness during the *Oz* magazine trial, one of the three young hippies accused of 'conspiring to corrupt the morals of the youth of the realm'. At the time, the judge described him as 'the least intelligent of the three'. It was the late Judge Argyle, now considered a poor judge, on most matters, who was probably prejudiced against Dennis for being uneducated, uncultured and working class.

After that, Dennis seemed to disappear from the newspapers for a couple of decades, then in the early 1990s there were occasional references to him as being a wealthy publisher who did the odd mad gesture, such as paying for three kids from the island of Eigg in Scotland, plus their teacher, to have an exchange visit with three kids from the island of Mustique.

I didn't know, till I arrived, that he had his own house on Mustique, nor that he was in residence. His house, Mandalay, used to belong to David Bowie and is probably the most stunning private house I have ever been in.

Yes, I do make rash generalisations, so let me think. I did once visit Noël Coward at his lakeside home in Switzerland: very chintzy. Also John Lennon's Weybridge mansion: rather suburban. The Duchess of Devonshire at Chatsworth: far too overpowering, not to mention cold and internally dull.

Mandalay is exciting and exotic. It is built in a Balinese style, mainly out of wood, with all the furniture and ornaments hand-made and distinctive, artistic and tasteful, yet at the same time wild and original.

Felix was busy on the phone to New York when I arrived so a man-servant took me round the house. Room after room, bathroom after bathroom, wing after wing, each more amazing than the one before. All different but all beautiful. The garden was equally exotic with streams and fountains, tropical trees, flowering shrubs, gardeners everywhere. The swimming pool, with its waterfalls and cascades, seemed to be floating in the sky, yet on a level with the sea which I could see clearly, down the lush hillside, about a quarter of a mile away.

He has a permanent staff of thirteen, plus a manager, even though he only lives in the house thirteen weeks a year. The costs must be enormous. Only a multi-millionaire could afford it, but of course having money is never enough, despite what people without money think. You have also to be energetic, tough, determined, creative to run and care for a house like this.

My first sight of Felix was from afar, sitting in one of his outdoor reception rooms, a stocky, bearded figure in a kimono, looking a bit like Rolf Harris. I half expected him to have an Australian accent, still thinking back to the *Oz* trial, till he started speaking, effing and blinding in broad estuary English, telling off a servant because the crisps were not to his liking.

He was born in Kingston upon Thames in 1947 where his father was at one time a greengrocer. Felix has no memory of him. He left his wife and children for Australia when Felix was four. 'I never knew the reasons, or what happened. I just knew that at grammar school there was only me and one other boy who didn't seem to have a father. The idea of divorce was unusual in those days.'

I said that Felix seemed a rather poncy name for someone of his background. 'I think it was my mother and her sister. When they were little girls, they said that when they had boys, they'd name them after Roman emperors. So I was Felix and my brother is Julian.'

Felix left school at fifteen, determined to be a rock star. 'I did tour in various groups, as a singer and drummer, but after four years, I realised the life was killing me. Oh, you know, fucking overdosing on drugs and sex all the time. Drugs are fucking brilliant. Don't let anyone tell you otherwise. The only problem is, they kill you.

'When I realised I was never going to be famous or make money, I started selling *Oz* on the King's Road. That's how I met Richard Neville [editor of *Oz*]. I was never a hippie really. In fact I thought they were a bunch of wankers. I just helped him with the design and headlines on *Oz*. One day he gave me the cheque book and said, here, you can be our publisher. I didn't really know what was happening when we got arrested and ended up in prison for a few days. John Birt, later boss of the BBC, went bail for us. John Lennon helped pay our legal fees. He said here's £20,000, then sent a limo for us to go and see him at his house at Ascot. He was working on "Imagine" at the time.

'We won our appeal, and our conviction was quashed. I wanted to keep *Oz* going. My idea was to turn it into a rival to *Rolling Stone*, but Richard had lost interest.

'So I set up on my own in a room in Goodge Street, publishing underground comics like *Fritz the Cat*. I thought those sort of comics were going to be really really big. It was a complete fucking flop.

'One day in 1974 I was walking down Soho, going past a sex cinema, when I saw hundreds of young kids outside. I thought, what the fuck are they all waiting for? Turned out they were queueing to see a Bruce Lee film. I'd never heard of him. They said oh yeah, he's really great. I went back to the office and we produced a one-shot Bruce Lee magazine. It sold out. I then sent my pal, Don Atyeo to Hong Kong and we produced a Bruce Lee biog. Then we did a Kung Fu monthly. That ran for eleven years – in eight different languages. And that's really how the Dennis Group began. Now where are those fucking crisps I asked for? Oi. You. Yeah, that's much better, ta.'

The Dennis Group now has 450 employees in the UK and the USA and publishes some twenty different magazines. They include *Computer Shopper*, the UK's biggest-selling computer mag, selling 170,000 a month. *Maxim* is his latest success, a glossy mag for men, recently launched in the USA, where it sells 2 million a month. In the UK, it sells 300,000 copies a month.

'A lot of British magazine publishers sell out the minute they get a hit. It's partly because they can't think of a good follow-up. I did sell one of my early successes, the US edition of *MacUser*, the magazine for Apple Macintosh users. I got $23 million for it in 1986, but I kept all the European rights. I used the money to go into the USA. Not many UK mag companies have made it in the USA. I have. *Maxim* is a massive fucking success in the USA.' It was the biggest launch of a consumer magazine for 25 years.

He was working on several new ideas, still secret at the time, but he told me about one of them in some detail, not that I could understand it properly. It was all to do with having magazines available on the Internet, all magazines ever published, anywhere in the world, including back issues.

'One of my companies does nothing but think up new ideas.

I call them the skunk works. They're boys and girls out of control.

'Why am I bothering with new stuff, when I have so much money already? Why does my dog scratch its balls? Because it can. I'm fifty-two, in the prime of my life. I know I can do this, and I know of no one else who can do it.'

All the same, he says he has lots of time for his hobbies, such as planting trees, reading poetry, looking after his houses. He has a Tudor-style manor and 5,000 acres in Warwickshire, a lake house in Connecticut, apartments in New York and London, plus his Mustique home. Which is what I'd really come to talk about.

'I was tricked into buying this,' he said.

From what he'd been saying so far, he didn't exactly sound the sort of person to be tricked by anyone.

'Oh, I was. I was tricked by my mother and my companion, Marie-France. In 1994 we were staying on Young Island, off St Vincent, when they announced they'd hired a helicopter and were all going to Mustique to look at a house. I should have suspected something when I saw they were all decked out in their best frocks. I think they were hoping they would get to meet David Bowie – that's why they wanted to look round his house. He wasn't here, but I fell in love with the house.'

Although he only stays twice a year, for seven weeks and six weeks, he has thrown himself into island life, serving on various boards and committees. 'I'm the firebrand. I stir things up because I don't give a fuck whether people like me or not.

'I told them it was diabolical having all the construction workers living in slums and shanties. It's not only unhealthy, it's political dynamite. It just takes one newspaper to get a photo of them in the work camps, then use it with a photo of one of the beautiful villas, and the shit will hit the fans.

'I don't want that to happen.' Two million EC dollars have now been spent upgrading the work camps. You could take your aunt on a guided tour of what used to be a hell hole.

'I value the Mustique experiment. Look at the village school, the village houses, the roads, the desalination plant, the reliable electricity, the library, the adult literacy courses. I don't want all this ruined.'

Mustique's Community Library is Felix's creation, which he mainly paid for and organised – a very attractive, gingerbread-style building, next to the island's school, housing over 4,000 books, plus computers, available for everyone on Mustique. It's now the best-equipped library in the whole of St Vincent and the Grenadines, so the two resident librarians told me.

When not in residence, Felix's house is always occupied.

'I run it as a free hotel. It's used by friends, or friends of friends, sometimes people I don't actually know. I also use it to reward my staff. If they've done something bloody good, they can have a free holiday here. Each year, about 150–180 people stay, all for free, with full use of my staff.

'One reason I do it is to keep the house on its toes. It means when I come everything is working perfectly. I get better service than I would do otherwise. For example, I keep a proper pharmacy, always fully stocked, with everything a visitor might need.

'I've also got my own football team. I had some fun with that. When I first began it, I told everyone at a company meeting that I'd bought Man United. Hold on, I'll show it to you.'

He came back with a framed photo of his football team: Mandalay United, or Man U for short. They include three men who work at his house. They all looked very smart in their red and black strips with a serpent logo. The serpent is the icon of his house. 'Bowie did that. The serpent is the god of music in Indonesia.'

He has never married, but there had been several references to a girlfriend, so I asked if he still had her.

'Oh, yeah, Marie-France. She's my companion, really. She goes with me everywhere. I have lots of girlfriends and she checks them out for me. Yes, I'm a lucky bastard. Most blokes would shoot me out of jealousy, if they knew the life I led.

'No, I have no children. I love children, and I have ten god-children, but I'm too cowardly to have any.

'I only have one problem in life: I'm going to die. Apart from that, I have no problems. Now fuck off. I've got phone calls to make...'

One does meet some interesting people when one travels abroad. But how surprising that such a small island should attract such big characters. Colin Tennant was first, with a christian name that didn't fit him, or betray his background. Now Felix, with his unsuitable name. Both originals in their different ways.

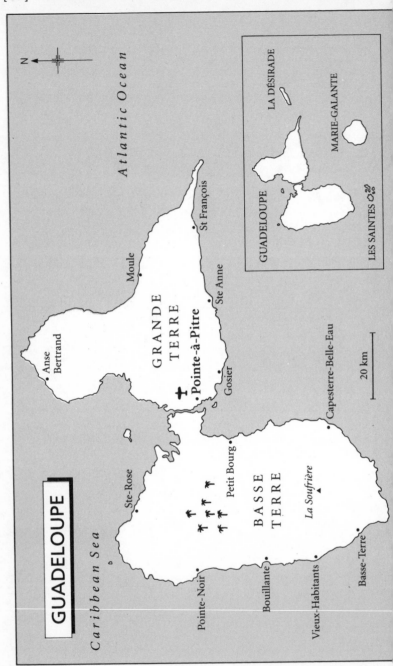

GUADELOUPE

Caribbean Sea

Atlantic Ocean

N

Anse Bertrand

Moule

Ste-Rose

St François

GRANDE TERRE

Pointe-à-Pitre

Ste Anne

Gosier

Petit Bourg

Pointe-Noir

BASSE TERRE

La Soufrière

Capesterre-Belle-Eau

Bouillante

Vieux-Habitants

Basse-Terre

20 km

GUADELOUPE

LA DÉSIRADE

MARIE-GALANTE

LES SAINTES

CHAPTER FOUR

Guadeloupe

Not many Brits visit the French West Indies, despite what Dr Bunbury had said about its excellent hospitals, but there again, not many French people visit the British West Indies. It's a matter of history. Different cultures, different systems, different languages, different attitudes have kept the two neighbouring nations apart in Europe for many centuries, or at least at sparring distance, while their offspring in the Caribbean always went their separate ways.

I have been twice to St Barts, and so have many other British travellers, but then visiting St Barts is not like visiting the French West Indies, nor even the West Indies. It's a white island, for a start, and very small. There was no history of plantations, so no black population. Today it looks and feels more like the south of France than the Caribbean.

The two true French West Indian islands are Martinique and Guadeloupe, both big enough to be classified as 'departments' of France, which means their inhabitants are all full French citizens, with the same legal and political rights as anyone in metropolitan France. Guadeloupe is also responsible for St Barts, St Martin and some even smaller islands. All together, the French West Indies, or Antilles Françaises, has a total population of 1 million.

I chose to go to Guadeloupe because of its shape. It looks like a butterfly, about to flutter away, with two definite wings which you feel must be awfully pretty, multi-coloured and exotic in real life. I'd also been told it was less developed than Martinique.

There are no direct flights from the UK, no packages I could see in the brochures, so I picked what looked like the best-sounding hotel from a French guidebook and asked my trusty travel people in Chester, Elegant Resorts, to book it for me. I'd get there myself, internally, flying from another island.

From the air, I could see that the wings are in fact separated, if only just, by a tiny stretch of water over which I could see at least two bridges. I could also see what appeared to be something ominously like a motorway.

We landed at the main town Pointe-à-Pitre, which is near the join between the two wings. It too looked ominously busy. I suppose French people, coming from France, know roughly what to expect, having been brought up with a vague idea of their colonies, the way most Brits have a rough idea of what Barbados or Jamaica must be like. It did happen to be the rush hour, not a good time to arrive anywhere, but my first impression was of metropolitan French bustle. None of that Caribbean, laid-back calm.

The Indian driver sensibly decided to avoid the town centre, doubling back before we got into the worst of the traffic, and took a round-about way, looping north, cross-country, rather than taking the main motorway along the southern coast. We were on the right-hand-side wing, known as Grande Terre, as opposed to the other wing which is Basse Terre, heading for St François, down in the far south-east corner.

The countryside was quite pretty, if rather flat and dusty. I amused myself by looking out for signs of traditional Frenchness, at least what Brits think of as traditional signs. Mad racing cyclists in full gear with their heads down and their bodies covered with French adverts. People in berets; yes, I did see one or two, standing at their front gates holding French poodles. An awful lot of people smoking. Very old men on very little old puff-puff motorbikes. Some dreadfully erratic driving.

St François was bigger than I expected, filled with cheap seaside-type souvenir shops and guest houses, but the hotel I'd booked blind, the Cocoteraie, turned out to be most attractive, all pastel shades, just fifty suites with a swimming pool the size of Wembley and a lot of très chic-looking French couples.

We were the only British residents, which was nice. It is hard to feel abroad if everyone is from your own country. In any year, so Fidel Montana, the general manager, told me, British guests amount to only 1 per cent. Over 85 per cent were French, from metropolitan France, 4 per cent from the USA, 4 per cent from South America. It's one of his running concerns, to try to achieve a proper balance, as with any hotel company, in case for political or economic reasons the country they are relying on most decides not to come.

I didn't realise that Fidel was the manager at first. He was dressed so casually, not like those besuited managers who sit behind the scenes and never appear. I don't think I've seen a manager so in evidence in his own hotel as Fidel, for ever bustling around, talking to guests, stalking his domain. He was aged fifty-seven, but looked thirty-seven, full of energy and enthusiasm. Not that a fifty-seven-year-old need be without energy or enthusiasm. Certainly not. Enthusiasts, among whom I like to number myself, tend to remain enthusiasts, often tiresomely so, regardless of age.

I was also impressed by his command of so many languages: English, French, Italian, Portuguese and Spanish. Spanish is his first, as he was brought up in Colombia of Brazilian parents. His wife Michelle is British, though brought up in Monaco. At home, with their four children, they all speak Spanish.

He worked for a while in London, as general manager of the Chelsea and Curzon hotels, which is where he met his wife. After that he managed hotels in St Martin, Bolivia and Brazil. 'I like to work abroad. I don't want to be a king in my own country.'

They were worried, when moving to Guadeloupe from Brazil, about schools for their four children, aged twenty-one to six. 'In Brazil they went to private schools because Brazil is a poor country with poor schools. I thought here would be the same, but no. They all go to the French state schools, and one to college in Paris. In Guadeloupe the state schools are tougher and the teachers more qualified than in the private schools. French education is solid, very solid. All my children are doing well. In fact all my children are brilliant. All of them are top of their class.'

That was another thing I liked about Fidel, his youthful boasting. He also bragged about how he ran his hotel. 'It's always been my rule not to stay in my office. I get in very early, spend an hour on paperwork, then the rest of the day I am out and about. One day a week I eat in the staff canteen. You have to, to keep an eye on it. It's often one of the things staff moan about when they are unhappy. They say they don't like the staff lunch and you can say yes, I had it today, and I'm changing the menu.

'All my staff have cars. Oh yes. When they got their insurance claims paid after the Hurricane Hugo, a lot of them bought cars instead of repairing their damaged houses.' So that's why the traffic is so appalling.

'I was invited to dinner the other week by one of our cleaners, a woman who does the lavatories. She lives in a shack on the beach with wooden poles and a plastic awning, but she had the biggest TV set I've ever seen – and her own car.'

Fidel's four children have British passports, but their hearts were in Brazil. He expected to go back there eventually, but for his next move, which might be his last, he would quite like Cuba. I said that was on my list of places to go. It sounded very exciting.

'I was in Cuba, as a student. So I know it. And of course having a name like Fidel could be helpful, if Granada ever buys a Cuban hotel.'

Granada? Yes, the British company. His hotel, which had seemed so wholly French and chic, turned out to be British-owned, which I'd never realised. The Granada group, apparently, had acquired it when they bought Trust House Forte.

The only disappointment was the hotel's beach. It was small, very enclosed, poor for swimming as it was so shallow, and very busy with boats and windsurfers.

On the first morning I bagged a beach chair right at the front and settled down for a quiet sunbathe, only to be awakened by the sound of aeroplanes. I could hear two, buzzing above my head. Then one crashed into the water, just yards from where I was lying, in amongst the swimmers.

Strewth, I thought. Have I walked into a little local Guadeloupian war? Are the two wings fighting each other? Or are they shooting an episode of *Biggles*? The planes, once I looked at them properly, did seem rather old-fashioned and toy-like. Both were little sea planes, with an open cockpit, out of which stepped the pilot and a woman in a bikini.

I have been on a sea plane before, as a form of transport, getting from Fiji to the little remote island of Vatulele. I've never seen sea planes used as a form of fun entertainment, right on a busy beach. They are another import from metropolitan France where they are known as ULMs – Ultra Léger Motorisés.

The pilot came across and asked if I'd like a go. Just 200 francs – about £20 – for a ten-minute flip round the bay. Or I could go longer, to one of the outer islands, for £100. I waded over and had a look. It appeared to have a sort of microlight engine, flimsy-looking wings, as if they might be held together with sticky tape. I said no thanks. I'm resting.

I lay down again, closed my eyes, and the next interruption was human. Through a half-open eye I could see a naked woman, standing in front of me, posing and pouting, smiling alluringly. No sex, please, I am English; well, Scottish actually. But I slowly opened both eyes and could see she was not quite totally naked but was wearing a little thong.

Having got my attention, she pulled on a bikini bottom and top and did a few twirls in front of me. Then she stripped down again, naked but for her thong, and put on another swimming costume.

I then noticed that another four girls, just yards away, were doing the same, strutting up and down the beach. They had turned the sand into a catwalk. But unlike a normal fashion show, where they change behind the scenes, all the stripping off and putting on of new outfits was being done right there, on the beach, in front of everyone. Being French, of course, used to toplessness, most people totally ignored them.

They were then joined by two young men modelling natty shorts and swimming cossies. They too stripped off each time they put on a new outfit from the large gaily covered canvas bags each was carrying.

It took me a while to realise that every new outfit had a label on, flapping away – the price tag. It wasn't just a fashion show. It was a fashion sale. And they all took credit cards.

Eventually, I managed to get a few words with one who appeared to be a leader of the little group, a blonde called Nathalie. Only a few words, she said, but I could have her mobile number. She was working. And if I wasn't buying, she couldn't really spare me much time at the moment. But for someone interested in buying, she had endless time.

I watched as she helped a French woman, rather on the plump-ish side, try on several outfits, each bigger than the other, getting out a mirror from her canvas bag so the woman could see herself. She bought a swimsuit at 550 francs and a beach wrap at 955.

'They are an exclusive line,' explained Nathalie, 'made by Janine Robin in Paris.'

Nathalie and the other girls are all from France. Each year they come to Guadeloupe for four months at the height of the season and rent a house where they all live together, and work together on the beaches of the better hotels. 'We can't do it in France, but it has been going on here for some years.'

They must do quite well, as she didn't seem to do much in the rest of the year. I asked one of the boys how much he made, but he wouldn't reveal it. 'But I can tell you I used to be a waiter. I now make more in three hours on the beach than I made in eight hours as a waiter, including tips. It means I can spend the rest of the day windsurfing, or just enjoying myself.'

Just twenty-four hours in Guadeloupe and I had seen two things I had never seen before in the West Indies, or anywhere for that matter: the *vendeuses de la plage*, as they are called, and the little sea planes. Perhaps the French West Indies were going to turn out really different.

After a few days of sunbathing and wandering round St François, which was more interesting than at first glance, with an excellent open market and lots of good restaurants, we got a driver for the day to take us round the other half of Guadeloupe, Basse Terre, which is hillier, less populated, not as touristy as Grande Terre.

We whizzed through Grande Terre, taking the main road this time, and I soon had the most awful headache. Not just with the mad traffic but our driver, who insisted on shouting everything in my ear. Mostly he was moaning about the cost of living. Either in English, which he could speak quite well, or French, which he spoke slowly, and loudly, me being a foreigner.

'Education and health, is very good here, and all free. Social security, is good also. And the roads, they very good. But the taxes, they are *huge*. Everything costs so much. Furniture, food, everything. We are now getting a lot of thieves. No, not from Guadeloupe but illegal immigrants from Dominica.' Funny how all over the West Indies, and the world at large, the baddies or scroungers always seem to come from elsewhere.

'Worst thing of all is the strikes. Workers strike all the time, for nothing. First it's postmen, then lorry drivers, then everyone.

Just like France. We have copied all this striking from France. Terrible...'

When we got across the bridge connecting the two islands, the dual carriageways ran out, our speed slowed down and so did his moans and I got him on to rather less noisy topics. Number plates, for example. I go through life noting number plates, working out the codes, or making names out of the letters, a disease really which began when I was in the Boy Scouts and was told a good Boy Scout noted everything, just in case. I'm not sure what the case might be, as so far no one has asked me to recall even one number plate. For those interested, 971 stands for Guadeloupe and 972 for Martinique.

He was of Indian descent so I asked him what he thought the proportion with Indian blood might be. He thought 5 per cent, most of them driving taxis, if they couldn't afford a shop. They came originally from the East Indies to work on the sugar plantations, after slavery had been abolished in 1848. He could take me to a Hindu temple, if I was interested, or to watch bullock cart racing, very popular with Indians, but I said no thanks. What I was really interested in was a drink.

We were passing a rather attractive house on a hillside beneath La Soufrière, the highest point on Basse Terre, some 4,813 feet high. It was a *gîte*, the French form of B&B, i.e. a house with rooms to let, so I went in and asked to have a look round, thinking it might be a pleasant place to stay, if I ever wanted to stay on Basse Terre.

It was run by a neat and slender woman of about sixty called Nicole – a Frenchwoman, a white returnee for a change, who had been born on Guadeloupe but taken to France as a young girl.

'This was in 1945, just after the war. All I knew about France I had learned from books. There was no TV in those days. I thought France was over there somewhere, behind Soufrière. I was surprised when we had to get there by boat.

'It was very strange arriving. I had never seen a train before, or an elevator. I had come with my parents and a black servant. I spoke Creole with the black servant, though my parents forbade it. In the eyes of the French I was a little savage. Our French accents were terrible. When I later decided to train to be an actress, I had to learn diction from scratch.'

She went on to spend thirty years in France, working as an actress with some well-known companies, so she said. I didn't know the names, but I had heard of Peter Brook with whom she once worked. 'I also worked in the Abbey Theatre in Dublin, doing a play by Molière. I met Brendan Behan and Eamon de Valera.'

She came back, she said, after she got married for a second time and decided to move here with her new husband.

'It was really *mal du pays* – homesickness. I felt like Scarlett O'Hara in *Gone with the Wind*. I increasingly felt a romantic love for the country I had been born in. As I grew older, I began to miss it – probably because I was missing my youth.'

Now she is back, and for good, she naturally misses the French theatre. 'There is no professional theatre work here. I miss seeing French movies, in their original form. I also miss the culture and the history generally; not just of France, but being able to go to Rome or Greece, to smell the past.'

France gave her a career and independence, both of which, for a woman, are still restricted in Guadeloupe. 'A woman here is still not totally free. She is told, "You can't do that, you can't do this." You have to get away to be yourself.'

Very true. Both expats and returnees would agree with that.

By chance, at lunch-time I met another Frenchwoman, who was also a white West Indian returnee, with a similar sort of French colonial life story.

I'd seen a signpost indicating a coffee plantation, Cafeire Beauséjour, not knowing what to expect, or if I'd translated it properly, as I thought coffee was finished in the Caribbean. I went to investigate and found it was doing modest lunches.

It was run by a woman in her fifties called Bernadette. She appeared to be doing everything herself, running the little plantation as well as cooking the lunch which she was serving under an awning. It was all rather makeshift, with wooden fittings, battered sofas and chairs, but awfully charming.

She was born in Guadeloupe, though her parents came from Martinique. Her family were long-time French West Indians who had emigrated from Normandy in 1700. 'They came by boat, looking for gold, that's the legend in the family.'

Aged seven, she went to France for her schooling. 'Arriving in

Paris was terrible. It was so dark, no blue sky, no colour at all. I was sad a lot of the time. Other girls would laugh at my accent. I felt so sad. You see things in black and white when you are young. When I was in France, I wanted to be here. Then when I came back here in the school holidays, I missed Paris.'

She trained as an architect, working in France and the West Indies, getting married along the way and producing four daughters.

'I bought this place in 1991, just four hectares. It had been a coffee plantation, but not for forty years. Young people had no memory of it as a coffee plantation, so I wanted to revive it, to let them know about their history.'

She does grow some coffee, with the help of two workers, but not enough yet to sell it, or even get any usable coffee beans. Almost all her energies have gone into the plantation house.

After lunch she took me round it – and it was exquisite, lovingly restored, not all that large, a house rather than a mansion, all made of wood, dating back to 1764. It was derelict when she bought it, so almost all the woodwork is new. She has her own electric generators which power her computer.

She appeared to be living alone, as no partner was mentioned. All four daughters are now married – two in France, one in Guadeloupe and the other in St Martin.

Like Nicole, she appeared so cultured, so artistic, unlike some of the expats and returnees who fetch up in the British West Indian islands. She had also travelled extensively in the Caribbean during her years as an architect. So I asked for her favourite.

'Oh, my favourite island in the West Indies is Barbados.'

That did surprise me, coming from a chic French West Indian woman. But why?

'Purely for the old houses. I do love that British colonial style.'

Back in the hotel, I went to the manager's party, which was like managers' parties in most Caribbean hotels, with drinks and nibbles, guests in their best casuals, the sixth formers with the best tans, and ever so confident, the newcomers looking confused and out of things. Except of course they were all French.

I talked to one of the receptionists, Isobelle, who was from Savoy in France, blonde, aged about thirty. She had come to

Guadeloupe seven years ago with her boyfriend, whose parents had come from the island. 'I didn't understand their accent at first and there was some resentment. "Why are you here, taking our jobs?"'

She was still careful when dealing with the locals. 'They are slow people, but you have to be careful not to boss them around. You have to ask them to do things in the right way.'

I went over to a group of French guests, and got talking to them in my halting French, when one of them broke into fluent English, with a Welsh accent. His name was Davies, so I said snap. He turned out to be a proper living speaking Frenchman, Didier Davies. His father was a Welsh soldier who married a French girl at the end of the last war. Didier was born in Wales, but his parents returned to France when he was aged two and he's lived there ever since. He is a French citizen, has a wife who speaks no English, but he has cousins in Wales whom he visits, which keeps up his Welsh-accented English. I asked who he supports in international matches. 'If it's France versus England, I support France. If it's France versus Wales, or England versus Wales, I always support Wales.'

He and his wife have a small hotel in Calais and take their holidays each year in January, usually to Mauritius, which they love. They have tried the Seychelles, but didn't like it. This was their first holiday in the French West Indies. 'Yeah, I love it, but the traffic is amazing. Never expected that.'

How about *les vendeuses de la plage*? Had he come across them in France? 'Not near where I live. They'd bloody freeze to death if they tried it on the beach at Calais.'

I then talked to another receptionist, Joel, rather serious, with rimless spectacles. At all hotel parties, if stuck for conversation, always find a member of the management staff. They have to talk to you. They might even get you another drink, or order a waiter, as they consider themselves officer class.

Joel was born in Paris of black West Indian parents, immigrants from Guadeloupe. He was brought up in an immigrant ghetto, but doesn't think it was anything like Brixton, and he didn't feel at all prejudiced against while growing up.

'It was only after I had left university I felt any prejudice. I found it very hard to get a decent job. I wanted to go into the aircraft industry, but I ended up selling clothes. I had to put up with racist insults all the time. It was very difficult. I began to feel like a foreigner in France, even though I had been born and brought up there. French people have an image of all West Indians being lazy, slow, taking their time.

'Ten years ago I decided to come here. My parents followed me a year later, but I came back first. They had always intended to, but didn't expect me to do the same.

'I feel at home here. I won't go back to France. I speak French to French guests, but with my friends I speak French Creole.'

Apart from English, he can also speak German, Spanish, some Russian and was learning Portuguese in his spare time. Fidel, the manager, had encouraged him to learn Portuguese, then he might use his contacts to get him a job in a hotel in Brazil.

I asked what he thought of the other French West Indian islands. 'In Martinique, they think they are more French than the French. That's their image of themselves. And they think people in Guadeloupe are primitive. That was probably true a few years ago, but not any more. St Barts is just a white island. St Martin is American. They have lost their culture. Guadeloupe still has its own culture.'

Walking round the harbour one morning at St François, watching all the little boats setting off for offshore islands, I decided I'd do the same. But which island? The choice seemed to be between Marie Galante, Les Saintes and Désirade, all about five to ten miles away.

I quite fancied Marie Galante. It's named after Columbus's boat, the one he sailed in on his second voyage, the *Santa Maria* having gone down on his first voyage. It was the sort of place I would definitely have gone to while researching Columbus. It could be interesting, historically. Then a French couple in the hotel said that Les Saintes, a little cluster of islets, were the prettiest. So, that might make the nicest trip. Then a waiter told me that Désirade was where Thierry Henry, now an Arsenal star, had originally come from. Well, that settled it.

As a football fan, I had noticed how the majority of France's 1998 World Cup stars were not in fact French. Most were from immigrant families, originally from North Africa, like Zidane, or Central Africa, like Desailly, or the French West Indies, like

Thurman and Henry, both of whose families came from Guadeloupe.

Guadeloupe doesn't have a professional football league, which
must be a handicap for any aspiring players. Even worse, if you
come from a titchy island like Désirade, cut off from everywhere.
So I came back to the hotel and told my wife I had booked two
tickets for the next day. They happened to be on special offer –
100 francs each, reduced from the normal 150 francs. I soon
discovered why.

The boat was old and battered and appeared to have been a
fishing boat at one time. It was almost empty – just twenty on
board out of a capacity of 110 – which indicated that other people
had done better research than me. The minute we left the shoreline
of Guadeloupe, the waves were enormous. A young woman beside
me was soon clutching her stomach and being violently sick.

My wife accused me of having gone for the special offer and I
said no, honestly, it's the Thierry Henry connection that interested
me. In that case why hadn't I got on a better boat? Two others,
much more modern, were soon whizzing past, riding high over
the waves.

We got there in just under an hour, landing at the only harbour,
Grande Anse. It reminded me of a Scottish island, in the Outer
Hebrides, especially some nasty concrete-looking houses by the
quayside. There were some older, more attractive if rather battered
wooden houses, all of them with double shutters, heavy doors,
indicating this was an island with strong winds, probably strong
characters, though most of them had no doubt long since left.
There was an air of abandonment and isolation, a feeling that the
locals, if any, were all inside, watching or crouching, again very
like a remote Scottish island. The main difference was the occasional palm tree and the 80 degrees. You rarely get that in Scotland.

The day was hot, but with an overcast Scottish sky and a fresh
breeze. Which was good. Our plan was to walk the island, end to
end. Before setting off, I tried to buy a map, but had to make do
with a postcard of the island.

Désirade is some eight miles long, with a population of 1,600.
It was the first part of Guadeloupe that Columbus spotted, on 3
November 1493, on his second voyage. This second voyage was a
magnificent affair, compared with his first speculative trip. First

time, he'd had only three little boats and ninety men, going off into the totally unknown. On the second, he had a veritable fleet: seventeen ships, 1,200 men, all heading into the relatively known, and all hoping to make their fortunes.

When they landed on Guadeloupe itself, so it was recorded, 'they took 12 very beautiful and very fat women aged between 15 and 16, together with two boys of the same age.' They didn't land on Désirade, just spotted it in passing, naming it because it looked desirable – but not desirable enough to land on. Probably very wise. More chance of fat women on lush Guadeloupe than on wild and scrubby little Désirade.

As we walked along the coastal road, the heavens opened and we were soon soaked through. A bit annoying, in case we found anywhere half decent to have lunch, but not unpleasant. Getting wet in the Caribbean is not like getting wet in Scotland. We passed a couple of nice-looking beaches with picnic tables, as if expecting tourists, but they were empty. The road itself was deserted, except for a few cyclists, tourists who had hired bikes for the day. One of them was the girl who had been sick on the boat. She gave a faint wave as she cycled past.

We came to some holiday homes, little bungalows, all empty, with the owners' names written in chalk outside, all of them French names. I wondered if they were people from Guadeloupe who had holiday houses here, to get away from the mad traffic, or even from French France, people who wanted to get away from everything.

I'd been given the name of a café at the end of the island, but when we got there we were told it had closed four years ago. We did find another place, above a little beach, which was very modern with a newly tiled floor, plastic-type bar, all clean and tidy, and all totally empty. A languid young man of around thirty eventually appeared, turned on a boogie box on the bar at top volume, then disappeared. On his return, I asked if he could turn it down a bit. After all, we were the only guests. He asked if we had booked. Seemed a dopey question in an empty restaurant, on an empty island, which appeared as if it always had been and always would be empty. Perhaps in his mind he was expecting a Jumbo-load of Japanese tourists to descend from the sky.

I ordered some drinks and the menu and we sat in emptiness

looking out at the sea and the beach below. The rain started again and this time it turned into a mini-hurricane. The barman's wife flew out from wherever she had been hiding and they both started banging down the hatches, closing windows, moving awnings, but despite their efforts, the whole floor was soon swimming in rainwater. Good job it was tiled.

Behind the woman, while she rushed about, was a toddler of about two years old whom she shouted at to keep out of the way. He was called Kevin. When she'd settled the shutters and came to take our order I asked if he was named after Kevin Keegan. Who? She'd never heard of him. Kevin Costner, I said, the American film star? No, not heard of him either. She just liked the name.

They had run out of bread, she said, which made my wife groan, as she is a bread freak, and had expected at least decent home-made bread on a French island, however isolated. There was only one thing she could offer, fish, and only one way she cooked it, which was grilled. We said fine. One does like to help. Hmm, she said, but it will take some time. Two customers, one simple dish, how long? Half an hour, perhaps.

While we waited, we went down on to the beach, as the storm had now blown away, and had a swim. The waves were quite big, so I worried about my ears getting bunged up again, not wanting to put Dr Bunbury's claim about French hospitals to the test. The swim was exciting and exhilarating, giving me a hunger for my grilled fish. Which turned out to be horrible. I pride myself on finishing everything, however horrible, but I just couldn't manage it, even eating very very slowly.

While we struggled with the fish, the café remained totally empty, no sudden coach parties, except for a local man aged about forty who arrived and sat at the bar, drinking beer and chatting to the barman and his wife.

When they had disappeared, to wash up or recycle my horrible fish, I asked the man if he was from Désirade. Thankfully not, he said. He was from Guadeloupe, posted here to work as a nurse. What's it like then, living on Désirade? He thought for a long time. 'Like living on Alcatraz.'

The rain came on again, lashing down all the way back to Grande Anse where we caught the boat back to civilisation, to *vendeuses de la plage*, our luxury hotel, chic French guests, gourmet cuisine. The image of a Caribbean island, any Caribbean island, is of blue skies, perfect weather. That's what most people think, sitting at home in Europe. It's good now and again to experience a bit of reality.

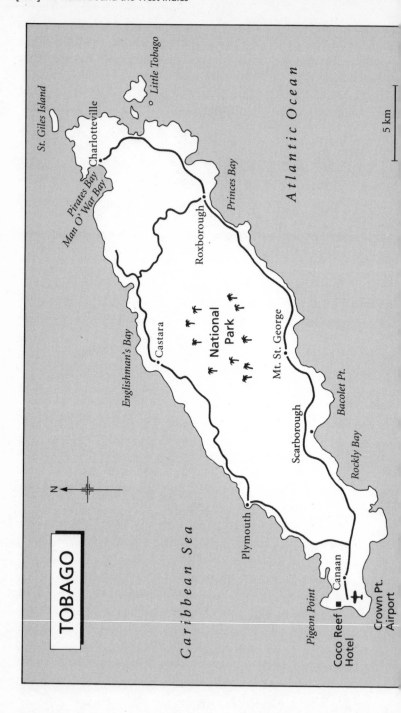

CHAPTER FIVE

Tobago

I never did discover where on Désirade Thierry Henry's family had come from, but I had no problem on Tobago with Dwight Yorke, Manchester United's star striker. Every Tobagonian can point his birth house out to you, which is a bit hard on his mother, who still lives there. And almost every person boasts they were at school with him, which must mean class sizes of about 500.

Dwight was born in Canaan, not far from the airport. As a poor boy, from a poor family, unable to travel far, he himself never realised on what a beautiful island he had been born.

It's a great shame, for the Tobago tourist people, that the area round the airport is so boring. At first glance, it all seems so dry and dusty, concrety and tatty. The lush parts, with the perfect beaches and tropical rainforests are to the north.

My expectations of Tobago were high because in my mind I had seen it as a completely natural, bijou little island, just twenty-seven miles long by eight across, with a population under 50,000, unlike big brother Trinidad next door, some twenty-one miles away, which has 1.3 million and is fairly industrial.

I was with my wife again and we had booked a hotel, Coco Reef, almost beside the airport, which is always a worry, as I am obsessed by noise, but we had been told it was the best on the island. The short drive to it was most unpleasant: lots of nasty concrete cheapo eating places and guest houses, some unmade pavements, quite a lot of litter, little sign of the loveliness of a tropical island.

A rep from our travel firm, who had kindly picked us up herself, said our room wasn't quite ready, as we had arrived early in the morning, so she was going to take us for a short drive to, short pause, the Famous Pigeon Point. I think the response expected was Wow. I couldn't quite manage that, but I did say, oh really. I enquired about the nature of the Famous Pigeon's fame, after which the point had presumably been named. A talking pigeon, a pigeon that had released a rap record or had perhaps starred in a Disney film? No, she said, it's just Pigeon Point, but it is very famous.

All countries, all islands, all towns of almost any size get it into their head that some location, some place, some person has achieved international fame, just because everyone in their village has heard of them. The Yanks are of course masters of this self-deception, being assured of their own worldwide fame in every known field.

Pigeon Point is a spit of land, a bit scruffy at first, then once through a barrier, where you have to pay, it is a bit prettier, in a metropolitan park sort of way. We got out, walked to a bar which reminded me of Butlin's, had a beer, which was very expensive, looked at what seemed a fairly nice but ordinary stretch of beach. If this is the famous but of Tobago, what can the un-famous bits look like?

We also did a short drive and quick look round Scarborough, the capital of Tobago. At first sight, another awful disappointment, with nothing apparently to commend it, not in the way of architecture or situation. The harbour, such as it was, looked scruffy, cut off from the town, with a scraggy bit of beach where no one would ever want to swim, surrounded by half-built roads. It's on the Atlantic side, which is strange. I couldn't think of another capital of a West Indian island which is on the rough Atlantic side.

My wife disliked the hotel straight away. It was on a scruffy bit of the airport road, so that was off-putting, but once through the gates, I thought the gardens were most attractive. At the imposing front entrance was parked a white Rolls-Royce which made me smile but Margaret curled her lip. Inside, the main entrance hall was enormous and rather dramatic. You look right through at the turquoise sea, as if nature had done the framing. It was the hotel's beach she really disliked – just because it was man-made. I said you couldn't have known it was man-made unless you had been told. Just look at the lovely white sand and all those marvellous palm trees, right on the beach. She said she could. Look at those ugly rocks. They had quarried out hundreds of tons of black volcanic stone and dumped them like an artificial barrier reef, about a hundred yards offshore, so that the new beach was on a lagoon, perfect for children or people learning to windsail. Yes, but horrid for swimming in, she said, taking one look at it. I won't be swimming there. I'll swim in the open sea. And how are you going to get there? She looked down the beach and could see that our hotel was totally enclosed – hence the reason it calls itself a resort. You couldn't actually get out on either side without swimming through the lagoon.

But she did admit our room was amazing – Sunset Villa, their best suite. There had been some mix-up, so I learned later. There wasn't a room for us as the hotel was full, in fact over-booked, but after one of the bosses of Elegant Resorts in Chester got on the blower, they moved us into the best apartment, the only one free. I use free in the vacant sense. At the height of the season, the charges are $2,000 a night. I reckon it must be the most expensive hotel suite in the Caribbean, if not the world. I take that back. There's bound to be one more expensive in Texas. Sylvester Stallone had recently stayed there, so had Luciano Pavarotti, several Prime Ministers and Presidents.

It does have total seclusion, being on its own rocky point, at the far end of the hotel, surrounded on all sides by its own gardens and sun decks. We loved it, but then we should have done, at that price, with those amenities. Two marble bathrooms, two televisions, endless phones, full working kitchen, fridge, bar, massive bedroom, massive sitting room, plus three gardens around us, a 100-foot-long sun deck all to ourselves, where we could look straight down at the fish swimming, out to sea, back to the hotel's artificial beach, or across to the famous Pigeon Point. Seeing everything, but not being seen or overlooked. Just what superstars always want.

When we were invited to dine with the managing director, John Jefferis, I was delighted. I wanted to hear how he had created the hotel, and the beach, what his problems were, what his aims were now. His visiting card, which had been sent to us, described him as owner. You don't meet many owners, living on site, not in big hotels. Coco Reef, with 140 rooms, is big for the Caribbean. Owners tend to be more outspoken, have more character, or allow more of their character to emerge, compared with hired-hand, rotating managers. Mr Jefferis was also the current President of the Caribbean Hotels Association, a big cheese amongst his peers. So someone worth seeing.

He said he would meet us first upstairs in the bar where we found a waiter already fussing over a bottle of champagne in a bucket and three glasses, already iced. Oh no. Neither of us drinks champagne, never liked the stuff, regardless of how good it is. Give me plonk any time.

Mr Jefferis arrived limping, his foot all bandaged. He'd injured it while playing squash, at which he is hot stuff, having captained the Bermuda team which won the Caribbean Squash Championship held in Barbados in 1983. He looked fit and tough, despite the limp, aged in his mid forties, not a person to be messed around, someone who speaks his mind, knows his worth, knows his power. He was casually dressed in a polo shirt and slacks, so that was a good sign. Swiss-trained managers always wear dark suits.

So I said, actually, I'd prefer some ordinary wine to the champagne, if that's all right. No problem, said Mr Jefferis, calling the waiter to take it away, then he ordered the wine list and a beer for himself.

He comes from Bermuda where his father was a bus driver. He graduated in business studies at Birmingham University in England, did a further course at Cornell in the USA, before going into hotels. From hotel managing, he moved on to owning a small hotel, then a bigger one, then another, then sold up, looking for a new opportunity, elsewhere in the Caribbean. Do you count Bermuda as Caribbean? They do, and the Caribbean Tourist Board does, and the Caribbean Hotels Association does, but in my mind, despite never having been there, I don't think of Bermuda as Caribbean. More mid-Atlantic, sort of offshore USA, but I didn't say all that, not wanting to slow down the saga.

'I wanted to build a hotel in an undeveloped place, yet one which could grow its own food. Bermuda is developed, but we don't grow our food. It didn't matter about the people's lack of experience in hotel work, or how unsophisticated they were, but they had to be the right sort of people. You can build a hotel anywhere these days, anywhere in the world, but if you haven't got the right sort of people working in it, it won't work. All I really wanted them to do was smile.'

He looked around at other islands and in 1990 arrived in Tobago. Along with government support, he bought an old hotel, Crown Reef, which had been closed for five years. He knocked it down in order to start again, deciding the site had potential, even though it didn't have a beach and was on a nasty road.

He got the nasty road moved back and now they have the lush gardens and a long driveway in front of the hotel. I found this hard to comprehend. How could a foreigner get all the right permissions and agreements to move a main road? He shrugged. Took a long time, lots of meetings, lots of arrangements, but it was done. The main road was moved. As for the beach, all that took was money and vision.

'There was no beach, just pure black rock, which had to go. We brought in 10,000 tons of sand from Guyana. I was told palm trees would never grow, I was mad, because the base of the beach was rock, but I brought in 200 palm trees, all well established, and all of them grew. I didn't lose one.'

Once they were ready to open, they advertised for staff. There were riots as people queued overnight. I later saw cuttings from the local papers, showing the fighting as people broke down a wire fence to be first in the queue.

'I told them all, as I still tell them, that you are actors and actresses – and this is your stage setting, which I have created, on which you will perform. I don't want to know about your problems at home, your family and domestic worries. When you put on the costumes, which I will provide for you, and get on that stage – you perform. You act, you smile, you do exactly what the script and what the job demands. Is that clear?'

If not, what? Well, they don't last long, that was also clear, though he says he has got an excellent staff, who have done him proud. I had heard, though, that he has been known personally to slap a few who step out of line – whether staff or guests.

'This very evening, I did reprimand a guest. He was only about ten, and no one else was watching, I made sure of that. I was walking behind him, down a corridor, and I saw him deliberately ripping the leaves off a plant. So I tapped him. Not very hard, just a tap, so he knew what he was doing wrong. I blame the parents, not him, for allowing that sort of behaviour.'

The opening year was a disaster. 'Nobody came. I just hadn't put enough energy into marketing and publicity. I thought as I'd performed such miracles, and the hotel was so beautiful, people would come – but they have to know you exist. We lost a lot of money. My partners were very worried.

'But now we are a huge success: all 140 rooms and suites are full. We're turning people away. I bought out my partners, so I am the sole owner. The total cost was £22 million. I borrowed a lot from the bank, but they'll get it back. Last week I was offered £50 million, but I'm not selling. A hundred million, well that might be hard to refuse...'

So what's next? Having walked on the water, or at least moved the water around, what are the new challenges?

His immediate object was to a build a bridge across to his breakwater. I had seen him earlier that day, not knowing who he was, limping around at the end of the beach, directing various labourers and carpenters building some steps, taking the odd swing of the pick himself. I thought it a bit strange, for a white bloke of his age, with an injured leg, swinging a pick.

I asked about the white Rolls-Royce. From observation, it would seem to be the most photographed object in the hotel, if not the whole island, yet I hadn't seen it move. Did it really work or was it just a gimmick? He was rather upset at the suggestion, denying it didn't work.

'Of course it works. I wouldn't have bought it otherwise. I bought it to take guests back and forward to the airport. It's a 1957 Rolls and once belonged to Errol Flynn. I bought it in California. It's just that, er, it's not working at this moment. We're waiting for a part, but it will be soon...'

Once he's got Coco Reef into its final shape, he'll look for another grand project. 'I have been offered a site in St Lucia to develop, on Cap Estat. Do you know it?'

Don't do it, John, I said. You'll have all the environmentalists, artists and Nobel prize winners after you. He just smiled. Someone who can take on governments and get them to move their roads can presumably deal with most factions. At Coco Reef he has made a big point of using environmentally sensitive materials and followed historical designs in the architecture.

'Then I am also interested in a development in Cuba. That could be very exciting.'

But why go through it all again? You've done it once, spending four years creating this. You'll just be repeating yourself, even if the scale is bigger, the location different. You must be worth a bob or two by now.

'Yes, but I started from nothing. If I'd been born into a wealthy family, I'd be much further ahead by now. I'd have a chain of hotels by now, if I'd had more capital earlier on.'

Sad in a way, that he would appear to be so interested in money.

'I have to be. I've been married five times. Each year I have to find around $1 million in alimony.'

Good gracious, I said. What made you do it?

'Hormones,' he replied.

Margaret had packed up by now and gone to bed, so we were left, man to man, finishing off the second bottle of Fleurie.

I asked what sort of women they were, I mean where did they all come from? They included a Cuban, American, Trinidadian, a Bermudian and I can't remember the other. It also turned out he has seven children. He is close to them all, the children and the wives. In fact he had stayed with one the previous week while seeing a surgeon in Florida about his leg.

'None of them has married again,' he said, 'which is interesting.'

Because you were such a special person they could never find anyone as wonderful again? Or because you were so awful they've had men up to here for ever?

'Probably more like the latter.' He smiled.

I woke Margaret up when I got back to our villa. I said guess what, he's paying $1 million a year to five ex-wives, isn't that an incredible amount.

'Good,' she said, turning over and going to sleep.

I then went to see two recent expat arrivals, Chris James and James Vaughan. Hard to believe, as they sat in the sun by their own pool, the palm trees waving, that just five years ago, Chris and Jim had been slogging away with British Gas in the West Country. You don't somehow think of gas-fitting as, well, a fitting preparation for running a fashionable eating place in the Caribbean.

Chris is thirty-seven, Jim twenty-nine, and they'd spent most of their working lives with British Gas. Jim was more on the accounts side, but Chris had gone on a course in Stoke to become a proper gas engineer. While there, he first worked evenings in a nightclub and found he loved it. Jim in his spare time had also done a bit of bar work. But their real careers, so it seemed to both of them, would always be in gas.

'Five years ago,' said Jim, 'we heard about these redundancies coming. About 25,000 might be paid off. Chris said why don't we take this chance, take the money and go off together to the sun for a new life.

'I was a bit sceptical, as I'd been thinking in terms of a career in gas, but Chris was getting more and more fed up, wanting to go off to the sun. He'd spent some time as a child in Kenya and loved it. I think that was a factor.'

They sold their respective flats, their cars, added up their redundancy payments and found they had a total capital of some £150,000. Not much on which to start a new business in the UK. But enough, they thought, to open a nightclub in the West Indies. That was their fantasy.

'We got a LIAT round-the-islands plane ticket and looked at eight different islands: Martinique, Guadeloupe, St Lucia, Barbados, Grenada, Antigua, Trinidad and here. Some of the little planes we went in were dead scary. I remember one with a canvas door which flapped and another where the pilot wasn't listening to his radio messages because he had his Walkman on.

'We wanted the least-developed island with the least crime. In Tobago we got lost in the rainforest, but this poor old bloke, living in a shack, was fantastic. He did everything to help us. In other islands, we had been hassled a bit. So we thought that's it, we'll stay in Tobago.'

Work permits and suchlike took a long time, and the red tape was confusing and time-consuming, but they bought a plot of land and started to build their nightclub – only to find that it was better to build rooms.

'The government has a scheme whereby if you create at least ten new rooms for tourists, you don't pay tax for five years. So we decided to start with some little villas, which Chris designed, plus a restaurant and swimming pool.

'We opened on 1 April 1995. I told the local paper we got the building wood from the wreck of the HMS *Bonkers* which had sailed from Plymouth, and that's how we got our name. They printed it. I don't think they have the concept of April Fool's Day over here...'

It was an instant success. They haven't had to borrow a penny and now have a staff of twenty-one. They've even had takeover offers. Profits have been ploughed back to buy more land. Next stage is to build a nightclub – to be called Bonkers Too.

'The real reason for the name was that everybody we knew at home in Bath and Bristol said we were bonkers.'

They admit it's been hard work, working seven days a week since they arrived. Chris did the cooking for the first six months. They still hadn't built a proper house for themselves, sharing a small, wooden, one-room cabana between them.

'My dad came out on a visit,' says Jim. 'He said where's my son? It wasn't just the tan – I'd lost so much weight.'

Getting supplies is a problem. Things like toilet rolls take for ever to arrive. 'What would be a real godsend would be a Sainsbury's down the road,' said Chris.

Jim misses British sport and British newspapers. 'But that's about all. Oh, Bass. I'd give a lot for a good pint of Bass...'

I had booked lunch at the Black Crab restaurant which Alison Sardinha runs with her husband Ken. She gave me a smacking kiss when I walked in, though I had never met her before.

'Ooh, you smell nice. I like a man who smells nice. In fact you smell like a baby...'

Actually, I said, I've had a bit too much sun since I arrived and I've been using Johnson's baby lotion.

'I knew it,' she said, clapping her hands and dancing round.

She had to go off and see to the kitchen, but Ken came out and sat down with me. From time to time, she rushed back to take over the conversation.

They are both in their sixties. Ken is thin and grey-bearded and rather studious, while Alison is small and exuberant. Both are from Tobago, from fairly middle-class families. Alison left at nineteen to study at the Pratt Institute in New York.

'I cried buckets when I left,' said Alison. 'On the plane, the air hostess tried to cheer me up by saying "I like your shoes." What she didn't know was that I was crying because I'd left Ken behind.

I'd met him a few months earlier, but all we'd done so far was kiss. I thought, now I'll never see him again.'

Not long afterwards Ken also came to study in New York. Alison graduated in design and Ken became an engineer. They married and had four children. They always planned to return, once they were trained, but time went on and they spent sixteen years in New York, returning to Tobago in 1977. 'I felt it was time I had a few sea baths again,' said Alison.

Ken got a job as an engineer on a building project while Alison opened a clothes shop in Scarborough. The shop lease was coming up, so she either had to pack up her shop, or buy the premises. They decided to buy the premises and open a restaurant – with Ken at first doing the cooking. 'Oh, he could always cook sweet,' said Alison, giving Ken a cuddle.

It's doing well, and my lunch was excellent, but they see it as much as a social centre, a focal point for their neighbourhood friends and all the worthy causes Ken supports.

On their return, they made a vow to themselves not to compare and contrast, not to go around saying, 'When I was in New York,' or 'In America they do it this way.'

Naturally, they do see differences, after so long away, but keep quiet about them. 'It's unfair to compare places, but life in Tobago is slower and predictable. America is a great place for equalising opportunity. If you were aged twenty-four or thirty-four in Tobago, your chances of getting an education would be limited. In New York, you can go to college at any age, any time of the day or week. It's all there for you. All you have to do is be willing to apply yourself. An education is never a handicap to anyone.

'We enjoyed the West Indian community in Brooklyn. You could get everything we have here – and all the year round.'

Their four children are now aged between twenty-one and thirty-one. Only one so far, the oldest, is in Tobago; the others stayed in the USA. 'They are citizens of the world – and the world is a shrinking place. They should be free to go anywhere, live anywhere, able to survive anywhere. People are people, everywhere. It doesn't really take a lot to be satisfied, as long as people count their blessings.'

In the restaurant, I was introduced to a woman who arrived for a late lunch – very impressive and attractive in a black suit, white blouse and fashionably close-cropped hair, aged about forty.

She was Deborah Moore-Miggins, LLB (Hons), LLM, LEC, Notary Public and Attorney at Law. So her card said, when she gave me one. I could see by her appearance she probably had a pretty high-powered job, but I couldn't have told that, unlike Ken and Alison, her background was working class.

Her father was a truck driver and she got her education by winning lots of scholarships, going from school in Tobago to the University of the West Indies in Trinidad to read law. She went on to Canada to do her Masters at York University, before being called to the Bar. She worked in the Caricom Secretariat in New York as a legal officer, got married, then decided she wanted to come home to Tobago.

'I set up on my own in 1983, which was stupid. I was inexperienced and made mistakes. I was young and green and lost cases. I didn't understand things like income tax. I left all the financial side of the office to an accountant, and that was a mistake as well. But anyway after a year or so, I soon learned and improved.'

Today she has a thriving practice, in partnership with another lawyer, plus two secretaries and a clerk.

Her double-barrelled surname is made up of Moore, her maiden name, and Miggins, her married name. 'My husband went to Sandhurst; now he's a fisherman. Turns out that's what he really wanted to do in life. Oh yes, we're still married.' They have two children aged fifteen and eleven who go to local school.

She is also a well-known local politician. In 1995 she was appointed a senator, joining the upper house in the Trinidad and Tobago parliament, but she resigned in 1996.

'It was mainly because the party which had nominated me as a senator expected me to vote in a certain way. I disagreed fundamentally with their mindset. When I was told to vote against a certain motion, I refused. That's when I resigned.'

She then stood for the Tobago House of Assembly, where members are elected by the populace. She won a seat, but as an Independent.

'It was my husband who suggested I should stand as an Independent. He was not impressed by the way things were being done in my old party. If you are in one party, you have to rant and rave against members of the other party. That's politics. I couldn't do that. As a lawyer, I have clients from all kinds of lives. Anyway, I know almost everybody, so it's hard to attack people. Except of course the male hierarchy in both the main parties. Some are deadbeats. I despair so much about my country. There is no structure, no plans for the future. Look at tourism, they just don't know what they are doing. It causes me such pain. It's helping my clients as a lawyer, that's what really keeps me going.'

Since arriving in Tobago, I'd heard some talk of the island becoming independent from Trinidad. As a politician, did she have a view?

'Financially, we gain by the union. We have had a lot of money for our roads. Trinidad is wealthier than we are, with all the oil money. But because we rely on them so much, we tend to blame them when things aren't so good – instead of ourselves. Perhaps we should do it all for ourselves.'

Her partner in her law firm is female. Was it a sign that women were coming to the fore generally in Tobago?

'I think it is happening all over the West Indies. I don't know about elsewhere. Men are losing their will to strive, as women acquire more power and position. Now I think that's good of course, that women are coming into their own at last, but what happens with men is that they give up, they lose their self-esteem. If a woman fails or makes mistakes or doesn't get promotion, she doesn't give up, she doesn't think that's it, I'm not trying any more. She can accept criticism – and will try harder. Men seem to lose their self-esteem. There should of course be a balance. We want women and men to be equal, with equal opportunities.'

I asked if she ever thought of going back to North America, or Britain, somewhere bigger, with more opportunities.

'I'm sometimes surprised I've stayed here so long. Aries women are restless. I loved the USA. There are so many things I could do if I lived in New York.'

Such as?

'Well, at this moment I've been thinking I would like to do some classes in interior design. I'd also like to know more about taxes. In New York I could go to evening classes for them, at a time that suited me, even at ten at night. Here, we do have classes, but they finish at five in the evening. I can't get to them, can I, not when I'm working so hard...'

She is in fact now going back to the USA, having been accepted at Harvard to do a Masters. 'All I need now is the funding.'

Tobago does have one new and surprising institution, offering local people the sort of training you would expect in a big city rather than a little rural country of just 50,000 people. Tobago now has its own Hotel School.

It isn't quite called that – the official title is more of a mouthful: The Tobago Campus of the Trinidad and Tobago Hospitality and Tourism Institute. Its purpose is to train people for jobs in the hotel and tourist trade, plus basic French, German and Spanish.

The director is Agnes Webbe, a formidable-looking Trinidadian woman in her late fifties. On her wall was a framed print of a bridge over the river in Shrewsbury, England, one of the many places she lived in during her years in England.

'I left Trinidad in 1960, when I was nineteen, on a boat called the *Venezuela*. It was August but my first impression was that it was bloody cold. My sister met me and I went to stay with her in a flat she had in Russell Square. I did a three-year diploma in business management at North London Poly, which of course is now a university. My first job was at Guy's Hospital, as an assistant superintendent, then I went back to do some studying.'

She got married to a fellow West Indian, Howard, originally from Nevis, whom she met in London. He was serving in the British army. She moved with him for a while to Berlin and then to Essex. They have two daughters, one born in Berlin and one in Essex. After some more studying, and more qualifications, she became a Senior Lecturer in Food Technology and Tourism at Birmingham. It was a good job, with a decent salary, and she was able to send both her daughters, Sarah and Trisha, to Millfield School, about the most expensive boarding school in England.

'They chose it. We took them round various schools, such as Benenden. They liked Millfield best. It seemed very open, with good sports facilities. They were about the only West Indians in the school at the time, but there were a few Nigerians.'

In 1991 she and Howard decided to return to the West Indies. He had left the army and was fed up with the cold weather. They moved to Trinidad first where Agnes got a government job, but didn't like it. 'I'd thought I was coming home to relax and retire, but found I was into a lot of politics.'

So she set up on her own, as a consultant, organising training programmes, till in 1997 she was asked to start up the hotel school in Tobago. It's a private enterprise scheme, backed by the Hotels Association, but with government support.

So far they had eighty students. Average age twenty-four. Around 40 per cent have already had some experience of hotel or tourism work, but have decided to improve their skills. Tuition, which goes up to degree level, has to be paid for, but most employers pay or give grants.

'I had hoped for 150 students in this first year, that was my target, but we should make that next year. I hadn't quite realised how new Tobago is to tourism. Tobagonians are very friendly, so that is a big plus, but they are also very comfortable with their existing way of life. Most own their own house, often one passed down to them, and they can get by with a few sheep and goats, a bit of fishing, growing vegetables in their own garden. The need to go out and work is not so great. Over in Trinidad, people need jobs to live. Here the culture is different. It's very African-centred. They keep their heritage alive with dances and festivals, songs and traditions.'

She misses the sorts of things from Britain many miss: punctuality, sense of order. 'People here wait to be told what to do. I've had to get used to that, though my whole way of life is English. I have had to adjust. My accent confused them all at first. They said I sounded weird. In Trinidad, when I first came back, I did sense some jealousy, people thinking, "Who do you think you are?" Here in Tobago it's been fine. I do miss the support systems I was used to, such as good hospitals. Here things are a bit, how shall I say it, more lackadaisical. I also miss things like *Yes, Minister* and *Mr Bean*.'

Unlike her husband, the Caribbean weather was not a reason for coming home. 'Oh no. I find it far too hot here.'

Her two daughters have elected to stay behind in England. 'When we decided to come back, we spoke to both of them, and they said they preferred to stay. They are both excellent young women. One is now training to be a solicitor and the other wants a business career. They're doing well for themselves. They each have a car and their own flat.'

Do they feel West Indian or British?

'I don't think either likes to be identified as West Indian; at least they don't seem to have any West Indian friends. I suppose they are British. They do come out. They like it for hols, and the weather, but I think they find things a bit disorderly here.'

I started my tour of Tobago at Scarborough, but didn't stay long, except to note a notice outside a fruit shop: 'Kids must go to school or you will loose out.' The spelling didn't worry me, as I can never spell that word either, but I wondered why a fruit shop should display such an exhortation.

On the way out of the town, I stopped to inspect the Tobago Museum, and add it to my collection. I never miss a museum, anywhere, on any topic, even if I give it only five minutes. As a collector of dopey things, I do enjoy anyone else's collections, the dopier the better. This was in a fine historic building, dating back to 1777, at Fort King George overlooking Scarborough with some panoramic sea views.

I skipped the usual stuff about Columbus, landing or not landing, seeing or not seeing. I went straight on to the colonial period. Every island has stirring accounts of battles between the Spanish, British, French and Dutch, but on this occasion the first leaflet I picked up didn't mess around with any rosy views of their colonial past. 'An infamous period of Western history – the annihilation of the aboriginals and the enslavement of Africans to foster European plantation economy.'

Tobago is one of the more consciously 'African' of the Caribbean islands. There is at present a growing movement to revive and revere their African connections, in festivals, music, food and crafts. Over on big brother Trinidad, the population is much more mixed: 40 per cent Indian, 40 per cent African, with Chinese and assorted Europeans making up the rest. In Tobago, almost the whole population is descended from African slaves.

One of the most interesting displays in the museum was a collection of West African costumes and furniture, with a list of African surnames and first names still in common use in Tobago – Quashie, Quamie, Quaccoo, Kwame. You rarely find such names in the rest of the West Indies as freed slaves usually took on the names of their plantation masters.

The museum had some fine collections, but had obviously been arranged by someone convinced the public was not to be trusted. On every table, every display, almost every inch of the museum, were fierce warnings: 'Don't Lean'; 'Don't Sit'; 'Don't Touch'. Unless of course they were a collection in themselves. Somebody somewhere is probably collecting warning notices.

Helene, our driver and tour leader, then headed across to the Caribbean coast at Castara Bay. Oh, if only we had not arrived in the south of the island, my first impressions would have been so much better. Once above Scarborough, it's all beautiful, whether inland in the rainforest or on the Caribbean coast. And all of it so empty and unspoiled.

Helene is English, married to Mike, a Tobagonian. She was brought up as an army brat, her phrase, daughter of a soldier, so they moved around a lot while young, and that was how she met Mike. He was then serving in the British army. We might meet him later, she said. We couldn't miss him. So she said.

Further up the coast we came to Englishman's Bay. I immediately decided I had to have a swim. No problem, said Helene. She'd wait. I said come on, have a swim as well, but she said no, she didn't swim. And she didn't like sunbathing either, not with her pale, very English complexion. She wouldn't even walk on the beach. Never liked the feel of sand in her feet. She'd just sit in the car. Foony woman, I thought.

Helene was of course working, taking us on an island tour, but I thought of all the other expats I have met who never seem to take advantage of the natural facilities which we passing tourists gobble up. They take them for granted, or ignore them, or, in some cases, actively dislike them. You wonder how they came to be there.

Margaret joined me in the swim. It was so perfect, the sand so pure, the water so fresh, none of that limpid lagoon feeling of our hotel. The beach itself was perfectly curved, perfectly framed with pretty rocks at either side like book-ends, placed there by God to complete the pretty picture.

She decided it was her favourite beach – not just in the Caribbean, but the whole wide world. Steady on, old girl.

Was it mine? I tried to get into my mind's eye a beach in the

Seychelles, which was equally remote and empty and divinely framed: Victorin beach on Fregate island. Pretty close.

We swam out and along the length of the beach, then walked back on the sand. We might even have held hands. We could see no one, observed no signs of modern life, no human developments. It was as if we were the first ever day-trippers in paradise.

Only when I got back along the beach, to where I had left my bag, did I realise we were not alone. There was a young woman under a mango tree, sitting at a primitive stall with some bottles. She was smiling and waving. A mirage, I thought, or I've stumbled into a television commercial.

My wife went back to join Helene in the car but I went over and bought a beer from the young woman. Rather expensive, but she had carted the beer from miles away. She said she lived in Castara, hitch-hiked here and back every day, with her food. Food? She showed me a little calor gas stove and a pot of soup she was making and patties she would be heating up, when the rush started. Rush? Well, later in the day there might be five or six people. She hoped to sell them a few beers and patties. She showed me a little concrete bunker, hidden under some bamboo, which her boyfriend had built for her. She locked it up at night with her heavier utensils, to save humping them home. Her stall was prettily and naturally decorated with palms leaves and bamboo.

I admired her enterprise, her skills, her determination. Dwight Yorke showed equal determination to succeed, but his field happened to be football, where success can earn you millions. Creating a beach stall on an empty beach would never make her rich, though her expenses must be few. Not quite. She showed me her licence badge. It costs 100 dollars and allows her to sell stuff on this beach.

Business might get better in the next year, she said. A new development had been agreed, inland, just behind the beach. It would bring more people on to the beach. But of course the developers might build their own beach bar. So she might not get any more customers. I said I was sure she would. She didn't look convinced.

I assured her there would be tourists who would prefer her pretty little home-made stall. Then she might make some proper money. Enough perhaps to do a course at the hotel school.

What? Where? It was her turn to throw question marks around. Hotel school? she asked. In Tobago? Oh yes, I said. I went to my bag and gave her a leaflet. I do like to help.

As we drove on down the coast, I thought of the dilemma created by all tourist development, everywhere. It does seem appalling that such a truly natural and perfect beach was going to be spoiled by some development. On the other hand, why be elitist? A perfect beach is there to be enjoyed, as long as it's not ruined. Nature belongs to all of us, should be open to all. It's surely good that the young woman with the stall would have a chance to make a decent living. Have what we all have. Aspire to what we all aspire to. Discuss.

The road up the coast was amazingly good, and even better inland, through the tropical rainforest. The verges were neatly cut like a municipal park. Oil money from Trinidad, said Helene.

At regular intervals along the empty roads were home-made painted notices, nailed up on trees: 'Almandoz for Forks'; 'Almandoz for Buckets'; 'Almandoz for Rubber Boots'; 'Almandoz for Tinners'. That last one foxed Helene for a while, till she realised it should have read Thinners, meaning paint thinners. Almandoz was a hardware shop in Scarborough. Seemed strange to me that he should bother to send someone out to the back of beyond to put up a load of home-made notices on empty roads.

We had lunch at the far end of the island at Speyside in Jemma's Bar, a little beachside restaurant which appeared to have been built out of a tree. It was surprisingly full, considering all the roads had been empty. A party of German tourists in a minibus had got there ahead of us. The meal was excellent, but there was no alcohol available. Jemma was a strict Seventh Day Adventist, said Helene, and won't serve alcohol, but she didn't mind customers bringing in their own beer.

I noticed a very tall West Indian bloke at another table, at least six feet five inches tall, in smart shorts and T-shirt, looking very relaxed, very smiley, very confident, speaking fluent German to the party of Germans.

'That's Mike,' said Helene. 'I told you you wouldn't miss him.'

Mike Grant left Tobago aged eleven in 1961, along with his mother and aunt, brothers, sisters and cousins. 'There was no father around. He left the scene when I was born. I never met him. My mother thought we would have a better life in England. We were British citizens, so we didn't need a passport.

'We sailed on the TN *Ascona*. I think it was a Spanish vessel; anyway all the crew spoke bloody Spanish. I couldn't understand them and they gave us funny food and wine with every meal. It was just plonk of course, though I didn't know what plonk was at the time.

'I loved the voyage, being a child. It was all an adventure, though I didn't like being put in a cabin with kids I didn't know. We were three weeks at sea altogether. In Guadeloupe the propeller fell off and we went into dry dock in Martinique.

'At Southampton we changed into long trousers and jumpers which my mother had brought with her. I remember putting my nose out of the porthole and feeling coldness – the first time I'd felt coldness in my life.

'We went to live in New Malden, in a semi which I think my aunt had bought. Her husband was a teacher. We all lived there, about nine of us. I got up the first morning and saw snow. We couldn't get outside, to the outside toilet, because there was snow behind the door. When we did get in, we found the toilet seat had frozen. My worst problem was chilblains on my toes. They gave me a headache for three months.

'I went to a local junior school where I was the only black boy and was very homesick. I did have one slight racial problem. It hadn't really bothered me at the time, but my mother, she was so perceptive, she got it out of me. Some boy had called me a name, so she marched me straight away down to the school and saw the headmaster. He warned all the kids. I had no more problems.'

At fifteen and a half Mike left school and became a boy cadet in the army. Over the next twenty-six and a half years he served all over Britain and in Germany, progressing from corporal, sergeant, staff sergeant, up to Warrant Officer Class One, the highest he could get.

'That was my career ambition, to make it to WO1. I was then recommended for a commission, to be an officer, partly I think because they were trying to get more black officers. I had all the qualifications, but it would have meant starting at the bottom again, as a junior officer. I'd have been fifty-five by the time I'd got anywhere. I thought I'll get out, when there's still time to have another life. But what else can I do?'

By this time he was married to Helene, daughter of a fellow soldier, with two young boys, Mark and Adam. They thought of going to Spain, as they wanted a warm climate, but worried about the language and education problems.

It had always been in the back of his mind to go back to Tobago one day. 'But it was Helene who said let's do it now, while the boys are still young, and get them into local schools.

'I'd not been in Tobago for thirty years. Yes, it had changed, but not a lot. I felt at home, straight away.'

But hadn't he changed, after a lifetime away? He'd struck me immediately as British, the moment he started talking, but from his relaxed, amused, casual manner I would never have thought he'd been a regular army sergeant for so many years.

'That's because in the army I adapted. I fitted in, to get promotion, but it never really suited me. The pace of life here is my pace of life. Anyway, Helene has enough energy for both of us.'

Together, they run a little tour firm, Elan Tours. Helene handles Brits mainly while Mike specialises in taking German tourists round the island. He had to learn German while serving in Germany. So thank you, British army. He was also doing some German teaching at Tobago's new hotel school.

'I've felt no resentment against me or jealousy since I've been back. After twenty-six years in the British army, I know when to bite my tongue, when to hold back. I never say, "This is the way we did things in England." That would be fatal.'

Their two sons, now teenagers, are settled at local schools, though it took a while to get them into schools of their choice. They hadn't realised there is such competition. One of the boys took a long time to settle and suffered a few racial remarks, just as Mike had done, all those years earlier.

'I never had any of those problems in the army; well, just from one person. I tend not to have problems. It's other people who have problems. That's my attitude to life. I'm also a grass-roots man. I like to start from the bottom, and work up.'

Their little travel firm is doing well, with enough work for both of them, but Mike is beginning to find it very tiring. 'My back aches after ten hours in the car or the minibus. And with talking to people all the time. I still enjoy it, but I feel trapped. I don't want to do it for ever. I fancy working in a hotel. It doesn't pay well, though I feel whoever employs me will make money.'

I told him what Deborah the lawyer had said about West Indian men – about them losing their self-esteem as the women take over. Was he aware of this?

'Yeah, I was surprised on my return to see how many women there were with good jobs. You see them walking down the street, looking gorgeous, all dressed up, taking their kids to school, then they're off in their cars to work in some bank, or some office. When it comes to HR, I think women are better than men.'

HR?

'Oh, that must be the influence of the USA. We're all picking up American ways now. Human Resources. Dealing with people. Women are good at all that. They can get on with people. Mind you, there are some ball-breakers, who are very powerful. Some of them even do lift weights. I think it would be a shame if women lose their womanness.

'I have seen local men who think if their women are doing it, there's no need for them to work so hard. Men do give up easily.

'But it's the modern world. Men's traditional jobs and roles have gone. There's no money in fishing any more, but they think, I'm not being a waiter, I'm not doing that sort of job. I'll go and dig potatoes instead. Not realising that nobody wants his potatoes any more. Men haven't got a grip yet.'

How about the other supposedly traditional activity of the West Indian male, fathering lots of children? Was it just the same as in his father's day?

'I think the arrival of Aids has done a lot to stop that. More men, when they get married today, do think that's it, no more women. But I suppose the attitude is still there.

'I had a boy of about sixteen helping me the other day on a tour. I told him to go across and tell some people something, and he wouldn't go. It was just a simple message, but he was too shy, too nervous. I said, "Be a man, go and do it." He said, "But I'm not a man." I said, "What are you then, a frog?"

'But I knew what was in his head. He didn't have the status of a man. He hadn't fathered any children, so he couldn't be a man.'

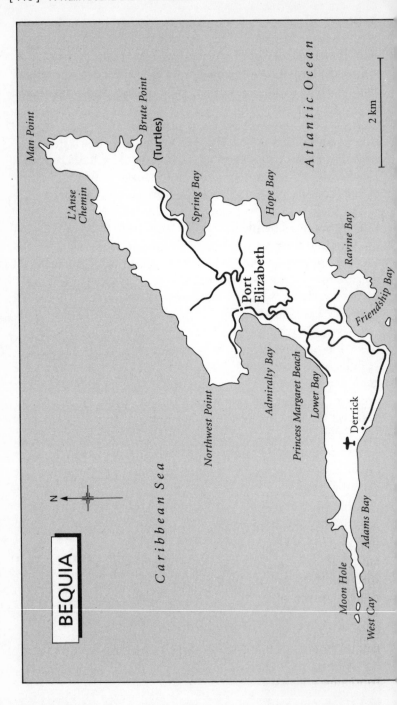

CHAPTER SIX

Bequia

I flew on Mustique Airways to Bequia, a charter flight on a small plane, but on board we got an in-flight magazine, which I always read, if just to spot the sponsored features and the cross-references between the ads and the places recommended. This was quite a good one, ninety pages, nicely printed, and it gave all the airline's services around St Vincent and the Grenadines. Lots of flights, by the look of it.

There was an introductory letter from Jonathan Palmer, chairman of Mustique Airways, welcoming us on board, telling us about some exciting joint venture with another Caribbean airline, Trans Island Air.

At the end of his letter was his photograph. I studied it carefully and thought, that's funny, from his side view, our pilot looks very like the chairman of the airline. Can this be possible? Does Lord King fly the occasional BA plane?

When we were getting off, I was able to see the pilot, front view. And yes, it was the said Mr Palmer.

'You are the chairman?' I said to him on the tarmac, the way people used to approach Nobby Ludd and get a prize for spotting him. (An ancient newspaper stunt, too ancient to explain now.)

'Yes, I love flying. And I can't stand being in the office all day long.'

I've had some interesting inter-island flights in the Caribbean. LIAT's their medium-sized planes shuttle back and forward all day between most of the English-speaking islands. The letters are said to stand for Luggage in Another Town, which of course is very unfair. A lot of the bigger islands, like Jamaica and Cuba, have their own lines, about which many unfair things have been said, some of them all too true. Then there are titchy airlines, flying titchy planes, like Mustique Airways, but trying to do regular services. Finally there are little charter companies.

On one little charter plane I had a pilot who insisted on having his door open all the way down the runway, saying he was too hot and wanted the breeze, but he'd close it when we got airborne. On a flight to Barbuda from Antigua the pilot turned out to have flown Diana, Princess of Wales and her two sons three times on her Caribbean holidays.

The worst was arriving in Tortola to catch a Virgin Islands Airways flight to Nevis, a service flight, not a charter, to find the airline had gone bust three days before. I was absolutely stuck, and had to get somewhere or other, by a certain time, so I hired my own plane and paid by Visa. The cost was only £80, which you could pay for a taxi to Gatwick.

Bequia, despite being an island only five miles long, has its own airport, exceedingly modern and smart, built out of the sea, an amazing piece of reclamation which must have cost millions. Some smart politicians must have got some smart grants from somewhere. And it was totally deserted. Not one other passenger. No sign of there having been any other passengers, or ever would be in the future, which naturally did not stop the bossy, fancily uniformed official from making us open all our bags. Would drug-runners really be bothered bringing in stuff by air, into a spanking new airport, when the seas are filled with yachts, scurrying all over the place, from island to island, carrying loads of dodgy stuff?

Bequia is a sailor's paradise. At one time, it was a centre for whaling but now it's mainly yachties, who harbour and replenish in Bequia's huge and safely enclosed harbour, in Admiralty Bay, some of whom arrive and never leave. Which is why the population is 5,000, quite large for a small island. Some of the older families are descendants of early Scottish and French settlers.

Bequia is the largest of the little Grenadine islands, which stretch for about sixty miles from St Vincent, its capital island, to Grenada. Mustique is one of Grenadines, hence the name of the little airline. But Bequia is a public as opposed to a private island, the Caribbean in miniature in some ways, with a range of beaches, harbours, restaurants, landscape. My wife fell in love with it almost from the moment we arrived, saying it was her best favourite so far, but

I started with grave reservations, mainly to do with where we were staying.

Plantation House, again booked blind, was said to be the best hotel on the island, certainly the most expensive, but it turned out to be not a patch on our Guadeloupe blind booking. It was almost as empty as the airport, which is not necessarily a bad sign, but a sign of something, as clearly a lot of money had been spent on the hotel and its handsome, colonial-type, main building. There were lawns filled with statues, nice villas in the grounds, two restaurants offering Italian and French food, lots of reception areas with expensive furniture and a big swimming pool. I could see the money. Where were the guests? Was it all a film set, or a cover for something?

In our little villa in the grounds, which was very pleasant, I found a welcome letter – badly printed and smudged, with no signature or name of any manager, done on a computer by someone who was clearly not very used to a computer. There was a blurry illustration at the top showing what appeared to be some sort of vehicle, possibly a hearse. Very cheering.

No bloody kettle in the room, or any tea- or coffee-making tackle. That does annoy me, being a true Brit, so I went back to reception to ask for one. They didn't have one, and could not understand why anyone should want one. I said there was a TV in the room, which I never ever want, can never understand anyone wanting, but come on, surely you must have had Brit visitors wanting tea over the years.

Then I asked for a map of Bequia. No, they didn't have one either. They did eventually find a free guide to Bequia, produced by the Bequia Tourist Committee. That's something, I thought, I'll be able to find someone to help me. It gave the name and phone number for the chairman of the Bequia Tourist Committee. I asked the reception girl if she could dial it for me, putting the call on my bill, of course.

She rang the number, and I could hear her starting to explain she had a British guest, then getting what sounded like a mouthful. 'Oh, sorry, were you asleep? Did I wake you up?' I could hear the phone being slammed down. It was about two o'clock. Must be siesta time in Bequia.

Over the next twenty-four hours, leaving constant messages, I still failed to make contact. 'We haven't got good relations with the tourist board,' said one of the reception staff, but wouldn't explain. I never discovered what it was, either the hotel had fallen out with them or the tourist board didn't really exist. Small islands can be full of mysteries and feuds which outsiders can never understand.

I don't know why you love this place so much, I moaned to my wife. How am I going to write anything about it if I can't find anyone to talk to? More fool you, she said. I'm on holiday. Why don't you try it for a change?

Next day I bought a book on Bequia, which looked quite good, and discovered the woman who wrote it lived locally and was running a restaurant and guest house. I thought, she's bound to be helpful. People who run restaurants welcome publicity. I rang her up, asked if she could spare a few moments for a chat. She gave me a rum punch, which was kind, then she said no, she didn't want to be interviewed or written about. And she wouldn't answer questions about her ex-husband. I hadn't realised she had been married to a well-known local politician. I said I wouldn't do that. I just wanted to chat about running a business in Bequia, that was all. 'Oh, I can't be bothered,' she said. Well, that was honest anyway.

We ate in the hotel the first two nights, in a posh dining room set for about forty people. Nobody else came. Yet the service was so slow. We were still waiting for our first course when an assistant manager walked past and said, 'How was it?' walking on before I could say, actually, it wasn't, we're still waiting.

I went first to explore Port Elizabeth, the little capital on Admiralty Bay. Right along its curving waterfront are scattered pretty restaurants and guest houses, little piers, quaint shops, ship's chandlers, little boat yards. You can walk the whole front, either on the beach, the waterfront or wooden duckboards.

There were about 200 yachts in the bay, plus a large ferry boat which had come in from St Vincent and a smallish cruise ship tied up at the main pier. Back and forth across the bay, little motor boats were zipping in and out, taking provisions and services to the yachts. Not just ice and water, but less obvious things like delicatessen goods.

As I sat and watched, I noticed two different firms of laundry boats, Daffodil Laundry and Lighthouse Laundry, each with their little fleet of motor dinghies, picking up dirty washing from the yachts then rushing back with the clean clothes. On the Daffodil Laundry boats, all the girls were in yellow uniform. Few people in Bequia, or anywhere in the West Indies, can ever see a daffodil growing. I wondered where the name came from. Then I wondered if the competition between them ever led to dirty tricks, carving each other up, outright warfare. How could it, in a sweet little harbour like this, with their sweet little boats? It could have been a Mediterranean setting, on a Greek island, perhaps, except it was all so clean, tidy, toy-townish.

When I got to the far end of the bay, I came across an Englishman; well, a white bloke with an English-looking T-shirt, who was mending a boat on a little slipway. He was tall and thin with a greying beard, his T-shirt rather tatty, his shorts worn, but he looked fit and lithe. He was more than willing to break off and have a chat, especially when I suggested a drink in a bar on one of the piers.

His name was Neil Saunders, aged fifty-four. In the late sixties he was a research scientist in England, working for Unilever, married to a statistician. When he'd got married, he had told her his real ambition in life was to sail round the world.

Eventually they did, buying a twenty-two foot sailing boat, and in 1971 they set off, going first to the Canary Isles, to La Gomera, then following Columbus's route across the Atlantic.

'I took my guitar and tape recorder and my wife took her sewing machine.'

What for?

'Well, she ran up courtesy flags on her sewing machine and I tape-recorded the noises.'

What noises?

'Oh, there are lots of noises at sea – the boat, the sea, the sails; you can tell a lot from noises. We woke one morning, came on deck to find there was no horizon, just a huge expanse of white. It was a massive merchant ship which we were about to crash into. My wife was naked at the time, so she rushed below.'

They got across safely in twenty-five days, landing first in Barbados, then moving round the islands till they got to Bequia.

'Everyone knows this harbour. There's nothing like it in the Caribbean. We'd bought the charts before we left England.

'When we arrived in the bay, a bloke came out to us in a dinghy and said there was a white man on the shore who wanted to talk to us. I said we don't know anybody here, and sent him away.

'Next morning, he came again, this time saying the white man wanted to buy our boat. He'd guessed from all our gear, the extra navigation stuff, the water containers, that we must have crossed the Atlantic. He wanted to buy our boat to sail on an inland lake in Peru.

'He offered me $7,000. I said we were actually going on, through the Panama Canal, round the world. But his price was good, so we told him that after we'd done the Panama Canal we'd come back and sell it to him. We shook hands on it. When we came back, we'd sold all our possessions along the way – to find the bloke had disappeared. We were stuck in Bequia. But we liked the island so much, we decided to stay.'

They both got teaching jobs, settled down in a house and had two children, a boy and girl, Ralph and Rachel, who went in due course to the local primary school.

'When Rachel was about seven, I was giving her some extra maths lessons to keep her up to scratch, though she was top of the class. She stopped and sucked in her teeth in the Vincentian way. "Choops", it's called. Don't know how you spell it. It's not a very polite thing to do, almost like saying to someone, "Fuck you." I told her off for doing it, and I tried to start again on the maths.

'Then she said, "Dadee, you wanna me bust me brain. Dat too much work, man."

'That was when I realised we had to make a decision if we wanted our children to reach college level. They wouldn't do it in Bequia. We couldn't afford to send them home to school, as we didn't have any money, so we decided we would all go home, give it ten years, till they had done A-levels.

'We both had to retrain in order to get jobs. I sold life insurance and my wife learned to be a computer analyst.

'After ten years, I said now it's time to go back to Bequia. My wife decided she wanted to stay in England. This was 1994. I've been here since, on my own. I don't know what we'll do. Separate probably, but nothing has been finalised. Ralph is now here, working as a diving instructor. He'll probably stay as well.

'I love it here. I suppose I'm irresponsible. But I like to feel free. No, I haven't got any money. I own this slipway with a partner who lives in St Vincent. He's a sleeping partner. I do the work, on my own. It was a rubbish dump, so I cleaned it before I could start mending boats. I don't make much. You would never come to Bequia if you wanted to make your fortune. I have two rooms in a guest house – I live in one and the other room is my office. I eat out every evening, as cheaply as possible. I live on roughly £5 a day.

'Every day I'm brought up sharp by the natural beauty of the place. I live outside and wear hardly any clothes. At night, the stars are crystal-clear, something you never see in England. I love the people. I love dancing. When something threatens, like a hurricane, or when a boat is being launched, everyone helps everyone, all together. In England, you can't get close to people. There are too many layers.'

He misses an English spring morning and good-quality shampoo, but that was about all. 'I still find this place stimulating. When it doesn't, I'll move on.' Talking of spring, I asked about the name of the Daffodil Laundry. 'That's the woman's name who runs it.'

There was, he said, only a small expat community on the island – a handful of Brits, six at most, with an equal amount of Germans, Americans and Canadians. 'It's a good mix, with no one dominant nationality. Of course we're all a bit weird. Expats usually are.'

We went on a tour of the island with Gideon's taxi service and got Gideon himself, a white Bequian, whose family has been here for decades, one of those who can trace their ancestors back to French and Scottish settlers. White settlers in places like Barbados, Jamaica and Antigua were originally rich plantation owners, and some have managed to hold on to their money, if not their plantations, but the whites in Bequia were always relatively poor, working as fishermen or farmers, just like everyone else. They were always a minority, and like most minorities they tended to marry amongst themselves and live in their own area, not always welcoming outsiders, white or black.

Gideon had a four-wheel-drive taxi, with outside seats, which meant it was pretty bumpy, once we climbed up the hill behind Port Elizabeth. On the map, the island is laughably small, easy enough to walk across, so why the need for all those taxis which hang around in Port Elizabeth? Once out of the little town, you can see why. The hills are quite steep, the roads poor with lots of steep bends and zigzags, so the map gives no idea of time or distances. We passed quite a few walkers, blond young Scandinavians on hiking holidays, striding cheerfully across the island, and young, muscular, sad-looking black workers, carrying their picks and shovels, off to mend some far-flung potholes.

Once over the top of the island, and there is only one top, it's the other side. We went down to Friendship Bay, not quite as pretty as the Caribbean side, but well sheltered and the beach was quite attractive.

There were some clear views of Petit Nevis, a rocky island a few miles away, uninhabited, but with a good bay where at one time the whaling station was situated. Now it's little more than a ritual sport, with young men going out once a year in sailing boats and using hand harpoons. In the last four years, Gideon could remember only one whale being caught. No need for Save the Whale campaigns on Bequia.

The night the rich woman was murdered in Mustique was a night on which a whale was spotted and chased. Ken Will, the security chief, had told me how that had complicated things. Young fishermen with dodgy characters, who might have been called in for questioning, were not at their usual haunts, but had very good alibis.

Much of the Atlantic coast of Bequia is sheer cliff, so we had to head inland for a bit, before coming down again to Industry Bay. There is no industry, or any signs of there having been any, though Gideon said at one time there was a sugar mill. The waves were high, the sea alarming.

Further on, with the roads even worse, and the beaches more storm-strewn, we came to Park Beach. No sign of a park – where do they get these names from? – but we did come to a strange-looking home-made building in which it looked as if people might be camping. Inside I could see what looked like a swimming pool. The Scandinavian walkers, getting ready for an orgy?

It turned out to be a turtle sanctuary, created by Orton King, known locally as Brother King. He was bending over the main pool, holding a large tortoise in his hand, inspecting its pink, fleshy bottom for any nasty signs. Homosexual tortoises? Not quite. But they can attack weaker members who have to be rescued and put in another tank.

Brother King is also a white Bequian, with a Scottish grand-mother whose red hair he can still remember. I found it hard to understand his Bequian accent at first. And he mine. Gideon was a bit easier, but then he spends his life taking foreigners around. White West Indians, naturally enough, have West Indian accents, even the middle classes. It struck me as strange when I first went to Barbados, hearing well-off white Bajans speak the same as everyone else, which shows me up as a Little Englander.

Mr King, now retired, spent his working life at sea, either as a fisherman or diver. Now he devotes almost all his time, and his own money, to rescuing turtles. In his working life, he spent a lot of time killing them.

When did you start saving them? He gave a grunt, which I couldn't interpret. I asked again and he pointed to the ground. I still couldn't follow. We have a right idiot here, I could see him thinking. Then I realised he was indicating the side of his main pool. In the concrete, he had scratched the date he had started: 14 August 1995.

'I've always been interested in things of the ocean, so I got very depressed when I read an article in the *National Geographic* about turtles being endangered all over the world. We have one breed here, the Hawksbill Turtle, which was disappearing fast, so I decided to save them.'

He was self-taught, reading as much as he could, picking up what he observed, remembering what he'd seen over his years at sea. 'When I was young, turtles were plentiful. I remember my grandfather catching them with hand-knitted nets. We'd eat the meat ourselves. There was no real market for it, though it tasted lovely, then we sold the shells. That was where the market was, in turtle shells. Before the invention of plastic, so much was made of turtle shells – combs, spectacle frames, oh lots of things.

'Now the trade in turtle shells is banned. People just have to throw the shells away, if they catch one.

'They started disappearing for many reasons, not just because of the trade in the shells. A female turtle comes up on to the beach at certain times of the year and lays her eggs in the sand. The depth depends on the size of her flipper – on how deep the mother can dig. Usually it's up to twelve inches, deep enough for any birds not to find them, but people did. Oh yes. People used to eat a lot of turtle eggs.

'After around sixty-five days' incubation in the heat of the sand, they hatch out and start making for the sea. That's when they are not safe. If there is a storm or high waves, they might never make it. When I first started observing them, watching them hatch out, there was a spring tide with heavy breakers. I could see they were never going to make it, so I collected as many as I could in plastic buckets. I released them next day, when the sea was calmer.

'When they do reach the sea, they tend to swim around on the surface and the seabirds like the frigates can pick them off. Thousands disappear every year that way – that's the real reason why the numbers got so low round here.'

So what Brother Orton decided to do was care for the baby turtles in his tanks. He has one large pond, thirty feet by twelve, and three smaller ones. In the main pond, the turtles looked enormous, swimming around like armoured battleships, lords of their domain. In the smallest pond, they were more like tadpoles, splashing around. Mr King checks each one each day, big and small, recording their progress and their size.

He built the ponds himself, mixing and fixing the concrete, and ran seawater into them via a home-made pumping system, using plastic pipes and a gasolene pump. He has no electricity on the beach. When they get to a size and strength where he thinks they can survive in the open sea, able to resist frigates and other predators, he releases them into the ocean.

'So far I have released 204 adult turtles. At the moment, I have 260 of all ages. At the end of this month, I'll be releasing another forty – on the same beach where I found them.'

During their stay with him, he has of course to feed them. In the ocean they eat jelly fish, but he can never find enough, so he feeds them sprats, minnows and tuna fish – tinned tuna which costs him 4 local dollars a tin. One of his ponds is a hospital pond, for sick turtles, those with fungi, or those who have been bitten on the bottom by other turtles.

'I use mainly gentian violet, from this bottle. It's a miracle the way it cures them.'

He doesn't know how long he'll be able to afford to run the sanctuary. Or if his wife can put up with him spending so much time with them. He camps out on the beach several nights a week if he's worried about any of them. He likes visitors to his sanctuary, and doesn't charge them, but hopes they'll make a donation. He gets several hundred a year, including schools. There are of course those who don't approve of his self-appointed, untrained turtle work.

I suggested that perhaps having so many together in a confined space might not be too good for them, hence the biting each other, though what do I know about turtles. He said he'd lost only twenty-four since he began – out of some 500. In the wild, he said, only one baby turtle out of 1,000 survives.

I said it must be tough for them, suddenly hitting the open, competitive seas after all this enclosed, luxury living. They've had matron dabbing their bottoms, then find themselves vulnerable and unprepared, like a public-school boy going into the real, nasty sharky world. But he had an answer to that as well.

'When I let the first lot go, I went snorkelling the day afterwards. I could see they had reached the coral reefs and were already feeding – and also hiding. I also put a mark on them, a little hole in their shell. So in years to come, I'll always know which ones were mine, which were the ones I saved.'

Mustique has its wonderful public library, a miracle on a miniature island, but it was money-bags Felix Dennis who created it. Bequia has a wonderful bookshop, a proper, self-supporting little bookshop, which somehow manages to survive on a remote island with a population of only 5,000. I know towns in Britain, twice that size, which can't support one real bookshop.

I had passed it several times, walking back and forth across the bay, and had even taken snaps, as it seemed so bijou, so pretty, so artistic, with its Caribbean chattel-house overtones, bright colours, nice woodwork. But I expected it to be all exterior and no content, merely a souvenir shop selling cards and gifts. What a surprise when I first went in. Rows and rows of classics of a definite literary nature, from Conrad to Doris Lessing. Not exactly up-to-the-minute fiction, of the sort you might see in Waterstone's, Hampstead, but all the same, real books. Naturally, they are strong on nautical books, with all those yachties on their doorstep, or duckboard step. And local stuff, for that was where I bought the book on Bequia.

It must be run by expats, I thought, but I was only half right. Heather Reynolds is a black St Vincentian. She was busy dealing with customers, taking orders, and couldn't spare much time for a chat first time I was in.

Her husband Patrick, a white American, seemed to have more time on his hands – till his wife suddenly reminded him he had not taken their daughter to school yet.

He is from Arkansas, a marine engineer by profession, which he has done since he was nineteen. 'I had a friend who came from Bequia, a member of my same union, and he said I should come take a look round the island, which I first did in 1987. All it seemed to consist of was a little mountain-top sticking out of the water. Then I discovered there were 5,000 people and more than half of the men were seafarers of some sort. I liked it so much I bought a piece of land here. Then I met Heather. We have a house now. This is our home.

'I still spend about six months of each year at sea. I'm just about to sail from Seattle to the Far East.

'Heather had been working here as the assistant for some years, working with the previous owners, the Gales, a couple from Barbados. They began the bookshop about twenty years ago. Mr Gale then died and eventually Mrs Gale decided to return to Barbados and give up the shop. We decided to buy it. I have always loved books myself. On long voyages, I always read several books. On my last trip, let me see, I read the *Mimic Men* by V. S. Naipaul. Heather is voracious. She usually reads two novels a week.

'We couldn't really run it without my other job. We might perhaps just survive, modestly, but not if we want to save a bit for our old age. You wouldn't run a bookshop to make your fortune anyway, not on an island like this.

'People who read books are pretty nice people. I don't think you'd meet such nice people if you had a shop selling rum.

'We do specialise in what I call contemporary classics – people like John Fowles. We sell a copy of *Moby Dick* about every week. I put two Kafka on the shelf last week – and they've both gone.

'If you go into a Barnes and Noble in any big American town, they'll have, say, 50,000 current novels on the shelves, but the chances are if you want a classic novel from the thirties you'll have to order it.

'What we've found is that our customers want a long, good read, the sort of book or author they always meant to read, when perhaps they were younger, but never got round to. A lot of them are on boats. They want something to last till the end of their voyage.

'They are all paperbacks. People want that, not to be loaded down on the boat with hardbacks. But the main reason is we can't afford to stock them. All our books are imported at vast expense. The heavier they weigh, the more they cost. We always choose the cheapest way, which means by sea. A quick order for us is six weeks. Normally it's two months. Even so, the cost to us is great, which means we have to charge roughly 10 per cent more than you would pay in America or Britain.

'The residents don't buy many books, nor the people on cruise ships. All they want is postcards or courtesy flags. It's mostly yachtsmen who buy books.'

They order direct from publishers, and in small numbers, so they don't get much discount. There are no wholesalers they can use. 'There is a distribution centre in St Vincent, but we buy more books than they do. We have roughly forty accounts with publishers, mostly in the UK.

'We like to think we have the best selection in the region.'

What does that mean?

'Well, let's say the southern Caribbean, from St Thomas in the US Virgins to Venezuela. That's about 1,500 miles. A big area, yes. But of course most of it is water.'

By best he means the choicest. 'I suppose there might be a shop in Bridgetown, Barbados, with a lot more books, but, to me, they are mostly selling pulp. I go into bookshops wherever I land, to check them out, and they are mostly selling cheap thrillers or romances. We don't stock any of them. No, not even Danielle Steele, though I know she is a world bestseller.'

So how many books do they stock? He wasn't sure, so shouted for Heather. She worked out they had 4,000 different titles with an average of four copies of each, so total stock, on show and in their stockroom, was 16,000.

Their bestselling current title was not a classic novel, or a maritime book, but a children's book called *The Caribbean Alphabet*. They hadn't got a copy left, but Patrick said it was very artistic, very well done. 'It's a neat version of the usual alphabet books, but with a Caribbean angle: A is for Auguti, for example, which is a local rodent. I is for Iguana.'

I asked Heather what books she was currently reading. I hadn't heard of any of them: *So Far, So Mad* by Maurice Patterson who is a Grenadian author; *Naked Justice* by William Bernhardt and *Outlander* by Diana Gabaldon.

Like all authors, the very first thing I'd done on entering their bookshop was look for any of my books. Not a sausage, curses. But they did have some books by my dear wife.

I offered to do a signing session when this book comes out, but Patrick seemed hazy about what this was. They'd never had an author session before. Nor had they ever had a publisher's rep visiting. But I promised I'd come, some time, if they stock this book. My ambition now is to be big in Bequia.

Another minor wonder of Bequia was the food. After the disappointment of our so-called luxury hotel, we ate out every day, and loved it, even the beach caffs. Friendship Bay Hotel, where we first ate out, was excellent, with live music, the waiters and waitresses dressed like sultans with embroidered waistcoats and white loons, for reasons not quite apparent. During the meal, a chef came out from the kitchen to dance with one of the waitresses, then went back in again to his work.

We also ate well in town at Timberhouse where they were turning people away in droves. Yet each time when we returned to our hotel, their dining room was empty.

Not far from the hotel are two very pretty, white, sandy beaches, which you can get to by taxi-boat from Port Elizabeth, or walk round to on foot. The first, Princess Margaret Beach, doesn't have a caff or any facilities, but it does have the royal connection, maybe, supposedly. It was formerly called Tony Gibbons Beach, till Princess Margaret allegedly took a dip there in 1958. It's Tony Gibbons I feel sorry for, whoever he was, or is. How rotten having your name cleared off the map just because of some passing royal.

The next beach, Lower Bay, is much bigger, with a good if simple restaurant, right on the beach, called De Reef. We liked it so much we booked a taxi-boat to take us there each morning. My wife decided this was her favourite beach, on her favourite little island, but I was still reserving judgement. It was about a mile long, easy for walking, excellent sand, with some interesting, unsophisticated beach life. On the surface anyway.

I met a tough cockney in his fifties who told me to take care about asking too many questions. He had come for two months every year for yonks, and yes, it was peaceful and quiet, but there were a lot of people coming in and out, moving money around, know what I mean, who had their covers, get my drift, and wouldn't like to think strangers were going around asking personal questions. I asked him one, such as what he used to do for a living, and was told to fuck off. Charming.

On the beach I met a Frenchwoman who was charming, Victorine Claude, an artist with a little studio nearby. She used to live on Martinique for many years, but decided it was becoming too dangerous for a woman living on her own. She found Bequia very safe and couldn't believe there was any criminal undercurrent. But of course smart criminals have things so well organised you never know about it.

Bequia did seem a safe place, with young women visitors walking on their own, either on the beaches or on the roads, without being hassled or pestered, everyone saying hello and being helpful.

At the end of the beach, near the Rasta Bar, a very kind rasta was particularly helpful, offering me a smoke. No thanks, I said, very primly. Why not? he said. He wasn't trying to sell me anything. I said I don't smoke, never have done, as I had asthma as a child.

'Oh man, dis is the best for asthma. My grandmother, she had asthma, but when she smoked one of these, it all gone, all gone.'

How kind, I said. Actually, I must go and meet my wife. We've booked a taxi-boat. In fact I think I can see Mr MacArtney now, coming to pick us up.

And it was Mr MacArtney, wearing his shades, looking cool, in his little motor boat which he steered with one hand. We were halfway across the bay when I heard the noise of female shouting. Two girls in a Daffodil Laundry boat were waving at him. He slowed down and they came alongside. One of them whispered something in his ear. He shook his head, then started the motor up again and we zoomed off.

'What was that about?' I asked him, though, being a stranger, I should perhaps be curtailing my inquisitiveness.

'Just gossip,' he said. 'She keeping me back.'

'Is one of them after you then?'

Mr MacArtney was about forty-five, I guessed, though hard to tell behind his shades, rather thin, rather worn and weedy, not exactly a hunk.

'I not time for girlfriends,' he said. 'I too busy.'

Our best meal on Bequia was at the Old Fort. We had actually been there before, which I had almost forgotten, four years previously, on a day trip by catamaran from St Vincent. Handsome boat, good skipper, very quick, just a two-hour sail, and utterly boring. Now could Neil or Columbus or anyone stand all those weeks on a little boat crossing the Atlantic? And big boats are just as claustrophobic. I did it once on the QE2 and was screaming by the end. The best bit about sailing is watching someone else sailing. Boats with sails do improve a horizon, but I never want to go on one again.

On that occasion, we had had a quick lunch at the Old Fort, all on its own, in the middle of the island, which I remembered as being run by a German couple with incredibly blond children. They were very friendly, but seemed a bit distant with each other. One senses these vague atmospheres, on a fleeting visit, usually getting it totally wrong. But the lunch had been very good.

We booked for dinner this time and arrived well before sunset, to have a drink and watch the sun going down. The building was as attractive as I remembered, built of stone, with turrets and towers and cobbles, very artistic, more like a Tuscan villa than a Caribbean hotel, yet fitting well into the hilly landscape. There was a swimming pool, which there wasn't before, and the gardens were now well established.

Otmar Schaedle joined me for a drink by the pool, looking very relaxed and rather professorial, with his beard and intellectual air.

In Germany he was a teacher, at a Steiner school in the Black Forest, where he had worked for twelve years. In 1978 he and his wife Sonia joined a three-masted, 100-foot-long schooner as crew members on a three-month round-the-world trip.

'We arrived in Bequia from Guadeloupe and the vibrations were so strong that we interrupted our journey and had a break here.'

They returned to Germany, and to work, then a year later he and his wife Sonia decided to give up living in Germany completely and move to the Caribbean.

'Why? I tell you. One, the noise was everywhere. Two, the hectic life. I was having a massage one day for pains in my neck and I was lying on a couch. Outside, I could hear people going past, pedestrians on the pavement – and they were all running. Everyone is running, running for something opening, running in case it closes. But why, what for? I felt trapped like a fly in a wineglass. Third, the grey weather. The moment I arrived here, I felt I had so much more energy.

'Bequia suits me because it has a little of everything. Not too lush, not too dry, not too cloudy, not too sunny, not too white, not too black, not too exciting, not too dull.'

They bought a plot of land, started clearing it, planting trees and building a house, living on their savings. 'My in-laws have some money, so my wife had a small income, while I used to go off in the summer to Italy and help in a business which they owned. In the winter, we would live here, and work on the house. Every week there was some sort of catastrophe, but it was exciting, doing it. The design came to us when we found that there had been a fortified French house on the site in 1763. Long gone, but it gave us an idea for the style of house.

'We had no intention of opening a restaurant or a hotel. It opened by itself. What happened was that friends came from Germany, then again, insisting on paying for their stay, and their food, so in 1990 we decided to open officially. I was tired of going to Italy by then anyway. It was being overrun with Germans.'

It has been a great success and he now has the house as he wants it with six rooms for guests and a large dining room. He tries not to have a concentration of Germans, despite his background. 'The German market is very demanding. They think because this is a Third World area, it will be Third World prices. It's not. The Caribbean is expensive. Then because it's First World prices, they still expect European standards, which of course they don't get. We are doing well, but a dynamic businessman would not come here to make his fortune.

'All the staff of six live in. They eat and sleep here in the staff quarters. I have found that otherwise, if you allow them to go home each evening, things disappear. They don't call it stealing, its called "rummaging for the family".

'I also don't employ any men. In the West Indies, it's a macho society. If you train a young boy to be a cook, which is not hard, as they are skilled people, when they become a chef they think they are head of the house, head of everyone else. He is the boss, so he won't do the ordinary jobs and thinks the girls are there only to clean the pots. Then at twenty-five, by which time he is married with children, he feels he needs a girlfriend for his image. He can't really do his job any more. He can't think of everything he has to do. That's the turning point, and he's no longer worth having. That's why I don't employ young men. Just young women.'

So he'd knocked the business into shape, and I could see it was doing well, but he appeared to be on his own. No sign of his wife. What, er, happened to Sonia?

'We are separated, but still friends. She lives in Port Elizabeth with the children, but I see them all the time. In fact the children are coming tonight, so you will see them.'

Their three children are now aged seventeen, fifteen and thirteen. The youngest, a daughter, who looked incredibly beautiful, later came and said hello. Her accent was pure Bequian. Two go to school on the island while the oldest, Kieron, goes on the ferry each day to St Vincent. What caused the separation?

'The building work. Sonia tends to float on a cloud and I am more businesslike. I want things done a certain way. As things progressed, we realised some of our tastes do not connect.'

His new girlfriend, a black Bequian, was the chef, whom he said we would also meet, as she was eating later with him and his children. Sonia did have a new boyfriend, but he thought that had finished. He stressed they were all friends. It was very civilised.

His girlfriend is also the mother of his two-year-old son. He was asleep, in the servants' quarters, so I didn't see him. 'I call him my Carib son. His mother is from Carib blood, but he has blue-brown eyes. His colour is café au lait.'

As we left, I asked Otmar what he missed from Germany, if anything. 'Pretzels and cheese. And fruit such as apples and cherries. That's about all.'

I said that British expats usually included in their list TV and newspapers. He didn't miss either. What about intellectual stimulation? He was clearly of a philosophical inclination, but the chance of meeting like minds, especially now his wife was living elsewhere, must be limited.

'Not at all. I am meeting intellectual people all the time. My guests are all intellectual. Sometimes too much . . .'

I couldn't quite work that out. I hope he wasn't thinking of me. I did think of him a lot later, and of all the other interesting things and places on little Bequia. A place, like so many in the Caribbean, where expat couples like to go to escape, and often end up escaping from each other.

ST. MARTIN

N

Atlantic Ocea

Petites Cayes

FRENCH

Pointe du Bluff

**La Samanna
Hotel**

• Marigot

DUTCH

Philipsburg •

Caribbean Sea

Point Blanche

3 km

CHAPTER SEVEN

St Martin

St Martin is a very unusual Caribbean island. Small, just thirty-seven square miles, but imperfectly formed. Its shape for a start is very strange, all over the place, hard to get a grip on. Politically, its formation is even weirder: the only island of its size in the world which is divided between two nations. One half is French, the other Dutch.

There are no customs posts or barriers, and people can move easily between the two parts all the time, to work, to shop, go to school, yet it sounds like a nightmare place to live in. How do they cope with two official languages, two currencies, two sets of laws, two education systems, different stamps, different electricity suppliers, different tax systems?

The day I arrived petrol had become cheaper on the French side, because of the different import duties. Even the telephone systems are different. It means you have to dial the international code, even when you are dialling the next house. Burglars can in theory do their burglaring on one side of the street, then escape to the other. Potty, or what.

It all sounds a suitable case for schizophrenia, or worse. And yet the strangest thing of all is that since 1664, when the division was made, the two nations have never been at war with each other. Not a drop of blood has been spilt. Would that other cohabiting nationalities had been so peace-loving.

One of the things they agreed, back in 1664, was that 'all birds, fish, salt pans, rivers, lakes, mines or minerals' would be held in common. So that was sensible.

They each have about 30,000 population, but the French chunk, which calls itself Saint Martin, is a little bit bigger in size than the Dutch side which calls itself Sint Maarten. The legend is that when the splitting up was done, a Frenchman and a Dutchman started off, back to back, to walk the island, till they met again. The Frenchman walked faster, because he drank only wine. The Dutchman was on the gin and took longer.

Until about thirty years ago it was very much a backwater, hardly developed, with 90 per cent of the 10,000 population of African origin. Now 50,000 or so strangers have turned it into a much whiter island. Most of the newcomers are from North America and Europe, as well as from elsewhere in the Caribbean, such as Haiti and the Dominican Republic. It has a young, cosmopolitan population, most of them attracted by opportunities in the new hotels, villas, restaurants, shops, bars and other tourist businesses.

As one might have expected, for an island dependent on the tourist industry, despite all the apparent national differences, the US dollar is accepted everywhere and the main language used is English, especially on the Dutch side. The French side is a lot more French than the Dutch side is Dutch.

The Dutch bit seemed to have more potholes than the French bit, which the French like to think is due to their natural pride. After a hurricane, so they say, the French are quicker to clean up, get themselves organised, not sit around bleating for outside help.

But it's probably more due to the fact that St Martin is in France – part of the French department of Guadeloupe. They are full French citizens, governed from France, so things get done quickly and efficiently. Sint Maarten is in a more complicated political state. It's not part of Holland, but the Netherlands Antilles, run from Curaçao, and not very well, according to those who would like complete independence.

In the meantime, it is a boom island, for both parts. The reason for all the new hotels and villas are the excellent beaches. It's almost impossible not to have a sea view of some sort, thanks to the island's strange shape, like a mad amoeba, or a demented octopus, with bits sticking out all over the place and some very confusing stretches of inland water which appear to be the sea but are totally enclosed. I was beginning to think I'd never see a pear-shaped island again.

Our hotel was La Samanna at the end of a two-mile-long beach, Baie Longue, one of the best hotels in the whole Caribbean, now owned by the Orient Express group. It was built as a private villa, so the entrance is low-key, with none of that over-the-top reception area, dripping with gilt. The original owners called it after the first few letters of his three daughters – Samantha, Anouk and Nathalie.

I went for a swim straight away, as I always do, but these days I don't rush straight in, especially if it's late in the day and the beach is empty, just in case I'm rushing into a nasty rock or something dodgy. The water was brilliant, so clear and deep. It's amazing how water can differ in the Caribbean. I've seen it grey, sluggish, pallid, muddy, lagoony, porridgy. I've seen it wild, fierce, noisy, crashing, tempestuous. But mostly I've seen it silken and translucent, warm yet fresh, smooth yet sharp. That's what I like best and how it was that day.

I could hear someone locking up the water-sports place for the day, the only sign of a human on the beach, so I went over, if only to keep him back from his work. He was a fit and angular-looking American called Mark. He'd done different stuff in the USA, he said, from running a Nautilus fitness centre to having his own little real-estate business. Seven years ago he sold up, tired of the pressures and the rat race, and took a long holiday in St Martin.

'I soon got bored being on holiday, as I'm a workaholic. So I took the first job I could find which was out on a remote part of the island, installing a water plant system, just me and three Haitians. We were in the middle of nowhere for six months, but I found I loved being here. When that job finished, I looked around for something else I might do and decided to use my fitness-centre training. I now have my own company which includes fitness training and also this water-sports centre. I've got six people working for me – a Swede, an Italian, a Canadian, a Brit, a Dutchman from Curaçao and an American. I work twelve hours a day. I'm not usually here at this time, as my staff generally look after this place.'

I hadn't come across expat fitness trainers before in the Caribbean, though I'm sure there are a lot, but then I would never think of having a fitness trainer personally or ever using a hotel gym. In fact I hate seeing them. All that money and space, usually empty when I've looked in, apart from the occasional overweight executive, sweating off a bit of fat in a horrible smelly enclosed room when he should be out in the fresh air, walking or swimming. I also never use any hotel's water-sports facilities, even when they are free.

'Then you are most unusual,' he said. 'Over 60 per cent of the hotel guests here use our facilities. We get a lot of high-end people – movie stars, vice-presidents. Some do go brain dead on holiday, and just lie by the pool, but most of them after two days want to do something.'

I'd never heard the phrase 'high end' before, but it was obvious what it means. Mark intends to stay on St Martin, now his business is thriving. He's a keen runner, and also involved in martial arts.

'There's a lot of work going on on this island – as long as you are good. Too many are lazy and careless. A lot of the people who come out here from Europe or the States come here because they screwed up elsewhere. They try to reinvent themselves. They usually screw up here as well, and reveal their true selves.

'You meet people from New York all the time who come on holiday and think, hey, I'll come back here and open a deli, just because they haven't seen one on the island. After two days, they close. They think they know better than the people here.'

I asked how he found working with two different nationalities. He groaned. 'This beach is on the French side and their laws dictate that to use a jet ski you must have a French boat-driving licence. On the Dutch side, there are no such laws.

'Over 80 per cent of the guests here are from the USA. Can you imagine how many of them arrive with a French boat-driving licence? Exactly. So I've had to give up jet skis on this beach.'

Hard cheese for him. But I was well pleased. I hate jet skis. So I should be having a peaceful time on this excellent beach. Where did he go for his holidays, or did he not take them?

'I have to get off the island every two months. Back to the US usually. I need to drive a car on a highway, go into a mall.'

To get back in touch with reality?

'I didn't say that. This is my reality. I just need a break, now and again, from this reality.'

The beach was brilliant, stretching for a couple of miles, with great walks in each direction, but after a few days I was keen to see the rest of the island, having explored as far as I could on foot, checking out the locality, trying to find hidden-away beach bars. Mostly I found hidden-away swarms of nudists, men and women, some of them not so hidden away, playing beach games, doing disco dances, watched by admiring local youths. This must be one of the attractions of the French side. The French do like to strip off on holiday.

I asked if a tourist board official could give me a tour, and she turned up in her own car, to take me personally. Which was nice. A very cheerful black woman aged thirty-seven, Maryse Romney, who works for the St Martin Tourist Board, i.e. from the French side. I could find no telephone number or address for any tourist people on the Dutch side.

Maryse was born in St Martin. When she was growing up, there were only 10,000 people on the whole island. 'We knew everyone. Now it's full of strangers, from eighty-seven different nationalities. But you have to go with it. It's where our future lies.'

We went first to Marigot, capital of the French side, which is very pretty, neat and tidy. She dropped me at the Arawak Museum while she went to do something in her office. The museum was well laid out, but I have seen enough Arawak museums in the Caribbean. They tend to label any broken pots older than last week as Arawak.

The best one I ever saw was in the jungle in Haiti, miles from anywhere, well off any roads, created by an American missionary doctor who had made it his life's work to excavate for the ruins of Columbus's *Santa Maria* which had gone down off the north coast of Haiti. He'd built the little museum himself, with donations, to display all the many things he'd found along the way.

I once had a bad experience after coming out of a very good Arawak exhibition in Kingston, Jamaica. All my fault. I'd stayed so long that the door I'd come in by was locked so I went out by another door, my mind elsewhere, and found I was wandering in a dodgy street near the docks. Two youths started following me. I walked faster and they seemed to disappear, till one was suddenly in front of me, flashing a knife. He tore my shirt, ripping out my wallet. I gave him all the money I had, which was just a few dollars, and persuaded him to let me keep my credit cards. He looked almost as nervous as me. I think it was his first mugging. But I was in shock for days, shocked by own stupidity.

I bought some postcards in the Marigot Museum, to show willing, then walked round the town. There was a street market, along the seafront, which was lively and colourful, though not quite as exotic as one I visited in St François, Guadeloupe. In the main shopping street there were some very chic, French-style shops. Not as chic as St Barts, but then few shops in the Caribbean can compete for expense with St Barts. Then I stopped myself comparing things. That's the trouble when you have been to so many islands. Not island fatigue but island rating sets in.

When Maryse had finished in her office, we drove to the north of the island. There are no hills to speak of, so no rainforest, and it's all a bit flat. Beach life is the thing in St Martin, with so many bays and inlets, though several are already becoming over-developed.

We passed a sign saying Butterfly Farm, my first so far, and I said let's stop. I went in, just in time to join a little tour led by a rather hippy-looking man with bleached hair and earring called Pete Reynolds.

'This butterfly farm opened in 1995, and has been blown away three times. We've got over 900 butterflies here, some forty different species, all of them tropical. Guess who we had here the other day – Yoko Ono and Sean. Oh, it was, it was. I recognised them straight away. But I didn't say anything.'

Pete came out three years ago, after the death of his wife whom he had nursed through a series of cancer operations. 'It was a beautiful experience.'

In England he worked in restaurants, but thinks he'll stay in the Caribbean, for a few years anyway. 'I don't miss much – English beef, pork pies and bluebells in April. That's about it.'

Thanks, Pete, I said, great tour, then I got back into the car with Maryse and we went for lunch at the Kontiki restaurant on the Baie Orientale. A bit like St Tropez, if not quite as swish, but very lively. I insisted on having a swim first, but the waves were very high and strong so I just had a quick dip, worrying about my ears getting bashed or bunged up.

Over lunch, which Maryse tucked into heartily, especially the pudding, saying that sweet things were her only vice, she talked about Diana, Princess of Wales, taking me blow by blow through what she was doing, where she was, on the fateful day.

'When I first heard about the crash, I thought she'll live, she'll live. She's in France, they have the best doctors in the world in France. Then when I heard she had died, I was so depressed. I was in tears. Part of me died that day as well.'

Maryse is married to an Anguillan who still lives in Anguilla. For seven years she herself commuted from Anguilla to St Martin. I found this amazing: living on one island, working on another. I have had a holiday on Anguilla, which I found flat and boring, but couldn't remember how far away it was.

'Oh, it's only fifteen minutes on the fast ferry. But now I live here during the week, in an apartment my father owns. I go home to my husband in Anguilla at weekends.'

She has two children. Her son aged twelve goes to school on the French side of St Martin while her daughter aged sixteen goes to school on the Dutch side. 'I want her to learn good English.'

On the Dutch side?

'Yes, they all speak English there, all the time.'

At the French school, which is the same sort of school she went to herself as a girl, they still learn French history. 'My son learns about Louis XIV and Joan of Arc, as I did, and all the other French heroes and heroines. On the Dutch side, they now study more Caribbean history.

'I would like my daughter to go to college in the USA when she is older, do business studies, learn how to be an entrepreneur, then return to Anguilla and run her own business. That's my fantasy.'

She said this with a loud laugh, mocking herself, but I could sense she meant it. And her son? Her hopes for him were not as grandiose as he's not as academic. 'I'd like him to go to the best culinary school in Europe, then come back and run his own restaurant in Anguilla.

'Kids in the Caribbean are still humble and respectful of their parents. When I was young, all grown-ups kept an eye on all the local children and they were obedient. We'd say to ourselves, "Mummy would not like that." And we wouldn't do it. I still respect my parents and would never raise my voice to my father, or anyone older than me. We are blessed on this island, not like other places.

'I have been to London, for travel trade conferences. I have seen your children – ears pierced, noses pierced, rude and swearing. I've been to Italy as well. All the children are smoking in Italy. Terrible, terrible. I will not allow my children to smoke or drink. I will know everything they do, all the people they know, until they are eighteen.'

I asked if we could go back via Philipsburg, the capital of the Dutch side. She didn't seem keen on this, as of course she was working for the St Martin Tourist Board, but I talked her into it, being a kindly, Christian woman.

It wasn't worth it. It was busy enough, with several massive cruise liners in the dock, but all rather run-down and scruffy, not half as pretty as Marigot. Or as interesting as Maryse.

I was wandering round the hotel grounds one day, poking into buildings, peering into corners, and came to what looked like a conference centre set in a lush tropical garden. I opened the door and found myself in a large, cool lounge. At the far end, I could see someone sitting behind a bamboo screen in a makeshift office, with a desk, filing cabinet and large computer. On the screen it said 'Dad's Army'. The man at the desk, large and shiny-domed, was smiling away. Must be a Brit, I thought.

Michael Davis, aged fifty-five, has spent almost all his working life, some thirty-five years, as an expat. Most expats I'd met so far were one-country expats, who had gone off to a particular place, or landed in a particular place, and stayed there. Michael is an intinerant expat. Been everywhere, except orbit.

He comes from Wales, brought up in the Midlands near Derby, qualified as an architect, not by going off to university but by going through the long process of studying while working. In 1969 he got a six-month job in Eire – and stayed sixteen years. He so liked being away from England that he's done it ever since. 'I have no problem working in England – just the tax.'

The places he has lived and worked in have included Malta, Indonesia, Cyprus and now St Martin.

'I was headhunted for this job in July 1998. I'd never worked in the Caribbean before, but my wife and I thought, why not? It's a strange job, for me. Usually I'm working on £50–100 million hotels, as the project manager, getting a project built. Here it's only a £20 million job, building nine new villas, but it hasn't even started yet. In the meantime I've been working on improvements to the swimming pool. We're starting on the main new work soon. My job will be to hire the architect and the builder, then manage the project.'

So what's he think of the Caribbean so far?

'Well, this island is amazing. It's about a tenth the size of Malta and, I dunno, about a thirtieth the size of Cyprus, yet there's more to do here than in either of those places for someone like me. I've never met so many different nationalities. I can well believe there are eighty-seven of them. You hardly meet the same nationalities twice. I've never made so many friends in such a short space of time.'

So what sort of things are there to do?

'All outdoors of course. The only culture here is in the yoghurt. Actually that's a joke I first heard about Cyprus. Where it was very true. Every Sunday here we are at some sort of beach party. We could be out at parties all the time, if we wanted.' Ah, that sort of culture. Expat sort of social culture.

He's been married to his wife Ann for thirty-four years and they have four children and three grandchildren. 'She loves it here. There's so much for her to do as well. Oh, you know, two days a week yoga, plus a lot of shopping...'

Workwise, he's not worried about finding good architects and builders. 'Wherever you are in the world, you are always rushed at the end of any building project. That's when you screw up, if you're not careful, when you rush the final touches.'

He hasn't felt any prejudice against him, being a white expat bossing local builders around. 'Not on this island. Normally when you are abroad on a building contract, and walk on to a site, the white guy is the one in charge. Here you are just as likely to find white guys laying the blocks, doing the manual work. Danish guys, Dutch guys, whatever.'

He does find the Caribbean very expensive, and wonders how locals cope with the costs of running cars, household bills, electricity. 'I'm okay. I've got a good deal here. My house and car are part of my wage package.'

Wherever he has been over the world, he has always thrown himself into local life, meaning local expat life, joining all the clubs, social gatherings, willing to serve on committees and organise things. 'It's the only way to enjoy working away from home. When I was in Ireland I got involved in the Boy Scouts. In Malta I was secretary of the rugby club. You assimilate by joining in.

'Cyprus was one of the places we didn't really like, and it's only now, looking back, I can work out why. There were two expat clubs there: one was called the British Residents Club where they played bridge and had cocktail parties. The other was the Travel Club where they played bingo and drank beer. One was sort of southern English, you might say, and the other was northern. We joined both, but didn't quite fit in either. I now realise it's because we're from the Midlands.

'I didn't like Saudi much. That's where you get the real boozers, because they make their own. Malta was about the most boring place, socially. I think all the expats were aged about a hundred. They even had jigsaw-swapping parties. No, it wasn't a cover. That's what they did. Meet up and swap your jigsaw.

'But the best thing to join, wherever you are, is the local Hash.'

'You mean cannabis parties?' Lots of those in the Caribbean.

'No, I mean the Hash House Harriers. Haven't you heard of them?'

I had to admit ignorance. From his drawer he got out a book called *Harrier International*, published in Bangkok, which listed Hash House Harriers in almost every country in the world, from Albania to Zimbabwe. 'It's also on the Internet. You can get updates all the time, wherever you are in the world.

'It began in Kuala Lumpur and the Harriers there are still called Mother Hash. In the 1930s, I think it was, the local tea planters and British army officers stationed there used to meet up every Friday evening and get smashed. They were doing this every Friday, getting smashed. Someone suggested, let's do something healthy and active – before we all get smashed. So they started playing hare and hounds, you know, old-fashioned paper chases. They used to meet up at a place called the Hash House, which was a pub, so they became the Hash House Harriers.

'The origin's very British, but you find it played by all sorts of nationalities – Brits, Ozzies, Americans, Indonesians, Malaysians. Mostly English-speaking nations. I've hashed in Saudi, Indonesia, Cyprus, everywhere. If you join the Hash, you'll meet like-minded idiots in every country. It's probably strongest in South-East Asia.

We had an Inter-Hash when I was in Cyprus and 30,000 people turned up.

'No, alas, there isn't a Hash in St Martin. The nearest is in Guadeloupe.'

I supposed, with thirty years of being an expat, they don't miss much about England, making do where they are.

'Oh, no. There's always something in each place we miss desperately, such as proper kippers. One of our sons lives in the Isle of Man, and while we were in Cyprus he sent us out a ten-kilo box of real Isle of Man kippers. He forgot to vacuum-pack them. Then a woman took them, thinking it was her package. What a saga that was. When they eventually reached us, they did pong a bit, but we put them in the freezer. Ate them all in the end.

'In St Martin we've been looking for Horlicks – and my wife's just found a place that sells it. It's in the supermarket – but on a shelf marked "Oriental Foods".

'We haven't found any white Stilton cheese so far. I love that. We'll probably have to have some sent out.'

I pointed to the name 'Dad's Army', still flickering on his screen. No, no, he hadn't been watching it, just sort of, well, checking, while he was working.

'I do most of my work on the Internet. The architect for these new villas lives in California. The interior designer is in Dallas, the landscape architect is in Aruba, the mechanical engineer in Cyprus. All the drawings and plans are on the Internet, so we all know what's happening. The Internet is brilliant. It saves the lives of expats everywhere. Their working life and their social life.'

How about yesterday's football results? In a flash, he had them printed out for me, so I could go away and study them at my leisure. We expats, even temporary expats, can feel out of things.

Michael Davis is an example of a traditional-style expat, the qualified person who takes contracts round the world. Alison Jones, aged thirty-three, is one of the newer, younger type, with no particular expertise, who just happens to end up expatting. On first meeting here, looking fresh-faced, rather bubbly, I thought she might be American, possibly in the personal trainer business, or managing a smart café. Wrong both times.

She comes from Burgess Hill in Sussex where she trained to be a nanny, but didn't finish the course. She worked in restaurants till aged twenty when she went off for a year in New Zealand. 'It was connected with having an Australian boyfriend at the time, but really it was because I had itchy feet.'

When that finished, she came out for a holiday in St Martin in 1990 to stay with a girl friend. By chance, the friend's partner, with whom she had lived, had just left. The girl was homesick, and decided to leave as well. Alison took over her apartment – and also her job. Not often that happens.

The job was working for a firm doing villa rentals. I should have guessed. I had seen adverts all over St Martin for estate agents, rental firms, property developers. So business must be good?

'Oh, it is. But very competitive. We have many rival firms. At this time of the year [January] I'm running around like a headless chicken because all our villas are full.'

She looks after sixty villas, all of the luxury class, with rents from $10,000 a week at Christmas down to $2,500 in July. Half are on the French side, half on the Dutch side.

'This leads to problems if we have to move people from one villa to another. We are always getting hair dryers blowing up, CD players failing. The electricity system is different on each side. People don't realise it or can't understand it.

'Then there's the problems of maids and housekeepers. If it rains, they often don't show up. they won't go out in the rain. "I catch cold," they say.'

Over 90 per cent of her villas are American-owned, and almost all the tenants are Americans, which explains why her Sussex accent has almost disappeared. She had a boyfriend who is Italian and also works in real estate. 'The Italian stallion, I call him.'

She misses Marmite, Branston pickles and English crumpets, but her parents bring out such essentials when they visit her once a year. She also goes home annually.

'In England, I usually sit for the first thirty-six hours watching television, especially all the adverts. I just love the adverts.

'I'll probably go back for good next year, which people here think is crazy. It is such fun here, and the work is interesting. But it's hard. I'm exhausted. Last night was the first night in six weeks I stayed in. I've been out till twelve every other night. Normal

Barbados, sometimes known as 'little England', and still one of the most popular Caribbean islands.

'Barbados is prosperous and at ease with itself; no antipathy to visitors, comparatively little crime and violence and the highest literacy rate of any country in the English-speaking world.'

Jim and Jill Walker, founders of
'Best of Barbados' shops.

Dr Colin Hudson, eco-warrior,
in his tyre herb garden.

Margaret and Theo Williams in their 'Pizazz' pizza parlour.

ST LUCIA

A volcanic island, St Lucia is famous for these two *pitons*, natural wonders known throughout the Caribbean.

Artist Llewellyn Xavier and his wife Christine.

The lawyer, Peter Foster.

MUSTIQUE

Mustique has eighty glamorous villas. Owners of such houses over the years have included Lord Glenconner, David Bowie and Mick Jagger.

The Hon. Brian Alexander, MD of the Mustique Island Company.

Above Dr Michael Bunbury, Mustique's GP. His patients on the island have included Princess Margaret.

Above right Felix Dennis with photo of his football team, Man United (Mandalay United).

Cardinal Simon, Chairman of the Mustique Indigenous People's Association. He spent twenty years in the UK as a chef.

GUADELOUPE

Top Guadeloupe, a French West Indian island, looks and feels more like the south of France than the Caribbean.

Above left Joel, hotel receptionist, born in Paris but with family from Guadeloupe.

Above right The author and sea plane.

Left Nathalie, one of the beach fashion models.

Top Tobagonian coastline. (Please don't say Tobagan.)

Above The 'famous' Pigeon Point – well, famous in Tobago.

Tobago lawyer, Deborah
Moore-Miggins.

John Jefferis, owner of Coco Reef,
and his white Rolls.

Chris James (left) and Jim Vaughan, ex-gas fitters who now
own 'Bonkers' in Tobago.

Top Bequia was once a centre for whaling but now there are mainly yachts in its magnificent harbour.

Above Neil Sanders who sailed the Atlantic to Bequia.

Right Brother King, with his turtles.

ST MARTIN

St Martin is the only island of its size in the world which is divided between two nations. One half is French, the other Dutch. Since the division of the island in 1664, the two nations have never been at war with each other.

Mike Davis, a British architect, who has been an ex-pat for thirty years.

Roy, bell boy at La Samanna Hotel.

GRENADA

Grand Anse Beach.

Graham and Leslie Drew on their boat.

The Hon. Joslyn Whiteman, Minister of Tourism, back in Grenada after twenty years in the UK.

ANTIGUA

Antigua boasts 365 beaches, one for each day of the year, as someone is sure to tell you.

Dr Peter Swan, scientist, millionaire, Jumby Bay resident.

Rita, German-born
receptionist at Jumby Bay.

Gilly Gobinet,
Brit ex-pat
and artist.

A beat-up, 1950s, American car
in downtown Havana.

A well-preserved
Cuban dancer.

Above left Jose, ex-engineer, selling t-shirts on the beach at Varadero.

Top right Nelson Hernandez, ex-vet and basketball star, now hotel manager in Varadero.

Above right Ernesto, organiser of the Beatles Conference with his son Dhani, named after George Harrison's son.

The author on the beach at Varadero. In the distance is Xanadu, once the holiday home of the Du Ponts.

social life is hectic, but at this time, there are lots of owners here. I have to have drinks with them or go to their parties.

'I am beginning to miss England very much. Having Christmas trees on a tropical beach just isn't quite the same thing, or singing Christmas carols in 80 degrees. I also miss my parents more than I thought I would. And England, sort of generally. I am very patriotic and beginning to feel out of touch.

'When I went home last year, I was on the train going to Brighton and I was reading an article about Kenny Everett. It gave the impression he was dead. That was news to me. I wanted to ask someone in the carriage, "Is Kenny Everett still alive?" but I thought they might think I was a weirdo.

'I've enjoyed it out here. Don't regret it at all. I've got so much more confidence than I had before. Or at least an air of confidence. You need that, whether you are dealing with multi-millionaires or housekeepers.

'Some time in the year 2000 I plan to be back in England. I then want to be settled, before I have children.'

With your Italian boyfriend?

'Oh no, the Italian stallion is just for here . . .'

West Indians from St Martin might find they have to go off abroad for an education or professional qualifications, but most of them these days don't need to leave to find work, not since the tourist and property boom on the island.

In La Samanna Hotel I got talking to Roy, a bell-boy, always around, always smiley, who seemed to know everyone and was clearly pleased that everyone seemed to know him. Not exactly a boy, as he was in his late thirties, but boyish in his cheerfulness, and very American in his outgoingness, with his constant 'How's it Going? Have a Nice Day.'

Roy was born in the French-speaking half of St Martin, one of those who did go off, only to come back.

'My mother was a maid to a wealthy American who had a villa here. He then asked her to come and work for him in the States. So she went off, leaving me with my grandmother. I don't have a father. When she got settled, she sent for me. I was aged twelve at the time. It was hard going to an American high school. But there was a nice French teacher. Like all Americans teaching French, he couldn't speak it very well. I helped out. That sort of gave me a friend and an identity.

'I had trouble getting a green card when I left school, as I was a French citizen. But I became a US citizen when I was twenty-one. I worked in the building trade, putting up framed houses. I came back to St Martin in 1993. No, I wasn't homesick. I got divorced. I didn't know what to do next. So I came home. I stayed with an aunt, tried to get a job, but the economy at the time was poor.

'I failed six times to get a job at this hotel. One day I met the manager and I pretended I was one of the guests. I do have quite an American accent. He found out I was kidding, so I said can I have a job. He says, "Okay, you got a big mouth, I'll give you a week's trial." I'd never worked in hotels before, so I was worried, but hey, I'm still here.

'I've been offered promotion, many times. I won't take it, not yet. If I was in reception desk, I wouldn't get the tips.'

All the time we were talking, he was smiling and waving at guests, shouting 'Hi', checking on things they might need. 'When there's problems, they send for Roy. They know I can calm people down, relate to them, make a few jokes.

'Yes, there are people in St Martin who are jealous of me. "You think you're so smart cos you been in the States, get out of here." You must never say, "This is the way we did it in the States." Some people do want to hear, when you tell them there's a tool for a certain job. Others don't. I have to live with it.

'I miss the fast movement of the USA, but I go back for two months every year. I'm staying here. I've got a girlfriend and a baby and my own house which I built. It's withstood two hurricanes already. See, I did learn something in the States...'

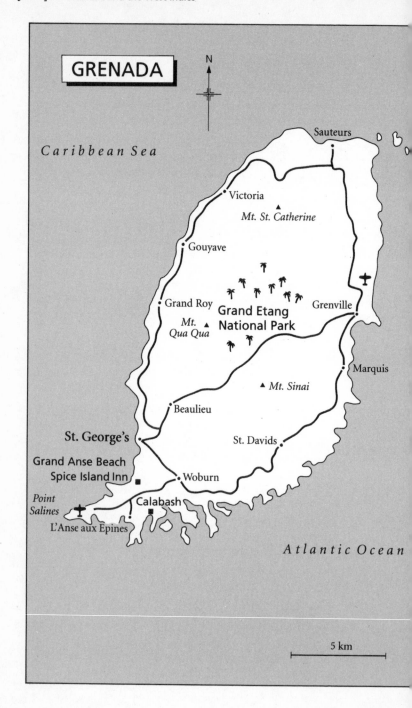

CHAPTER EIGHT

Grenada

It was late afternoon on a Friday, people about to pack up working or playing, the sun about to pack up shining. I'd spent the day on Grand Anse beach, the longest, biggest, busiest in Grenada. The end of another day could clearly be sensed and seen in the slow movements of the last holidaymakers, putting away their towels and their memories, and in the beach vendors, wearily plodding home along the sand with their unsold goods. Outside those hotels with beach frontage, staff who seemed to be in a trance were mechanically folding up their beach chairs, folding away another day.

I do like that time of day in the tropics, melancholic, moody, echoing. You can almost feel in the air the heat and activity of the day now gone. I save my last swim of the day for that period between five and six, to have the sea and atmosphere to myself, watching the light slowly go, and with it all beach life, then, wham, sudden darkness descends. In the tropics, there is a definite curtain which can be quite dramatic, especially if there's a good sunset, the sort that makes you think that's it, for ever, the sun has packed up for good. Then comes the best part. Time for the first rum punch.

This time I was going for a beer. I walked across the road behind the beach, heading for the little shopping centre called Le Marquis Complex. On a wooden bench outside Presents shop were sitting five middle-aged Grenadians in their shirt sleeves, drinking beer and gossiping. 'Liming', as it's called in the West Indies. A bit like 'crack' in Ireland.

I could hear voices raised, roars of laughter, and someone was saying, 'No, Heath was definitely before Callaghan.' I wondered for a moment if they were discussing cricket. Then an argument started about the exact route of the Number 24 bus. That's when I realised they must all be JCBs.

JCB is a local term in Grenada for West Indians who have Just Come Back. Grenada seems to have more than most other islands, especially the ex-British ones. All good judges. For Grenada is one of the nicest, friendliest islands in the whole Caribbean. A comfortably shaped island, just twenty-one miles long by twelve across, population 100,000, one of the pearish-shaped, not awkward like St Martin, which you can get your mind round easily, with the full range of Caribbean landscape, from empty beaches to tropical rainforest.

The five liming included Lincoln, short and stocky in a bright-yellow polo shirt. He had arrived in London in 1960 aged five and was very confused by his first sight of a double-decker bus. 'I thought there must be a driver upstairs, and a driver downstairs. But how did they know which way to turn?'

I asked if he'd gone by air or boat.

'Oh, by boat,' he said, then he put on a stage West Indian accent. 'We poor people from de country, man.' The others all laughed. Then he changed to a posh English accent. 'You see, I was being sent aged five to meet my mater and pater.'

He met them in Tottenham, where he went to local schools, and loved it. 'I had perfect attendance. I never bunked off once. I went to an excellent school, but I left early because I wanted to work on my own.'

I thought perhaps he might have become an actor, from his funny voices and camp mannerism, but no, he went into the courier business and ended up with his own firm, with vans and bikes. 'In 1990 I got an offer I couldn't refuse. I'd been married and divorced, so there was nothing to keep me in London any more. I took the money and ran. For the first three years I just travelled the islands, enjoying myself. Then I bought myself a house. I didn't look for a job. Well, would you employ me?'

More laughs. Was I being wound up? Probably, but I decided to carry on down the bench, asking the others about their UK experiences.

Sitting beside him was Wayne who also arrived in London as a boy, ending in the accounts department of a publishing house. I asked which one. 'Mills and Boon.' There were loud guffaws as they each put on silly voices, making up soppy romantic lines. Wayne let them all have their fun, then said no, he had a real one which was much better. 'He reached down into the delta of her womanhood . . .' Three fell off the bench with laughing.

Wayne first returned in 1977, and soon found himself in the middle of revolution when there was a left-wing takeover of the government. 'I was considered a counter-revolutionary and I was interned for forty-eight hours. Look, that's the marks the hand-cuffs left.'

'Oh yeah,' several others shouted. 'You've just painted the marks on.'

Wayne seemed a bit hurt by this very British style of mockery, but managed a weary smile. He went back to Britain in 1980, returning home for good in 1993. Today he is managing director of a local radio station and deputy leader of one of the opposition parties.

Next to him was sitting one of his political rivals, Mark. There had been various jokes at his expense which I'd taken as pure jokes, not realising he really was a politician. Every time a new round of beers was called for someone shouted, 'Mark will pay. He's rich. He's a politician.' He turned out to be the Rt Hon. Mark Isaac, Minister of Health.

Mark's a JCB from the USA, not the UK. He went to New York aged twenty, did various menial jobs, drove trucks, joined the US army. 'I was very disappointed by New York. I really did think the streets were going to be paved with gold.' However, he did manage to pay his way through college and qualify as a social worker. He then became a diplomat, serving in Washington for his gov-ernment, before returning to Grenada and becoming a politician. He misses nothing about the American way of life, whereas all the others, all ex-Brits, had fond memories of the UK. 'In New York, I was a black man. Here I am a man.'

The couple who own the shop, Marcelle and Peter Touissaint, had both been a long time in the UK. They were the ones I'd gone to see, not knowing that their shop is a focal point for other Grenadians who have lived in the UK.

Marcelle is the niece of the late Lord Pitt, Britain's first black life peer. She moved to London aged eleven. 'I hadn't seen my dad for about ten and a half years. I found I had lots of half-sisters and half-brothers, all over London. He was a very fruitful man...'

Collapse of stout parties, right along the bench. They had now been joined by another middle-aged man, this time much smarter, in a white shirt and tie, who turned out to be a banker. He sat down for only a few moments, when his mobile phone went, which caused cheers all round, but then he went off, so I never got his JCB story.

There was another minor interruption when one of the male benchers, despite his mature years, saw a girl of about seventeen going past, and got up to ask if she'd like a lift in his car. That led to lots of jeers. He sat down again, having failed to chat her up, deciding a beer and liming would be just as pleasant a way to pass the time.

Peter, Marcelle's husband, moved to London when he was fifteen. For a while he worked as a roadie for a reggae group and then ended up with a good job as an insurance broker. He met Marcelle in London. She was working in the rag trade. 'It was a blind date – that's why I've been wearing specs ever since.'

They married, had four children and returned to Grenada in 1990. 'I always planned to return,' she said. 'We owned our own house in Enfield, we'd done pretty well, but I thought we would have a better life here and our children would do better at school. We still have the three Rs in Grenada.

'I think West Indians get a better education in the West Indies than in England. In England the expectations for West Indians are that you'll be good at sport, and little else. You become a black man in England. Here you're just a person.'

They admit they are still seen as somehow foreigners in Grenada, after all their years in London. They have two shops, and are planning to open a third, a bookshop. They are not making much money, but are having an easier life than they did in London. 'We worked too hard in London,' said Marcelle.

On her return, she noticed that local people don't queue up in an orderly fashion for things like buses, the way they do in London. She also misses good plays and films, and kippers.

Wayne said what he missed was the pubs by the riverside in London. 'And draught Guinness. I really miss that.'

Lincoln said that West Indians left England a much brighter place.

How do you mean?

'Well, just look at the houses. When I first arrived, and was invited to a party, I often didn't have the right house number. So I'd walk down the street till I came to a house painted all different colours – I knew that would be the West Indian house. We gave colour to England. You can't say we didn't have input.'

'This is a beautiful island,' said Marcelle, 'but I do have a soft spot for London. I think we all do. That's why we meet up here, on the bench, to chat.'

There was just one bench at first, which Peter and Marcelle propped up outside their shop when they first invited a few friends to have a beer. Now they have two benches to cater for all who might turn up. There are some thirty to forty benchers, all JCBs, scattered throughout the island. A group of them is always there, on Mondays, Wednesdays and Fridays after work.

'The second bench, over there, was specially made by a local carpenter. The other benchers gave it to us as a surprise present, tied up with ribbons.

'The bench is a great leveller,' says Marcelle. 'We all have a go at each other, whoever we are, whatever our jobs, whether someone is a Rt Hon. or out of work. Everyone teases everyone else. Very English, really...'

I was staying on Grand Anse beach at the Spice Island Beach Resort. From the beach itself it looked rather horrid, simply a line-up of cheap concrete villas, but behind there were much better villas which had recently been upgraded. In our villa, classified as a Royal Suite – hotels do love these poncy titles – we had our own walled garden with a locked front gate. Inside the front garden was a banana tree, with real bananas, our own swimming pool, real enough, but not very big, and then something I've never seen in a Caribbean hotel before: our own sauna in its own little Finnish-style wooden chalet, plus an electronic exercise bike. None of these did I ever use, or would ever want to use. Likewise the massive TV set which we had in our sitting room. Why do they do it? Why do they think guests on a Caribbean holiday want such things?

In the Caribbean, there are only about three things I really want in a hotel bedroom. First a shower with decent hot and cold water.

I don't need a bath. I can manage without baths in the Caribbean, as I am in the sea practically all day long. I don't require a hotel pool either, unless the hotel is miles inland, because I'm swimming in the sea. In fact I groan when I see that a beach hotel has its own swimming pool, for I know there will be lots of screaming kids, or, worse, screaming drunks.

Second, I want a fridge, or at least a decent supply of ice. I don't want a mini-bar, stuffed with stupid things. I am too mean to pay hotel prices, but I like to have ice to cool any water, wine or beer I may bring into the room.

Third, I want tea- or coffee-making equipment for my morning cuppa. I don't like ringing room service, if they have any, and I don't like booking it the night before because I don't know what time I will want it in the morning. And when I do want it, I want it now. I don't want to wait till some dopey waiter arrives, half an hour late, with everything cold. Simple enough, you might think, yet rarely, even in the best and most expensive hotels, do I get all three to my exact satisfaction.

A minor extra, as you've asked, which I always like, is a free morning newspaper. In some of the posher hotels in Barbados and on the bigger, more affluent islands, they provide a faxed English-language newspaper at breakfast, a four-page digest which has come in overnight. I moan and groan when it's an American-language version, full of their boring baseball results, Wall Street prices and news of people I've never heard of, but I cheer when it's a Brit version and read every word.

My wife thinks this is appalling, to be so dependent on keeping up with the news, even on holiday. It's usually bad news or horrors, so who wants to know about that. I say famous people will have died while I have been away, footballers will have signed by other clubs, and I'll never know.

Failing a faxed foreign digest, I am just as keen, if not keener, on the local paper. I love local news, even about people and places I know little about, just to see how they handle it, and I read all the opinions of their columnists and leader writers. God plays a big part in West Indian leader pages, along with moral musings and philosophical homilies. They are also big on anniversaries, events that happened on this day. I even like the adverts, especially the classified, which give sideways insights into local life.

Naturally, I also require efficient air-conditioning in a hotel bedroom, but I won't go on about that again. I want a bed that is hard rather than soft, a bedroom big enough to be able walk round, peace and quiet at night. You should expect all of them in any half-decent hotel. I don't demand a sea view, as I'll be out most of the time, or a balcony, as I won't be sitting there. I don't need room service. I much prefer breakfast in the hotel, especially if they have it in the open air.

Not much to ask, is it, yet instead of concentrating on all these basics they insist on spending thousands on pointless, poncy so-called luxury extras which I'm sure are only there to look good in the brochures but are rarely used in real life. Or perhaps it's just to impress other hoteliers, make them feel macho. Ya boo, all our rooms have got their own swimming pool and 200-channel satellite TVs in every lavatory.

In the brochures they always show some young sexy-looking couple sitting in their personal jacuzzi, drinking champagne, with the bucket carefully balanced to hide their bollocks or their breasts, because we are talking good taste here. We all know they are models, posing, not flesh and bloody guests. Flesh and blood guests, from my observations, are more interested in getting on their best casuals, getting down to the hotel bar, getting stuck into the rum punches, meeting other guests, not lolling in their baths, stuffing themselves from the mini-bar or gaping at TV. They can do all that at home.

I have some friends with a small Lakeland hotel and they were thinking of how to upgrade, i.e. how to charge more. They asked what I would suggest in the way of luxuries. I said decent coffee-making equipment in every bedroom, no question. What did they do? They put in a jacuzzi in each bathroom. I could not believe it. Within a year they were fully booked, had won awards and had made their fortunes. Shows how much I know.

Spice Island Resort, along with all the luxuries I didn't want, did indeed have a proper coffee-making machine, so naturally I cheered when I first saw it. But I never got it to work properly, despite calling out a girl from reception who didn't seem to understand it either.

The room also had some excellent hotel notes. Not in my above list of requirements, or even essentials, but I always read them when they are there. I like to catch a flavour of the mentality behind the hotel, what they think they're doing, their own image of themselves. These notes were the best I've ever seen – for quality of writing and for content. Not only did they give a full account of the hotel's amenities, but a brief and well-written history of the island, including the 1979 revolution, a topic I would have thought many hotels would have kept quiet about.

There were also some Hurricane Warnings, something else you rarely see in Caribbean hotel literature. It made clear they should only be expected between July and September, and then rarely. But they did list what one should do. First stage, which would be announced by a thirty-six-hour warning, included paying the bill. Not stupid, these hotels. Then you put your belongings in plastic bags which will be provided and seal them with masking tape. All very sensible.

Another little extra I did enjoy at Spice Island was the uniformed waiter who came round to our villa at six o'clock every evening with little treats. The first night he stood there with a tray and said, 'Hot Dabs.' I said no thanks, sending him away. I thought they might be those stupid hot towels you get on aeroplanes which they hand out as if they were rubies, and always when you don't need them.

Next evening, my wife answered the door. She realised that what he had on his tray were little bowls of dippy stuff and little plates of hot savoury things and that what he'd been saying was 'Hot Dips'. They were delicious.

There was one thing at Spice Island I have never experienced in a hotel before: an invitation to a party. It is fairly normal in the Caribbean for managers to hold a weekly cocktail party in their hotel – but this time guests were invited to the private house of the owner, Royston Hopkin, where he was having a private party. He even laid on minibuses to get us all there.

It was absolutely crowded when I got there, with his family and friends from all over the island. One of seven brothers and sisters had returned from Montreal, so that was apparently the main reason for this particular party. There were masses of drinks and food, far more lavish than you ever get in the normal cocktail party.

Royston said he'd always made a habit of inviting hotel guests to his own parties. It went back to his childhood, when his parents ran a little guest house, and his father made a point of having his guests, four at a time, to eat at his table, in his own house. Royston has carried on the tradition, even now when he has a large and luxurious hotel.

No doubt it has helped his success. In his photograph, up in the hotel reception area, it says he has been awarded the GMG and also been President of the Caribbean Hotels Association and Caribbean Hotelier of the Year.

After I had thanked him for his party, complimented him on his house, and his hotel, I said now come on, Royston, was it really necessary to have a sauna and swimming pool in our suite?

'Since we've put in all those extras, those have been the most desired suites. The proof of the pudding is in the eating.'

I said yes, but I didn't believe people actually used them. Had he done surveys? No, but putting them in the brochures definitely made people think they *might* use them.

All the Grenadian women at the party were dressed to the nines, very colourful, very elegant, including his own mother who was sitting in a chair, very thin, very old, but as bright as a peacock and as sharp as a pin. She was one of the first people, in all the Caribbean, so Royston said, to create Caribbean dishes for visitors. 'Now every hotel offers them.'

I moved round the party, avoiding any of my fellow hotel guests, looking for locals to talk to, and found myself in conversation with a man of about sixty, casually dressed, compared with some of the sharp dressers. He said he was in the law. Doing well then? I said. Come on. We know lawyers always make a packet, wherever they are.

He considered this carefully and said the most lucrative legal practices were probably in Trinidad, because of the oil money, followed by Barbados. There they could make about 150,000 East Caribbean dollars a year. I worked this out at £40,000. No London barrister would put his wig on for that. He smiled and said that in small islands, such as Grenada, a lawyer made a great deal less.

He'd just been to Puerto Rico, on some conference to help standardise legal practices throughout the Caribbean, bring lawyers working in British-based legal systems closer to those in the Latin or Spanish-based islands. Nice little jaunt, I said, swanning off to Puerto Rico.

It only slowly transpired, as the conversation went on, that he was in the fact chief Judge of Grenada, a Dominican, trained in London, called to the Bar at Lincoln's Inn, before returning to Dominica where he worked as a lawyer for the next thirty years. Two years ago, he came to Grenada as a judge. I said how much I liked Dominica and asked if he knew the little guest house we had stayed at, Petit Coloubris. He knew it well, and the owners, whom we then discussed. Which was nice.

One of the most successful JCBs I talked to in Grenada, or anywhere in the Caribbean, was Joslyn Whiteman, a Grenadian in his late fifties, quiet and gently spoken with a greying beard.

I arranged to have a drink with him at the Nutmeg restaurant, on the waterfront in St George's. By chance, this was the very spot from which he had set sail for England in 1962 aged twenty-two.

'As I left the harbour, I held five fingers up to my mother who was standing on the quayside. It meant I'd only spend five years in London.' In the end, he stayed twenty-seven years.

He set sail on the *Ascona*, the same ship which Mike Grant in Tobago had sailed on, though a year later. He had a fairly decent job in Grenada, as a supervisor on a plantation which grew cocoa, nutmeg and bananas, in charge of forty men. The attraction of England was for the experience, the adventure, to see what it was like. His father paid his passage, £75 one way. He expected to have earned enough to pay his own return fare.

'When I arrived in London and saw all the factories and smoke I thought there must be lots of work here. I didn't realise they were ordinary houses.'

I'd heard this before, from other West Indians, and I'm sure it's very true, but I'm beginning to feel it's an observation more remembered afterwards than at the time, the sort of thing returnees tell those who never went.

'I had two brothers already in London, at 28 Linden Gardens, in Chiswick, W4. I shared with them, three in one room.'

Isn't it interesting how people remember first addresses? I can remember mine from 1959 when I arrived in Manchester: 22 Daisy Bank Road. No, hold on, that was my second address. I was in a horrible room in Cheetham Hill first, but I've forgotten the name of the street. Back to Joslyn.

His first job was as a ward orderly in the West Middlesex Hospital in Isleworth which he got through one of his brothers. Then he joined London Transport as a bus conductor. 'I can clearly remember the 27 route from Highgate to Teddington and also the 19 from Wandsworth to Heathrow.'

After that he worked for the Post Office, in the sorting office at Mount Pleasant. By this time he had been joined by his girlfriend from Grenada. They had been in the same class at school. They got married in London, thirty-four years ago. She worked as a nursing sister, then left to bring up their four children.

His next job was in a travel agency, specialising in sending West Indians back and forward to the West Indies. While there he found himself selling a lot of travel insurance. He discovered he was good at selling insurance, so he left travel agenting and went into insurance, full time, joining the American Life Insurance Co. in 1975.

'I started by selling life insurance to other West Indians, contacting Grenadians first of all. When they heard my surname, Whiteman, most of them immediately said, "Are you Althinus's son?" That was my father. No, that wasn't his real name. Just a nickname he had all his life. He only ever drank tea so he was called All Tea as a young man which became Althinus. His real name was Francis Ignatius.

'Yes, my surname did cause a few incidents during my years in London. When I was a bus conductor, an inspector jumped on my bus one day and said, "What's your name?" "Whiteman," I said. "Don't be clever," he said. He thought I was being awkward and he booked me.

'Another time, when I was selling insurance, to anyone by now, not just West Indians, I called on this house and gave the woman at the door my card. She burst out laughing and called her husband. They were a white couple – called Black. It was in Devonport Road, Shepherd's Bush. I remember it well. We all had a good laugh.'

Joslyn did so brilliantly as an insurance salesman that he was given his own unit, with his own sales force, and was soon turning over £1 million a year.

'In 1988 the UK Chamber of Commerce elected me Black Businessman of the year. I'm still getting commissions from that time.'

That was the year he and his wife decided to return to Grenada. At the age of forty-five, he thought it was time to give up England, and insurance, though he still has a flat in London, in East Croydon, which he stays in most years. One of his daughters, aged sixteen, is still at boarding school in England.

'My first thought on my return was to build a hotel. I did look at some land on Grand Anse beach, and made plans to start, but Royston from Spice Island told me that particular plot had water problems. So I backed out. I went into agriculture instead, buying a small plantation, growing mainly bananas.'

Just a year after he returned, he was approached to go into politics. During his years in London he had started a project to build and equip a library in Grenada, getting some fellow Grenadians in Canada and the USA, who like him had done well abroad, to put up the money.

He stood in 1989, and lost, but got in at a second attempt. In 1995 he became Minister for Agriculture. Now he had become Minister of Tourism and Civil Aviation.

He was very pleased that a Ritz Carlton hotel was coming soon to Grenada, making it the island's first big international hotel. The next problem was to get more airline services. 'In the past, our tourism has been ad hoc. Now I'm working on a ten-year master plan. At present, we have 1,700 beds. In ten years, I want to have 3,000 beds.'

Oh, no. One does like to see returnees doing well, and putting their experience and knowledge into helping their mother island, but steady on. I know what will happen with these 3,000 beds. Half of them will end up with jacuzzis.

And so to the tour. I always have one, as all visitors should, after about three or four days' lolling, just to get the lie of the land, find out if you have chosen the best spot or if there's somewhere much better. Caribbean islands are mostly pretty small so you can get round them in a day, or at least across and back, or do a good circle, convincing yourself that's it, done it, seen it. I hate driving, so I always find a way to be driven. Taxi drivers offering island tours tend to take you the route they took yesterday, and tomorrow, but usually for a good reason. Not just the craft shop and the beach bar where they get a back-hander, but they do know the accepted beauty spots. Once is usually enough for me, as I always come back knackered, especially on an island that appears small on the map, such as, say, Dominica, but takes for ever to get round as the roads are hell, the bends tortuous.

Grenada is one of those islands where the Island Tour is a joy. There's a satisfactory coast road, a real tropical rainforest in the middle and lots of alternate return routes. Best of all, for a beginning or an end, is St George's, the capital of Grenada, the most attractive capital in the whole of the West Indies. No, I can't think of a nicer one. Gustavia in St Barts has a fine harbour, but rather enclosed, with little grandeur. Kingstown in St Vincent has a good setting, but is too dusty and industrial. Port Elizabeth in Bequia is pretty, but lacks architecture.

St George's has almost everything. It's on a stunning bay, shaped like a horseshoe, with the town nestling on the slopes of the green hills behind, coming right down to the water's edge. There are no ugly, smoky, dockyard bits to spoil the views, no nasty road or dirty dockside factories to cut off the sea from the town. St George's is all of a piece. So you can walk round the whole harbour without fear of being knocked down or poisoned by fumes, enjoy uninterrupted sea views, gaze across to the ancient fort and buildings at one end, standing guard over the town, or look inland towards the handsome houses on the green sloping hills. There are cafés and restaurants and walkways along the front, interesting squares and markets behind. It's big enough, with some imposing 18th-century buildings and some fine churches, to feel like a capital, if only of a little island, yet small enough to walk round in a couple of hours.

Yes, I could live in St George's. How strange that most expats don't, cutting themselves off with their boring new houses, big wire fences and barking dogs in the fairly flat and featureless peninsulas on the south coast around L'Anse aux Epines.

Even stranger, for such a pretty little town, with such friendly people, on such a placid island, that they had that revolution, that mini bloodbath, not so very long ago. Those JCBs on the bench might tease Wayne today about the marks of his manacles, but at the time it was far from a joke.

It happened in 1979 when there was a bloodless takeover by Maurice Bishop who set up a socialist government. All went well for three years or so, with the new government being popular, despite economic difficulties. Bishop at first favoured Russian-Cuban aid, but in October 1983 he was in negotiations with the Americans, which so outraged some extreme left-wingers in his own party that they decided to stage their own coup. Bishop and several of his cabinet were assassinated. A joint US and Caribbean force mounted a fairly chaotic rescue mission, invaded the island and democracy was eventually restored.

The assassins were sentenced to death, but got life imprisonment instead. They are still locked up in one of the forts on the hill, so my taxi driver informed me, as we drove out of the town, heading north. There had been a request that week for one of them to be allowed out for health reasons, which had been backed by some cleric, but the population as a whole was still against them ever being released.

The taxi driver had given me his memories of the whole bloody saga, with graphic accounts of the tortures that had gone on, but once out into the country he was full of funny stories about the American invasion. He stopped to show me some mango groves where apparently American marines had tried to land – using a little tourist map of the island, out of date, and badly duplicated. They got totally lost and ended up bogged down in swamps.

Maurice Bishop is still a hero. His original socialist revolution had been bloodless, driving out a right-wing regime which was considered corrupt. On a rock by a roadside I noticed a slogan which said 'Maurice Live'. Underneath was a drawing of a gun.

The present-day dramas, often involving guns, revolve round drug trafficking, though my taxi driver said it was not as bad as it was. 'The Americans have these helicopters that fly over the ganja fields, up in the hills. They got a sensory thing that can spot ganja, then the police and the army come and burn the fields.'

So has that stopped it?

'Yes, many of the ganja fields have gone. But Venezuelan fishermen now bring it in on their boats, then private yachts take it out again.' Taxi drivers, everywhere, are of course terribly well informed.

We passed a settlement called Happy Hill, which he said was named after the fact that it was one big happy family, where people always helped each other. 'Not like that now. Not with the younger generation, ugh . . .'

I got out in Gouyave, a rather dusty, deprived-looking little town, which has a working spice factory, open to tourists, where naturally I bought a selection of nutmegs and spices. About the same price as in Camden Town, but awfully genuine. Grenada is of course known as the Spice Island. It still produces about one-third of the world's nutmeg and cloves.

In the far north of the island, round Sauteurs, the driver pointed out houses belonging to JCBs. He said you can tell them by their English-style balconies. About 75 per cent of the people he knew of his age, around fifty-five, were JCBs. He himself had lived in London for thirteen years, in Ladbroke Grove, working as a motor mechanic. 'I got fed up, man, being stopped by the cops in the middle of the night for nutting, just for walking down the street.'

Those who went to Britain, like himself, tend to come back with more money than those who went to the USA. 'Americans spend more money on their clothes. English people spend more money on their houses.'

West Indians in New York for thirty years, paying rent for their apartment, in the normal American style, often ended up with very little. West Indians in London or Birmingham, by doing what the normal Brits do, getting a mortgage on a flat, then a little house, then perhaps a bigger one, often ended pretty rich when they came to sell up, their original £10,000 modest property turning into something worth £200,000. On their return, many have enough to buy two houses in their home island, one to live in, one to rent out.

The new houses he was pointing out, with their three beds, garage, wrought-iron balconies, bay window at the front, could be bought for as little as £25,000. Some JCBs not only manage to buy two but a little block of flats as well which they fill with British holidaymakers. Nice to think that Britain has put something back in their pockets over the last thirty years, having taken so much out in the last 300 years.

I had booked lunch in the far north in a place called Mount Rodney, a very attractive old plantation house, owned and run by Norris Gurling, a stalwart of the JCB benchers, and his English wife Lin.

Norris's father was a successful shopkeeper in Grenada and wanted him to join him in the shop, but in 1955, when he was eighteen, Norris decided to get away. 'I could have gone to the USA, but I chose London because I wanted to be alone.'

Alone, in a place like London?

'Yes. I had a plethora of relations in New York, but I knew no one in London. I therefore had no obligation to live in other people's pockets. A big city like London is a good place to be alone.'

He went by boat, which he thinks was Italian, stopping at every island, although he couldn't remember where exactly. At Southampton he got a train to London and then looked for a taxi.

'I stepped into the taxi with my big case and the taxi driver said "Where To?" I said I was looking for a place to live. I left it to him where he took me. I can still see his face, and his look of astonishment. But he said get in. I got into that cab at 5.30 in the evening and it wasn't till 1.30 in the morning that he'd found a place that would take me.'

And how much did he charge?

'Oh, I remember that exactly: four pounds, ten shillings.' It didn't sound much, till I tracked back in my mind to prices in 1955, and remembered that a train ride from London to Carlisle cost that.

'The place where I eventually got a room was in Regent's Park Terrace, near Camden Town. The house was lived in by young men of my age, British men, most of whom turned out to work at the BBC. They happened to have a spare room.

'One evening, after I'd just arrived, I said I'd like a bath, but I was told the gas heater wasn't working. An Ascot heater, was it called? They had run out of money for the meter. Anyway, I said cold water didn't worry me. I always showered in cold water in Grenada. So I filled the bath, put my toe in – and my screams must have been heard all over London. I only put in my toe, but I don't think it thawed out for three days...

'But I was very comfortable in that house, after I got used to the noise of the trains. I'd never heard that noise before. Not at all like the rolling noise of the surf I was used to.

'I got on well with the BBC chaps. We used to go and eat in Soho, go to clubs like the Golden Slipper, the Talk of the Town.'

The Pigalle?

'Oh yes, I'd forgotten that. I saw some big stars there.'

He was in London to study, and went to a college in Hammersmith to train as an engineer. He then worked as a civil engineer on various building projects in and around London.

'I was happy in London. I didn't think for a long time about coming back. In my mind I thought of here as being claustrophobic.'

But in 1976, after twenty-two years in England, he and Lin went to Trinidad for a holiday during the Carnival. They liked it so much, they decided to stay in the West Indies. He got a job in Tobago for four years then in 1980 returned to Grenada and bought Mount Rodney.

'The house was built in 1890. It had been a cocoa and banana plantation, with sixty-four acres, but the previous owner decided to give each of his sixty-four workers an acre – then sell up the house and garden. So all we have is the house and six acres of garden.'

They have added bits to the house, all in the same Caribbean style, with wooden verandas and balconies. Lin, who is from Ealing, worked in a local hotel for a while, then began her own little tourist handling company, Serendipity. It now has a staff of six, but she works in the office only one day a week. Norris is retired. She is semi-retired. They do lunches for people touring the north of the island, which have to be booked. They don't do other meals, or take guests. They've had enough of working hard. Done all that.

Could I live in Grenada? That's usually my thought when I leave a pleasant place. The ocean views from their house and garden were wonderful, their house and gardens beautiful and artistic. I could certainly spend a long time in such a setting, but no, I think I'd still like to be nearer St George's, civilisation, as they know it.

On the other hand, I could never imagine myself living like the Drews, even for a day. They are an expat couple who live at the far southern end of the island – on a yacht. Not a smart, luxury yacht. A very basic little boat, where they live a very basic life, just managing to keep afloat, in both senses of the word. Yet, as so often happens with people with little, they were so generous. Not just inviting me to lunch but coming to my hotel to pick me up.

Graham, tall, bearded, angular, arrived in what appeared to be a home-made pick-up truck. Most of it is, he said, especially the wooden body which he did himself.

We bumped along various dusty unmade-up roads till we came to a modern house, on a rather swampy, reedy, lagoon-like shore.

At the water's edge we got into a little dinghy and he rowed me across to their yacht, shouting for Lesley, his wife, that we had arrived. We clambered aboard but she was nowhere to be seen. She soon emerged from the sea, in her swimming costume. She'd been looking at a lobster pot to see if anything had been caught.

Lesley's accent is pure Essex, even after all these years, while Graham has a rather refined English accent, though he left England when he was fifteen. He was born in Penzance, Cornwall, where his father was a motor mechanic. In 1955 he decided to emigrate with his family to Rhodesia.

'He couldn't stand another horrible British winter, lying on a slab of concrete under a car. I was quite excited. The Rhodesian government sent us this booklet which had a photo of a bare-breasted woman. Being fifteen, I thought this looks good. A country where women don't wear clothes...'

Graham qualified as an architect, worked for various firms in Africa, got married and then divorced. As a Rhodesian citizen, he was called up for national service, serving in the army and then the police. When independence came, and Zimbabwe emerged, he was not so keen on the way the country was going. 'I couldn't see a future for it.' Which was about the time he met Lesley.

She was born in Woodford Green, Essex and got married in 1963 to a motor mechanic. One winter, he decided that's it, he'd had enough of cold concrete, etc. Almost the same words as Graham's dad had used. So, aged nineteen, Lesley emigrated with her husband. The marriage collapsed, leaving her with a daughter, Kim.

'When I met Graham, he said he was leaving, building his own boat and going to sail from Mozambique to the West Indies on his thirty-foot-long catamaran. I decided to go with him.'

Their first problem was getting money out of the country and any of their possessions, including their boat. 'The negotiations about that took for ever.' But they set off, in 1981, all three of them, including Kim who was then six. 'We gave her lessons on the boat.'

After many adventures and near disasters, they eventually fetched up in Antigua in 1983 – where their boat was stolen and all their possessions. 'The British High Commissioner paid for our fare back to England. We landed with nothing and found there were no jobs. We spent three years fighting an insurance claim in Trinidad on our stolen yacht, and ended up with nothing. If you are a big man, you can fight them. If you are a small person, they just laugh at you.'

But Lesley's mother died, leaving a house worth £45,000. They spent half on another boat and set off again across the Atlantic. They ended up in Grenada this time, where they worked as a skipper and cook on charter boats, taking people round the Caribbean.

They then built their own house, Fiddler's Reef, the one I could see just a hundred yards away on the shore. Handsome-enough house, with its own little beach, but they can't afford to live in it full time. So for half of each year they live on their boat, renting out the house to holidaymakers. It's even on the Internet.

'White people in the West Indies usually have maids and gardeners. In our case, I'm the maid. When the house is let, that's what I do. Graham's the gardener.'

Daughter Kim is now grown up and married locally and they all feel they are in Grenada for good. 'I call myself Cornish, if asked,' said Graham, 'but I don't feel British at all.

'It's the weather and the people I love here. They don't have hang-ups here. There's no racial tension, not the sort we had in Africa. In the West Indies, Grenadians are known as fairly bolshie people, awkward people, but that's really because they are self-reliant, with self-respect. They march to their own drum.

'Expats usually say they miss British culture, the theatres and stuff, but I never had that, not in Cornwall. We get BBC World Service on the boat, and that's enough to keep us in touch.'

Their little boat has solar panels and a wind machine to generate electricity and charge their batteries. They have lots of local friends, many of them other yachties. 'I estimate there's about a hundred boats around the island with people living on them full time – Americans, Swiss, Australians, Brits. Some move around, with the trade winds, as we used to do. Some stay put.

'You get all types of boats. Some are small and home-made, some old and battered like ours. It's now almost thirty years old. I don't think I could even sell it now. But you also get the £250,000 jobs which are chromium-plated, all mod cons, air-conditioning, top of the pops. In a harbour in the Med, that sort of boat would get all the admiring looks, but not here. The top of the pops here is an Ozzie I know who has sailed from Australia in a boat he made out of old tea chests.'

I said I was amazed that anyone could even sail across oceans, especially Columbus, without any modern devices at all.

'Oh, it's not as hard as you think. I could sail the Atlantic with a compass and dead reckoning. You have the stars and the birds to help you, as Columbus did, to tell you where you are, and the swell of the sea and the trade winds. It's easier today of course. You can follow the shipping lanes or the direction of the jets overhead.'

I mentioned Otmar, my German friend from Bequia, who did the same cross-Atlantic sail with his wife, to get away from it all, and now they have got away from each other.

'Yes, we saw that sort of thing happening all the time when we were sailing round the world. They get to Cape Town, or the Canaries, and one says that's it, I've had enough. Then the bloke goes off and finds a dusky maiden. We've been together for twenty years now, though it's only two years ago we did the decent thing and actually got married.'

Living in such cramped accommodation means they obviously have to get on. When I looked inside, and saw where Lesley had made an excellent lunch, I couldn't believe she could boil water in such a confined space. Yet they even have a little lounge area, with a row of books, their radio for the World Service, and the local newspapers which Graham loves.

'I used to keep a collection of the better headlines. "Man Rapes Cow. Cow Dies." That was one. It was illustrated with a cow tied upside down to a tree. Of course you get bestiality all over the world in rural communities. The papers love religious homilies, but then people don't necessarily take a blind bit of notice.'

He asked if I'd noticed how so many Grenadian men are tall and thin while their women are, well, a bit on the fat side.

'Being fat is seen as desirable. They say it to you as a compliment. I am thin, as you can see, and always have been, but the other day in St George's a friend came up to me and said, "Man, you looking fat." By that he meant I was looking well and prosperous. I'm not of course, no more than I'm fat. But I'm very happy here.'

For the moment, maybe, both being very fit and healthy for a couple approaching their sixties, but what will happen when they get older or ill?

'Yes, that could be a worry. We have no pension or medical insurance. But I think people in the so-called First World go to the doctor too often, just because they have access to a doctor. We've never been able to. But what you find is that most illnesses run their course without medication. Anyway, life on a boat is very healthy. So fingers crossed...'

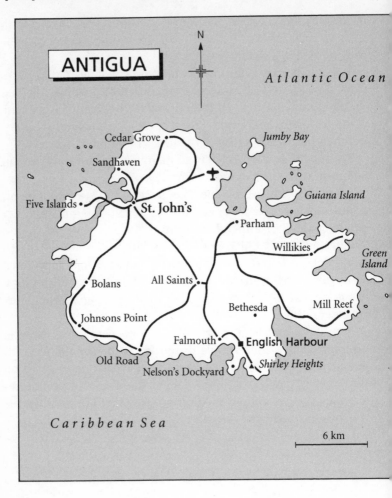

CHAPTER NINE

Antigua

Just before we were due to arrive in Antigua, Elegant Resorts rang to say we could cancel, if we wanted. They'd had some bad reports on Jumby Bay, where we were booked, so if we were worried, they would try and move us elsewhere. Oh no.

It's been one of our favourite places to stay for years – a whole-island resort, just off the north coast of Antigua. Much smaller than Mustique, about one mile across, covering some 300 acres. On the map it is often still called Long Island, which it isn't, as it's more round than long. It's all very kempt, with cut lawns, concrete paths, no wild or hilly parts, more like a park than an island, the sort of place we'd normally not care for, but it's always been so quiet, well run, with good food and a magnificent white beach.

It's a good base from which to explore Antigua, two miles away on the hotel launch. Antigua is just fifteen miles by ten across, with a population of 65,000, but it has become rather prosperous and developed in recent years. It boasts 365 beaches, one for every day of the year, as some Antiguan is bound to tell you, every day of the year. St John's, the capital, has little to recommend it, but there are some interesting historical and architectural buildings, notably around English Harbour and Nelson's Dockyard. Great views, handsomely preserved buildings, but now very much tourist traps. I am always very pleased to get back to the peace and quiet of Jumby Bay after the excitements of Antigua.

Jumby Bay can accommodate around a hundred guests, in a variety of luxury cottages and buildings, spread out, all very artistic, in landscaped gardens. Bikes are provided for getting around. There are also some twenty private villas, owned by rich persons, such as Lord Sainsbury and Ken Follett.

I've always liked the Jumby Bay staff. Being so near the mainland, most go home every night to their own homes in Antigua, which I always think is a plus. On a really remote island, however attractive it is for guests, staff begin to feel imprisoned, grow sullen, get caught up in petty feuds. I have stayed at one remote island in the Virgin Islands where the staff stopped serving, as they were so busy fighting each other.

Another attraction is that it is handy for the main airport on Antigua. Not so handy when the monster planes take off, and fly straight over the little island, hence the nickname Jumbo Bay, but handy for catching a direct BA flight straight back to Blighty. We have usually stayed at Jumby as our last island, after wandering elsewhere round the Caribbean, our final flop, before heading home.

Over the years, there have been several major refurbishments, often after hurricane damage, but sometimes for no reason that I could see, apart from a desire to spend another few million on new curtains and furniture. This time it had been closed for eighteen months, because of some complicated row between the hotel and the villa owners which I hadn't quite followed. It had just opened again, so presumably they were having teething troubles. When I asked Elegant Resorts what the problem was they said, 'Oh, clients have complaining about the food and the service, baggage being late at the villas, bottles of water not turning up when ordered.' Didn't sound all that serious, so we decided not to cancel.

The hotel boat which took us across was pretty scruffy and basic, not the luxury launch they used to have, as that wasn't ready yet, but we did get a rum punch. Dinner that night was poor. Seemed to be lots of soups and no fish. Quite a few staff appeared not to know what they were doing, though they were all smartly dressed. I asked a barman, a large muscular young man who was wearing a pink bow tie, if he'd worked at Jumby Bay before it closed.

'No, this is my first time in a hotel. I was a construction worker.'

I suppose it must have been hard, finding new staff when you've been closed for eighteen months. It was the height of the winter season so, in theory, anyone any good or highly experienced would have already been in work.

*

After another really long hard day swimming, sunbathing, walking and cycling, I caught the late afternoon hotel ferry across to Antigua. On board were a couple of guests, going to the island for the evening, and a chef. He was wearing chef's-type trousers, so that was a clue. He also looked pretty tired and a bit pasty, as chefs do. He was going for just two hours, a quick break between dramas, to see his wife and family who were living on Antigua.

I asked what it had been like, these last four weeks since the hotel reopened. He groaned. They should never have opened when they did, but all the marketing and bookings had been done, so they had no alternative.

'For the first week we had no flour. Can you imagine a kitchen not having flour? We had ordered it in time. It had arrived, by container, but it was stuck on the dock while customs refused to open it. Oh, it was all very complicated.

'We've been unable till now to get fresh fish. Yes, there's lots of it locally, but it's all pre-ordered, in long-standing deals. Most of it goes straight to the French islands who pay premium prices. I went round all the suppliers and some said yes, they would send fresh fish – but when it arrived, it was frozen. So I had to send it back. Then some people wouldn't deal with us at all because they said they were owed money by the previous hotel management. I've had to say I'll pay money up front, in advance, to reassure them. It seems to be working at last. Tonight you will have fresh fish. I assure you.'

I was heading into St John's to the offices of Price, Waterhouse. Accountants aren't usually a lot of fun to interview, and are too discreet, unwilling or too boring to say anything of interest, but I'd been told that the senior partner was an expat Brit. Not met an accountant before on my travels, so a first for my collection.

Don Ward, aged about fifty-five, was sitting in his plush, air-conditioned office in a new modern white block. Behind him on the wall was a large photograph of a racing yacht and a large silver trophy. Reverential staff came in from time to time with queries or for things to be signed. His blue shirt was crisp, his suit jacket off, but he was still wearing a tie. Relaxed formality, I suppose it's called. Dress-down day is Friday in the City of London but every day in the Caribbean. So, Don, how do you come to be sitting here?

'I qualified as an accountant in London. One of my first jobs was in Nairobi in 1969. When I came back, I was itching to get abroad again, but my wife wasn't keen. Till one day she woke up with a terrible dose of flu and said quick, get me away from this.

'I rang around and on 23 March 1973 I arrived in Antigua to work with a branch of a British firm called Pannell Kerr and Forster. There were two partners and twelve staff. I came as manager, one level below a partner, which means you don't share in the profits.

'I could not have chosen a worse time to come. The economy was at rock bottom. There was nothing doing. The hotels, such as they were, just opened in the winter season. There were only about 1,000 cars on the whole island. That year they harvested the last sugar crop in Antigua. There's been none since then.

'The actual day I arrived, one partner left. In July, four months later, the other partner resigned. I was given a choice. I could either close the office and be given my fare back to England, or pay £25 a year as a licence fee and I could have the firm and keep the name. I wanted to stay, having hardly arrived. So I took over the firm.

'This was in July 1973. By December, I was £2,000 in debt. A year later, I was still in debt; but in August 1974 we had a stroke of luck. That month Court Line went bust. You must remember them, big holiday and travel firm. They were involved in the original LIAT Airways which also went down. LIAT was based in Antigua and I got the job of liquidating them. A huge job, which took us three years, but we were well remunerated because we got a share of each aircraft we managed to sell off.

'There was a second stroke of luck that same year: an earthquake in October 1974. It only lasted thirty-seven seconds, but it resulted in insurance claims of £37 million. We got a lot of work out of that as loss adjusters.

'So yes, the results of two awful tragedies were wonderful for us.'

There was also another development, a bit more complicated this time, but in the long run more important than either of the tragedies in establishing his firm's success – and the present success and wealth of Antigua.

'Around 1976 I was asked by a foreign mining firm if I could establish an office for them Antigua. In doing so, I came across the International Business Companies Act. It had been passed here in 1967, but the lawyers didn't seem to know much about it. In looking into it, I realised it gave us the ability in certain circumstances to act as a tax haven. Foreign-owned companies, trading internationally, do not need to pay tax here.

'Since 1976, the International Business Act and subsequent legislation have provided us with one of our main activities – setting up tax plans.'

In 1983 his business was doing so well that he sold his interest in it to his new partners. At this stage, his three daughters were at school abroad and he wanted to take a break.

'The money I got was substantial in East Caribbean dollars, but my wife was soon spending it in hard currency. Permanent retirement was not an option.'

After four years not working, Price, Waterhouse was setting up its own Antigua office, so he joined them as partner in charge. Today, there are three partners and forty staff, mainly specialising in offshore business.

'It is more regulated now than it was. It was a free-for-all in the 1970s. Today there are many more regulations and controls. We won't accept anyone who just turns up, however rich. Thorough searches are made on the source of their money, just in case. No, we don't do the searches here. That's done by Price, Waterhouse offices in New York or London or wherever.'

So how's business in Antigua today?

'Terrific. No complaints. We haven't been wiped out by a really bad hurricane for some years. We get hit, but we recover far more quickly than we ever did. Experience has taught us how to get the infrastructure going again. Each time it happens, we recover more quickly. Hotels now reopen in just three months. It could take a year in the old days.

'There's also been a change of attitude. After Hurricane Hugo, we did sit around, waiting for people to come and help. Now we don't wait. We all join and get on with it.

'Jumby Bay closing was very sad. Not just because we lost the money and work it brought into Antigua but it sent out the wrong signals. It was very bad for our image.'

Now that it has reopened, Antigua's upmarket tourist trade is recovering again with a steady stream of wealthy foreigners wanting holiday homes in Antigua – which the authorities are encouraging.

'I suggested to the government that they should charge for residency qualification, which they now do. You have to pay 20,000 a year in US dollars. Expats also bring in a lot of money in other ways. You pay 7 per cent stamp duty on your house when you buy it. They usually import a car, so that's more duty, and bring in furniture. By the time a guy has set himself up here, a lot of money has been spent. We should be grateful to people like Lord Sainsbury and Ken Follett with houses here.'

Tourism and its related activities are now the country's biggest earner – but there is also a new arrival, already bringing in millions and boosting the economy. Something I'd never heard of: offshore gambling.

'It's all done on the Internet, by people all round the world. Some of it is gambling on sports results, but mainly it's just like casino gambling.

'Legislation was passed in various Caribbean islands to allow the people running the gambling to have their offices based in the Caribbean. St Kitts, Dominica, Jamaica and Antigua all passed the appropriate laws. Ours seems to have worked best, and been the best regulated. Elsewhere there have been some terrible scandals.

'The government now gives out these licences for a fee of $100,000, so that's how the government gains. The operators gain by not paying any taxes, though they are encouraged to support local charities.

'We as a firm are not involved and I have my own view on the morality of it all, but the fact is these operations do help the economy generally.'

I mentioned all the stories currently running about corruption in Antigua. Not just stories but actual cases, reported in the British press. He made no comment. So I bashed on.

Encouraging all these offshore investors, and now Internet gamblers, must presumably increase the chances of money laundering? Then with all that cash swishing around, people in high places must sometimes be approached to give favours. Did he think that might be happening?

I waited for him either to explode or refuse to answer any more questions.

'I can't say there's no corruption,' he said after a long pause. 'But don't believe all the stories you read in the papers. I know from the inside the details of several businesses where corruption was widely alleged – and I know that none of those allegations was true. So I take with a pinch of salt the stories about cases I know nothing about. A lot of them are lies, politically motivated.' He paused again. 'As far as money laundering is concerned, it's a Caribbean problem, but new regulations are making it tougher. Hopefully, we are on the right track. The realisation is sweeping through that these islands must clean up or be ostracised.'

He is in Antigua for good now, with no intention of ever leaving. 'I love it. As all male expats do. It's an exciting, stimulating place. Wives don't find it as stimulating, especially when their children go off to boarding schools, or grow up and leave the islands. The wives are left with cocktail parties and coffee mornings.'

So what's so exciting for men?

'Well, the opportunity to make tax-free money. It's heaven. You also meet an enormous variety of interesting people for such a small island. Then of course there's the climate and the sport, especially sailing and golf.'

Sailing is his big passion, as I could see from the photo of his yacht and his cups. He has a fifty-foot yacht and his own dock at the bottom of his garden. 'I can walk out of my house, get into my boat, turn right and sail to Guadeloupe or left and sail to Barbuda. What could be nicer?'

So what does he miss?

'It used to be strawberries and mushrooms, but in our super-markets now, you can get anything, all the year round. There's nothing we go short of. The only thing we brought back from England last time was a bunch of tulips.

'We don't have the theatre or concerts, but we do have BBC World Service and CNN to keep us in touch. I still miss the seasons, but travelling is much easier than it was. We are going skiing in March, probably Colorado. In May we're going to Verona for the opera and in August to London for the theatre. Antigua is a good place to be in and to get out from.'

*

Is expat life for a woman really all that boring? Marriages do seem to come unstuck, but that can happen anywhere. And wherever you live, it's an advantage to have some sort of career or outside interest in life once the family grows up. But of course when life goes wrong for the expat wife, being *ex-patria* makes it so much worse, stuck in a foreign land, cut off from family and friendship support systems.

I went to see Gilly Gobinet, a very attractive, lively woman in her forties living alone in a beach house. A most artistic house, beautifully situated, but through a window I could see a lot of tree debris on her bit of beach. Left over from the last hurricane, she said. She's been looking for a strong man to come along and help her clear it away, but hasn't found one so far.

She was born Gillian Holdup near Kew Gardens, London, and went to Sussex University where she read biological sciences. For twelve years she worked in Strasbourg with the Council of Europe as a biologist. 'It was very bureaucratic and very chauvinistic. I was the only female with a lot of French males.' She married one of them, a French physiotherapist.

'We had a holiday in Antigua eighteen years ago and both fell in love with it. My husband then managed to get a job here, as a government physiotherapist, setting up the physiotherapy department in the island's hospital. It took him about two years to get the simplest things, like a white coat and a bar of soap.'

Things didn't work out as well as expected, by which time they had three children and little money. 'I thought I had come here to retire to a life of leisure, but I then had to look for a job. I got one in an estate agency, but the pay was nil. It was all on commission. I was in the library one day and got down this book on self-fulfilment. Amongst other things, it said: "If you want to do something, you *can* do it."

'As a child, I had always wanted to paint, but my mother was against it. She wouldn't let me go to art school. That was really why I did science. Yet even when I was sitting in science lectures at university, I was doodling, illustrating my lecture notes. Since then, with working all those years, and bringing up children, I hadn't even doodled. I began to think that art is really what I like doing best – but how do I begin?

'The book also said that you shouldn't compare yourself with other people; just do what you want to do. I didn't know a thing about painting, so I started with pen and ink drawings.

'My husband wasn't at all supportive. He said I was a lousy artist, with no talent and shouldn't even try. But I did a few drawings and even managed to sell them. Then I moved on to watercolours, just teaching myself. They were a disaster at first and no one wanted them.

'Then I did some funny little Christmas cards for the expat community here to send home: Santa Claus on the beach in his shorts, drinking a rum punch. I moved on to calendars and prints. It's just built up from there, over the last eleven years.'

For the last seven of them she has lived virtually alone, since she and her husband separated. 'We just drifted apart. There wasn't anyone else, though I think he now has a girlfriend.

'I arrived here as a housewife and mother, supported by my husband. Now I am alone. Supported by no one. Just myself. And there are my three children to educate. But I've found I like having my own freedom and independence.'

She has two boys and a girl, aged fifteen, thirteen and eleven, who are at a boarding school in England. 'A comprehensive, state boarding school, near Gatwick. The education is free, but you have to pay for their keep.'

She has become not just an artist but a businesswoman, creating, printing and selling her own stuff. 'I began by taking stalls at craft fairs and sat there, trying to sell my prints. I did have an agent for a very short time, but it didn't work.

'I paint and print what I think will sell. I don't yet have the luxury of expressing myself. I think, now, if I was a tourist here, what scene would I like to send back or take with me?'

Her best lines are still her Christmas cards, which sell 10,000 a year, and her calendars, showing scenes from the Caribbean, which sell over 2,000 a year.

Two months previously she opened her own little gallery in St John's. 'It's still got an open sewer outside, which puts customers off. Not to mention the junkies hanging around. No, it's not exactly a prime site. But I sit there Wednesday to Friday and manage to sell a few things.'

At the beginning, printing was a problem, something else she had to learn about. 'I used a local printer at first, but the quality was lousy. Then I had a printer in Singapore, but things like Christmas cards and calendars would arrive months late.

'I now have a printer in Calne in Wiltshire who is wonderful. And I've got an excellent new delivery system – with Geest Line. The ships take bananas to England, and bring back freight, including my stuff. It works out quite cheap. It means I have to work to the banana ships' timetable, getting their arrival times here, then working backwards so I have all the material at the printer's in time.'

She had just had her first book, *A Caribbean Christmas*, published by Macmillan Caribbean. This has Christmas scenes from all the Caribbean islands, with jokey little symbols to represent each island. In Cuba, Santa is smoking a cigar. Ho ho. For the Cayman Islands, there's a shark behind Santa. I didn't get that. 'A lone shark, gerrit.'

Looking back at her life, she thinks it might have been better now if she hadn't got married.

'Coming to the Caribbean is a test of anyone's marriage. It has been hard bringing children up here. There were lots of problems. "What problems?" my husband used to say, when I was worried. That could explain a lot about him ...

'When we got here, everything began to change. When we were in Strasbourg, both working, I was aware of some of his attitudes, but I ignored them. I deluded myself. Once we were here, thrown together all the time, seeing each other more and more, I realised I was being turned by him into his mother. Oh, you know. He expected his meals to be always on the table, waited on hand and foot. That's how Frenchmen are brought up by their mothers. Yet I had to go out and earn a living, somehow.

'I suppose there were problems in the marriage already – and this was the worst place to come to solve problems with a relationship. We are not enemies. We just live separate lives. And he does contribute half of the children's expenses.'

Right, now for what I had asked all expats, what do you miss?

'The London galleries and theatre. But I'm now okay for books, since I started getting *The Good Book Guide*. I don't feel so out of touch. I love cooking and at one time you couldn't get butter here, except in a tin, which was horrible. And the meat was always awful. Now you can get anything. The supermarkets here are excellent.

'I miss the seasons, as all expats do, but I don't miss the light nights which many do. I am used to it getting dark at six o'clock. It was strange being in the UK last summer and it didn't get dark till ten o'clock.

'You have to get used to power cuts, which happen all the time, and of course the hurricanes. I've lived through Hugo, Luis, Marilyn, Sebastian, Bertha, Georges. We have been hit directly by two of them, hence the bits of the roof blown away and debris down on my beach.

'The big problem now is that the insurance premiums are so high that people can't afford to insure their houses.

'I am insured, at vast expense. I have to be because I still have a mortgage on this house. I have a friend who owns a restaurant but she can't afford to insure it. The cost of the premiums would be more than her income. So if she gets hit, that's it, she's wiped out.

'What's happened in Antigua now is that it's easier to get a loan for a car than a house. That's why you see so many cars, and why people are always washing them. It becomes their big thing, their prize possession. The reason why car loans are easy is that they can seize your car if you default. You can't actually drive off the island with it, can you?

'Will I stay? I dunno. I have a house here, I have a business to run. I don't relish going back to the cold of England. I don't think anyway I could earn a living in the UK. I am now a citizen. Yes, I don't pay any income tax, but because of import duties, everything is very expensive.

'I've got used to being on my own. You indulge so many of your own habits. I see just a few people because I've now decided that most social occasions are a waste of time. I want to establish my business, so that I can then have the time to paint what I really want to paint.

'I don't think I'd ever get married again. If someone came along, then that would be jolly nice as I do miss companionship. Otherwise, I am quite happy being free and independent.'

Mostly, on my West Indian wanderings, I'd been looking out for

British expats, for obvious reasons. I know where they come from, and can speak their language. Plus Americans, if pushed. On ex-British islands you are bound to find most of the expats are British or American, just as the French islands attract the French. You don't get many Germans or Italians, as they were not colonial powers, not in the Caribbean. I don't think I met one Italian expat. I am sure in the restaurant business there are some, but I was trying to avoid the restaurant business.

In Antigua I met my second German. Easy enough, as she was on the reception desk at Jumby Bay. I had assumed at first from her name, Rita, and her fluent English, that she was a Brit. She also had a rather haughty English look about her, the way you often get in posh hotels, with her dark hair severely swept back, and her stern expression. Until of course she smiled.

Rita was born in 1955 in a small village in rural Germany. At the age of eighteen she moved to the big city and got a job as a telephonist in Frankfurt. Through her job she had to make calls to British Telecom in London and found herself speaking frequently to a male telephonist at the other end. They liked the sound of each other and over the months became very friendly. Rita was unaware that the male was a black West Indian, and an actor, resting between parts, thought the parts were getting fewer and fewer. She came to London to meet him, fell in love and got married.

Her husband failed to get acting parts, so carried on as a telephonist. 'He's a very proud person. He believed people should seek him out. He didn't think he needed to go looking for parts.' So Rita went out to work.

'I was an air hostess for a while, on Freddy Laker's airline. They were looking for people who could speak German. But that went bust. Then I was a hostess on the Orient Express train to Venice, but was laid off when they started making cuts. I then did various other office jobs.'

She was eleven years in London, and loved it, by which time she had a son. Her husband then decided to take early retirement from BT, accept a small pay-off, and return to his home island. So all three went off to live in Antigua.

'I was all for it. I was interested in doing something new. My husband had a job lined up running a workshop for local actors.

But that didn't work out. He alienated himself from the government, not something you should do out here if you want to get ahead.

'So I had to look for a job. It took me three months, but I got one as secretary with a property company. I got quite bored, after two years, and saw a job advertised at Jumby Bay, secretary to the general manager. I got it and worked here for four years from 1993 to 1997. I left when I got offered a job at Jolly Harbour, on the mainland, which was handier to get to.

'So I had left Jumby, just before it closed down. "Rita, you should have told us." That's what all my friends said. "You must have known something." I didn't of course. I was just lucky to have been offered another job at the right time.

'But on 26 February 1998 I was made redundant from that job – for the third time in my life. I remember the date because it was the day of the eclipse.

'My marriage had also collapsed by then. So I was on my own, with my son Sven. I had no job, no husband.

'When we first came to Antigua in 1990, things had been fine. But after about five years, I started to feel he was becoming an Antiguan man. They don't hang out with their women. They do their own thing. In London, it had not been too bad. We hadn't actually gone many places together, but we'd still felt like a unit.

'The main problem was politics. I didn't lose my husband to another woman but to politics. After his workshop didn't get going, he started campaigning for the opposition party. He stood for them in an election, against Lester Bird, the Prime Minister. He got 600 votes to Bird's 1,200, so he did quite well. But I never saw him. He had no time for me.

'It was a lovely day, the day I was made redundant, but by then, with my marriage finished, there was nothing any longer to keep me here. What could I do? All I could think of was to go home.'

It was twenty-five years since she had left her home village in Germany. She had gone off to seek wealth and happiness. She returned home with nothing. 'I literally did have nothing, because I had sold my car, my furniture, everything, to pay our fares home.

'I went to live with my mother in the Saarland, to the smallest county in Germany, the place where I had been raised.

'I suppose I had returned a failure. Other people probably

thought that. But I told myself I did have something: I had a beautiful son. What is material wealth anyway? You can always get new furniture, a new house. I had had many experiences, seen many places. So no, I didn't look upon myself as a failure.

'It's a very small village, where I come from, so I was seen as a big-town girl in a small place, a bit flamboyant compared with people of my age, the ones I'd been to school with. They all seemed middle-aged to me. When I said let's go on a pub crawl on Saturday night, they looked shocked. They had to stay at home and cook the Sunday roast for their husbands.

'I managed to get a job, with Ford motors, and lived at home with my mother, but I felt like a fish out of water. I had no friends. What am I doing here? I said to myself.

'I realised why I'd left at seventeen in the first place, yet while living in Antigua, I had become homesick for Germany. I suppose the longer I lived away the more beautiful it became. You should have heard me before I left Antigua, running down Antigua. Once I got back to Germany, I knew I'd made a mistake.

'Sven adapted better than me. He enjoyed his new school, but his problem was the weekend. "No one invites me for sleep-overs," so he told me. All his friends did things with their families, so if the weather was bad, he was stuck inside, with nothing to do. In the end he said to me, "Mummy, you are right, we should not have come."

'I rang a girl friend in Antigua, told her I'd made a mistake, and she said come back at once. I said I've no money, but she said don't worry, use my credit to get a ticket and pay me back later. I didn't want to do that. My mother also offered to lend me money, or give me my inheritance in advance, such as it is, but I said no. So I worked hard and saved enough. I came back on 6 November 1998, six months after I'd left. My friends here were amazed. "Rita, Rita, you're not back are you?"

'I arrived back and moved in with my friend, an English, cockney girl. I had no job, nothing. Not even a pot to piss in.'

Rita lowered her voice at this bit of English vulgarity, in case any guests might hear. While we talked, she was running the reception desk, answering queries, taking calls.

'I found that Jumby Bay had reopened, so I applied for my old job, as secretary to the general manager. It had gone. But I was offered a job on the reception desk. I started just four days after I got back. So here I am, back to where I used to be.

'Sven has gone back to his old school and I have applied for citizenship. I'm staying this time. Oh yes.

'I don't see my husband. I have met him in the street, but he doesn't talk to me. I don't know what he's doing, except I know he's now left the opposition party. I don't know if he's got a woman or not. There wasn't anyone else involved, on either side. We just grew apart.

'When I left Germany, my friends there said I was being so courageous, going back again, on my own. I didn't feel courageous. I just felt I was going home.

'It's hard to explain why this feels like home, and Germany doesn't. In Germany I just seemed to worry about bills all the time, about the gas and electricity. The skies seemed grey, every day. It seemed like a grey country. All I could ever see was the next house. I never saw any horizon.

'When I'm here, I pick up the warmth and attitudes of the people. They are so friendly. It was only being away I realised how true it is. You live outdoors all the time. The warmth of the climate does seem to make people warm.

'They don't worry about tomorrow. So I don't. In Germany, my friends all the time were saying, "Rita, what are you going to do about your old-age pension?" They were so busy worrying about tomorrow they were not enjoying today. The West Indian attitude to life does suit me better.'

There are of course some things she misses. 'Nice German crunchy bread with sunflower seeds. Here the bread is mostly white and soft. I like bread with a bite.

'But I don't miss shopping in Germany. People are so rude and you get pushed all the time. I grew to hate the German department stores with the crowds and unhelpful staff. Here if you're looking at clothes, the staff will bring you as many things as you like, while you just sit there. No need to dress all the time then go and look for something.

'Actually I miss England more than Germany. I grew to love British TV, things like the drama series and comedies like *Smith and Jones*. I loved them. And *French and Saunders*. I don't miss German TV at all.'

So what about Sven, now aged twelve? Rita might have made the right decision for herself, but it must have been tough for him, moving back and forward. At his age, I had moved four times, but only between Scotland and England, yet it took me till I was eighteen to feel I really belonged anywhere. Sven has moved continents, with different languages, cultures and climates.

'He had to sit the Common Entrance exam on his return, to go to secondary school, and he came fourth in the whole island. Three girls did better, so he was the first boy.

'He got chosen to go to Edinburgh for the Commonwealth summit meeting. You must have read about it. They also had a children's summit as well, with school children from each of the different Commonwealth countries. Sven went as Antigua's rep. He met Tony Blair and the Prince of Wales.

'One of the things that amazed him was seeing his own breath. He hadn't lived in Germany at this time, and had never experienced cold. He was too young when we left London to remember anything. In Edinburgh, all the children were told one day they were going swimming – so he turned up in shorts, sandals and T-shirt. That's how he always dressed for the beach. He'd never seen an indoor pool before.

'I was so proud of him, going to Edinburgh. The children all made their own website. He's still in contact with a child from India and from Canada.

'I suppose he would get a better education in Germany. There would be more facilities and opportunities, but he's a clever chap. Even in less good schools, I am sure he will be okay. He's naturally ambitious. He wants to excel. He'll sit up half the night to finish a school project.

'The teachers here are appallingly badly paid, but they do have discipline, insist on politeness and they push the children. In Germany, he would not be pushed. It would be up to him, which of course in Sven's case would be fine, because he pushes himself.

'All children have to have uniform, and it has to be clean and tidy. In Germany, there is no uniform, but what happens is that children demand the latest styles, the latest Nike, in order to go to school. They exert such pressures on their parents.

'Here, you can't tell whether a child comes from a rich home or a poor home. That's what I prefer.

'So I'm staying this time, oh yes. I still don't own anything. I haven't got a house. I'm still living with my friend, but I have just bought a car, so I am making progress.'

So what had happened at Jumby Bay? Why had one of the Caribbean's best-known and most luxurious resorts been closed for eighteen months. I did eventually hear what happened from one of the main activists, Dr Peter Swann. He also turned out to be the only permanent resident on the island. So an expat, on my doorstep.

I had breakfast with him and his wife at his villa, served by his young English housekeeper. The house is very swish, with his own little beach, plus a pool, plus two little baby ducks who had recently arrived in his garden. Every time they appeared, he jumped up from his breakfast table to go and beam at them, just as I was getting the saga roughly straight in my mind.

He is aged in his early sixties, with a slight rural edge to his accent and a sort of rural, ruddy glow which might suggest he is an affluent West Country farmer who has spent all his life in England. In fact he is a scientist, who has spent almost all his working life abroad. He was born in 1935 in the West Country, but educated at Dulwich College in London.

He first fancied the idea of being a scientist at sixteen when he read Neville Shute's *No Highway*. At Cambridge, he read material sciences, did a PhD, then at twenty-five went off to do research at Alberta University in Canada. It gave him the excuse to travel, spending four months living off the land in British Columbia. 'I'd always wanted to get out of England. I found it too stodgy, people set in their ways.'

When he came back to England, he joined the brain drain to the USA, which many bright scientists did in the 1960s, attracted by salaries and facilities five times better than in the UK. He went to Pittsburgh to join US Steel as a research scientist which involved some time at Göttingen University in Germany.

After ten years he was tempted back, becoming a professor at Imperial College in London, the UK's leading scientific college. 'But I didn't really like the university life. There were too many committee meetings and I hated commuting into London from Petersham. The work itself was interesting, thanks to the development of the first million-volt microscope in the UK.'

He went on to develop instruments which enhanced the performance of this new creation, building them in his department's workshops. 'Colleagues started asking me to make copies of these enhancements, and orders came in. My workload was becoming so great that I had to cut down somewhere.'

So he gave up his job, his professorship. He returned to the USA to start his own company, making scientific instruments.

In order to use the new wonder microscopes properly, you needed to be able to slice your specimens as small as possible. He did it with instruments creating ions which accelerate at high speed through any materials to produce very very thin slices. I think that's it. Anyway, he'd got orders for $1 million worth of these instruments from various universities before he had even started.

I was just getting to grips with all this science when his two ducks appeared and he jumped up. 'They're West Indian tree ducks. Aren't they amazing? Sometimes they're known as whistling ducks, but I haven't heard them whistling yet. They nest in trees and are an endangered species...'

He called his instrument-making company Gatan. 'I wanted a name that meant nothing in the English language to give us the flexibility to branch out into any field. It's actually a misspelling of the German word *getan* meaning "done" and also happens to be Swedish for "street" and Japanese for "bump"!'

His brother joined him in the venture, looking after the manufacturing side. They soon had a research lab in California, plus the manufacturing base in Pittsburgh. 'In the electron microscope business, you have to attract the best PhDs in the field, and most of them at the time wanted to live in California.

'In our lab we made the first commercial digital camera for an electron microscope – similar to the ones on the home camera market today, but ours were used not only to capture digital images but also to align and focus the electron microscope automatically. Our cameras then cost $100,000 each, but we were only making one at a time.'

After ten years he was employing 200 people and turning over $25 million a year in sales, with offices in Munich and Japan as well as the US. 'It was becoming hard work. Once you get over twenty-five people, you have to find managers. Then over 100, you need a second tier of managers.'

In 1990, aged fifty-five, he decided, quite suddenly, to sell out. None of his children was interested or technically equipped to run the business. He sold out in two steps – 70 per cent for $35 million, then the remaining 30 per cent for $50 million – making $85 million in all.

Oh no, just as we were getting on to the money, a subject I can understand, the two stupid ducks, sorry, fascinating and endangered ducks had appeared again, this time heading for his swimming pool. He jumped up and we both went to look at them.

'I am trying to get them to swim in my pool but they have not yet learned how to waterproof their feathers. They are really filthy animals. I keep them overnight in the shower so it's easy to clean up after them in the morning. They think I'm their mother, because I saved them and look after them. When they eventually fly off, I'll be sad to see them go.'

He first came to Jumby Bay in 1988, on holiday, staying at the hotel. While there, he had a most dramatic experience.

'I decided to swim round a little island, Bird Island. On the lee side, it was easy, very calm, but when I got to the ocean side, it was frightening. I just hadn't expected such waves, such a swell. I was soon being bashed against a sheer cliff. I thought I'm going to drown, this is it. When you fear you are drowning, you try to keep your body up, so you push beyond what you can do, which means you lose oxygen. The pain was becoming unbearable. You use your brain to force your muscles, but all they want to do is relax. Eventually you don't care if you do drown, thinking it will be a relief from the pain. As a near-death experience, it was most interesting.'

And interesting to hear a scientist describing it, so analytically, in scientific terms. So what happened next?

'Just as I was giving up, I saw a tiny crevice in the cliff. I got one hand into it and managed to hang there for long enough to get my strength back. Then, about fifteen feet away, I saw a much better ledge. So when I felt strong enough, I watched the waves and managed to swim over to it. Eventually I clambered up the cliff. All together, I was in the water about two and a half hours.

'Over the next three days of the holiday, I began to think, why am I working like a maniac? What is it all for? Not for the money because I had earned enough. It was for the pleasure of accomplishment. That's when I decided to sell up, realising I still had a few years left to enjoy myself, but not push myself.'

On 8 December 1988 he bought two plots at Jumby Bay, one for himself, one for his brother. On his plot, he built the house in which he still lives. For the first few years of living here he was still working. 'I remained president of the company for three years, till they found a new president.'

Being so active, mentally and physically, he soon found himself caught up in the business of the island, which at first he'd thought would be very straightforward.

'The first problem had arisen when I found that the construction company which was going to build my house, part of the deal, so I'd thought, when I'd bought the plot, had closed down. I therefore had to find my own building company.'

Then there was the matter of who actually owned what. 'In buying my plot, and building my house, I got a share in the island, as did seventy-five other owners, plus some 500 non-residents who regularly used the hotel and were in what we called the Club. The deal was that we would eventually own the island and operate it ourselves. It was a wonderful concept. But as the years went on, the developer who had created Jumby Bay realised he was soon going to lose the island himself. That's when the trouble began. It became a war between us.

'On 4 February 1993 we stopped selling any more Club memberships and took the developer to court. I became the chairman of the Club. And thus began my legal education. It took us four years to win the case, and it was during this time the hotel closed for eighteen months.

'Yes, life was made very uncomfortable on the island. The Antiguan government was upset that the hotel was empty, for whatever reason. Oh, it was such a mess. In the end, it was settled at a meeting that lasted six days, in this room, negotiating with the developer's family. I had to form a company and raise £6 million in a matter of days. But we did a deal. The company then bought the island, the hotel, everything, though it later sold the hotel part to the owners of Half Moon Club in Jamaica.

'Today, it's like running a miniature city. We look after everything, water, sewage, our own generator. We've also got our written constitution, so we never get in such a mess again.'

Dr Swann, having retired to a remote island for a simple, quiet, stress-free life, found himself caught up in a drama he never expected, and a responsiblity that still goes on.

'I hardly ever leave the island. Since 1992, I have spent an average of ten months a year here. Pat gets off the island now and again and goes to visit her family.' Pat is his second wife and between them they have seven children.

'In some senses I am trapped. I made the commitment to the island to sort out the mess, get everything running properly. When the hotel closed, 200 people were immediately out of work. We gave them relief aid of $1,000 each. Now we have to get back to where we were. I wish there were more people to share the burden. Pat doesn't enjoy it as much as I do.

'But it does keep me occupied. We have divided the island into four management areas. I am Director of Public Works. I keep an eye on drains and sewage. At the moment I'm working on a plan to redesign the water distribution system.'

Not quite what I'd like to do in my retirement, but then he is a scientist. But even as a scientist, I'd find living permanently on such a small, artificial island stultifying.

'I came here to get away from stimulation. Now I get enough of it, thank you. I communicate with people all the time on the Internet. Part of my brain at the moment is working on a new design for the Jumby Bay garbage bin, to standardise them and ease collection. I've also taken up astronomy. I warned the Antiguan government when the eclipse of the sun was coming up, and did a little TV programme for them.

'Even on this little island there is enough social life. You could go to a dinner party every night, if you wanted.

'I miss nothing at all, except certain friends. But if I go on to the main island, I have friends there. For an island of only 60,000, there are some very interesting people living there. Antigua is a special place.'

He asked me how I'd found Jumby Bay, compared with the old days. I said it didn't yet compare with the old days, but I was sure it would. The new management was trying hard. Things were getting back to normal. And the new management structure for the island, despite all the agonies they'd gone through, might turn out to be a blueprint for other Caribbean islands, and elsewhere.

On my last day, a charming American real-estate agent called Don approached me over dinner and asked if I was interested in buying. That proved things were now back to normal. He could offer me a plot for $1 million, he said, then it would cost roughly the same again to build on it. Cheap, compared with Mustique.

But I declined his kind offer. I said I had to get on to Cuba. A veritable continent, compared with little Jumby Bay. And a place where no plots or houses are for sale.

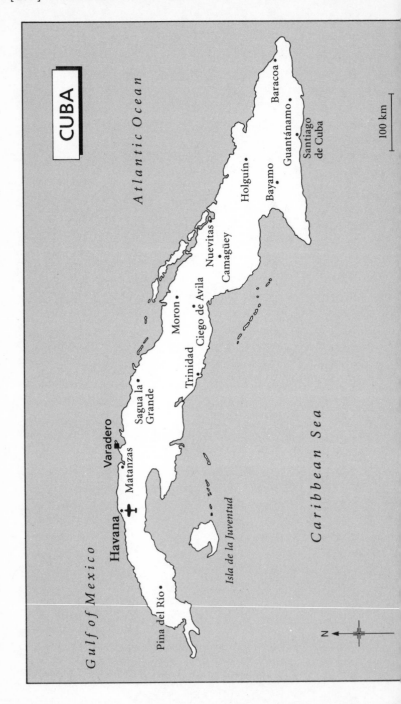

CHAPTER TEN

Cuba: Havana

'Cuba is full.' That's what I was told by everyone. I didn't quite believe it. You mean people are falling off the edges, into the Caribbean? Very unlikely.

I did try to go to Cuba about ten years ago, when I was on Columbus's trail, but there was no tourist industry then, no arrangements for holiday makers. You had to have a special visa, which took for ever, with very complicated conditions. I couldn't even get hold of a visa application form. So I gave up and never went. Did Haiti instead.

Now, Cuba is a tourist-taste thrill, easy to get into, all visitors are welcome; you can get a tourist visa in seconds from a travel agent. It's both trendy, attracting film stars and advertising people doing commercials, and at the same time cheap, attracting the mass market. All of them are fascinated to find out what is happening in Cuba, a country cut off from the mainstream for forty years since the 1959 revolution.

Ten years ago, only about four Brits a week managed to get in. Now the average is 1,000 a week, with the market growing all the time. I got a list of twenty different companies offering package tours. I rang five, and they were sold out, all saying the same thing: Cuba is full.

I eventually got a seat with Cubana, the only airline doing scheduled flights from London to Cuba (though BA has since started). Their economy section was full, sold to the package-holiday trade, but I managed to get a seat in club class and a room booked for me.

Cubana is Cuba's national airline. I hadn't heard of it before, but people likened it unflatteringly to Aeroflot.

While checking in at Gatwick, I heard people talking about the previous day's Cubana flight to Havana – forty had been turned away, despite having tickets. They were given vouchers for a hotel for the night, and told to come back next day.

I got my boarding card, heard my flight was on time, and even found that as a club passenger I could use one of the club lounges. It was totally empty, so I filled up with peanuts and biscuits to give to poor people I might meet in Cuba. It is a communist country after all, and they always have shortages. I had a few books with me, to give to people. I usually take a few Beatles badges or Man United badges as well. I find they go down better than beads these days with the natives in the USA or Europe, but I hadn't brought any, thinking that Cubans don't play football or like the Beatles.

As I waited to board, in the departure lounge, a young man came up to me and said hi, I'm Pete, we met some years ago. I looked into his face, but didn't recognise him. Then his girlfriend Janice came over. She was vaguely familiar, but I couldn't place here.

'Are you going to the Beatles conference?' asked Pete. The what? Didn't know there was one. Oh yes, he said. This is the third time that Cuba has organised an International Beatles Conference. It last three days, very well organised, very serious. He was going out to give a little talk.

Pete, who comes from East London, was a railway driver, till BR was sold off and he was out of work. He'd always been a Beatles fan, collected all their records and stuff, and now makes a living, of sorts, by writing little stories about the Beatles for things like *Beatles Monthly*. That's how I'd met him, some years ago. He's also a Beatles dealer. It doesn't pay well, but luckily Janice has a proper job, working in the offices of Carlton TV.

'It's our second visit,' said Janice. 'We love it. Cuba's healthy and the water's drinkable, unlike the Dom Rep. The crime rate is negligible. The people are friendly. You don't get ripped off or hassled. The worst is kids in the street asking you for soap. Oh, and there's no Americans. That's another plus...'

'You've missed out the rum,' said Pete. 'That's very good – and cheap.'

We parted on the plane, me to my club seat, then to economy with the other ranks, but we arranged to meet for a drink at their hotel in Havana. They wanted me to meet Ernesto, organiser of the Beatles conference.

The plane took off on time, and arrived on time. Club class was as good as BA's, for food and service. What has everyone got against Cubana? Their in-flight mag told me that Cubana had been formed on 8 October 1929, and was now celebrating seventy years of flying. Economy did look a bit, well, cramped, but I averted my eyes and concentrated on stuffing my face.

At Havana airport I was stopped by some frozen-faced officials at security, told to go over to a table, where some more frozen faces were seated. Just as it had been in Russia. They make this big performance of keeping you waiting, checking everything, till you feel like a criminal. Arriving in New York can of course be a similar hassle.

I had to empty my hand luggage. So out came my books, newspapers, sponge bag and other bits. They picked out a plastic bag and told me to open it. I'd forgotten about this. I'd bought a dozen tangerines before leaving home to eat on the plane, fearing that Cubana food would be uneatable.

'Against the law,' said one of the frozen faces. I thought for a moment I might be taken away for questioning. He threw my plastic bag in a bin and waved me away.

I got a taxi from the airport into Havana. It was after midnight, the streets deserted, as if a bomb had gone off. Surprising, for a city of 2 million. Surely they have some sort of night life or urban movement. The street lighting was poor, so perhaps there were people moving around I couldn't see.

Cubana had got me a room, the last room, at the Havana Libre, in the Vedado district, a few miles from the centre. It was formerly the Hilton Hotel, till the revolution confiscated foreign properties. It was enormous, stretching up into the sky, and looked, well, very Russian. In Moscow I had stayed in an equally enormous hotel, the Ukraini, grand enough from the outside, and quite grand inside, as our room even had a grand piano, but nothing worked, everything was broken.

Before falling into bed I checked the phone, and it was working, turned on a tap, and it flowed. Everything seemed boringly okay. Just like any other Hilton.

First thing next morning I got a taxi to the British Embassy in the Miramar district, the embassy area. The biggest embassy building by far is still the Russian, with a massive space-age tower. At one time it held thousands of diplomats, or people pretending to be diplomats. Now it looked like a ghost embassy, with most of the Russians departed.

The British Embassy is small, white, colonial, bijou, a little haven of air-conditioned tranquillity and quaintness. In the reception areas I noted a bust of Churchill, an exhibition about Shakespeare, some TV videos of *Middlemarch* and a selection of British newspaper, all two weeks old.

I had faxed a request to see the ambassador, whoever he might be. A few minutes would do. All I really wanted was to say I'd seen Our Man in Havana, though I hadn't said that in the fax. I then got a reply from the Foreign Office in London, asking if I'd like to come in for a briefing. No thanks, I said, not got that sort of time, but a quick chat on the phone might be useful, as I'd never been to Cuba before.

A jolly helpful FO official told me that the UK and Cuba were good friends, now that the Cold War was long over. We were doing great business with them though not, er, quite as good as Spain, Germany and France. They were well ahead of us, but of course their governments gave lots of subsidies. Yah boo. No, he didn't say that, just inferred.

His theory was that the Americans would soon change their attitude towards Cuba. They were still blockading it, refusing all political or economic contacts, but the American business community could see the enormous opportunities in a country of 11 million, right on their doorstep. They were not best pleased that the European countries had got in ahead of them and were cleaning up. It would be the business people, in both countries, who would eventually bring about political changes. But when? Ah well, nobody knew that. Perhaps not till after Castro goes. All the same, Cuba was a fascinating place to be in at the moment.

That was roughly what the ambassador, David Ridgway, himself said, though he had only taken over three weeks earlier and was still finding his feet. 'It's always a combination of pressures which changes things,' he said. 'Cuba needs tourists. Tourism needs an infrastructure. And infrastructures need investments, and that usually means foreign investment.'

He'd already met Castro and been impressed by the lack of corruption in Cuba. 'It's far less than in other Latin-American countries. Castro himself has said to all possible investors, such as Britain, that "If you come here, you will find no corruption. But if you find it, tell me and I will deal with it."'

Mr Ridgway was previously British Ambassador in Bolivia and has a long experience of Spanish-speaking countries, though he was a bit confused to find that *guagua* in Cuba means a bus whereas in Bolivia it meant a baby.

I thanked him for his few minutes and came away thinking, is Cuba Latin-American? Or is it Caribbean? The language is Spanish, but then so is it in the Dominican Republic and that to me had felt more Caribbean. Puerto Rico, where they also speak Spanish, is more North American than South American.

Cuba's architecture has Spanish overtones, but so mixed up with boring Russia-style housing blocks and pretend American, such as the Capitolio building, which is an exact reproduction of the Capitol Building in Washington, that it's hard to see an overall style. Salsa music is definitely Latin. Culturally, judging by the books in their bookshops, they look to South America rather than Spain or Europe.

Watching schoolchildren in the street, they seemed very Caribbean-clean and immaculate in their school uniform, something you see in even the poorest or smallest West Indian island, but rarely in Latin America. That of course is due to Russian conformity and equality of education.

As for the people themselves, they look on the whole South American, black, mixed, light, covering the whole range, with a surprising lot of white. It's quite common to see totally blond, blue-eyed Cubans. That doesn't happen in other Caribbean countries, apart from St Barts, which doesn't count.

There are no shanty towns or settlements, which you find in Latin America, and the people seem calmer, quieter, but then the regime has kept them pretty quiet, these last forty years.

I was wandering round the back streets from my hotel, a mix-up of the usual down-town concrete blocks and decaying houses, assembling in my mind all these huge generalisations. In some ways I could have been in any big city, except of course for the lack of commercialisation: no adverts or posters, other than political ones, which I carefully wrote down. '*Socialismo o Muerte*' (Socialism or death). '*Unidos Siempre Venceremos*' (United we always win), which was under a huge poster of Che Guevara. That was neither modern Latin America nor Caribbean. More like 1950s Russia.

When I went to explore Old Havana, everything changed. That is definitely Latin America, despite all the attempts to communise and conform it.

I went first to look at the Museum of the Revolution. Communist name, but set in a stoutly, grandiosely Latin-American palace. It hadn't opened yet, tut tut, these tardy communists, so I walked round the back to look at the motor boat *Granma*, displayed in an adjoining square.

The *Granma* is one of the best-known symbols of the revolution – and also the name of the official daily newspaper, a very boring, grey, propaganda sheet. The boat, inside a glass building, looked a bit more interesting.

Until the success of the revolution in 1959, Cuba had been almost a US colony, popular with wealthy American tourists and big-time gangsters. America pulled the strings, provided the money, controlled the economy, supported whichever politician appeared to be suitably strong. In 1952 this was Batista, a self-promoted general, who had led a military coup and was head of a corrupt, right-wing regime. Many Cubans lived in wealth and style, but 50 per cent of the population were unemployed and starving.

In 1953 Fidel Castro, a young bespectacled lawyer, born in Cuba in 1926 of Spanish immigrants, led an uprising against Batista. It was easily put down and most of the rebels were arrested, tortured and killed. At his trial, Castro gave a five-hour speech in which he said, 'History will absolve me.' He was sentenced to fifteen years in prison, but after twenty months he was released and went into exile in Mexico. This was where he met a young Argentinian doctor, Ernesto 'Che' Guevara.

In 1956 Castro returned to Cuba on board the *Granma*, along with his brother Raul, Che, and seventy-nine others. After two years of guerrilla warfare, during which Castro was at one time down to a gang of only twelve, Batista was overthrown, and in

January 1959 Castro assumed leadership of Cuba. He did not at first proclaim a communist state. During the revolution he had promised a return to democratic elections, but after increasing hostility from America, Castro aligned himself with Russia and communism.

I went across to look at the *Granma*, known today by all Cuban schoolchildren, but I couldn't get into the building. Work was going on and several guards eyed me suspiciously. The boat is about thirty feet long, small but quite luxurious, the sort of sedate yacht you see pottering around Windermere rather than leading revolutions. The name 'Granma' had always intrigued me. I'd presumed it must be Mexican or Cuban Spanish. But no, it is as English as it sounds. Castro bought it from a Texan – who had named it in honour of his grandmother.

The Revolution Museum had at last opened, so I went in with six or seven others, all young backpackers. The building had been the presidential palace till Batista's fall, with vast marble corridors but no signs or directions. I wandered round, looking for clues, and at the end of long corridors I came across little huddles of elderly female attendants, some half asleep, who looked as if they had been there since Batista's day. One of the boasts of communism is that they have full employment, even if it means fantasy employment, pen-pushing, paper-rustling, or simply guarding empty corridors.

In one corridor, to my surprise, I came across a bust of Christopher Columbus. In most Caribbean and Latin-American countries he has now become a baddy, blamed for the centuries of colonial oppression. In Haiti, the year I was there, his statue had just been dumped into the sea.

Nice to know that Cuba is not PC and turned against him, as he did put Cuba on the map. He visited Cuba on his first voyage of 1492, and again two years later, convinced he had hit the mainland. He never realised it was an island. He found the locals burning funny bits of rolled-up leaves, the first recorded evidence of what they called tobacco. Cuba was part of the Spanish empire for almost the next 400 years, apart from 1762 when the British captured Havana and held the island for a couple of years, before swapping it with Spain for Florida.

When I eventually found the display rooms, the photographs

and illustrations of the revolution all looked a bit faded. There were a lot of guns and uniforms, and a toga-like dressing-gown worn by Castro, so it said, when he gave his 'History Will Absolve Me' speech. There was a pair of jeans as worn by his brother Raul in prison and a cloth toilet bag given to Raul by Fidel, nicely if amateurishly embroidered with the initials FC. Rather sweet. I could see stains on a shirt as worn by Fidel, but couldn't work out if it was blood or sweat. It was all somehow reassuring that a communist country should be just as keen as any capitalist country to let us see the trivial personal possessions of their heroes.

In a little souvenir shop I bought two post cards of Che, then watched the girl assistant spend fifteen minutes filling in bits of papers, in triplicate, recording the details of this massive trans-action.

There is clearly a cult of personality in Cuba. The names of three heroes are everywhere on souvenirs and mementos. Castro and Che get top billing, but close behind comes an American – Ernest Hemingway. You can even follow a Hemingway Trail, round places and houses associated with him, but I restricted myself to the Hotel Ambos Mundos in Old Havana, where he based himself in the 1930s.

The hotel, in an elegant eighteenth-century house, has recently been restored but not modernised, very stylish, with a great atmos-phere, very Latin-American. I immediately wished I was staying there, rather than my hotel.

I asked at reception if I could see Hemingway's room, and was casually waved towards the lift, told to go up to 511. Catch them doing that at the Savoy or the Ritz. I walked down the corridor to room 511 and knocked. It was locked. A maid, whom I'd seen working on another room, came down the corridor and opened up 511 for me. An ordinary hotel bedroom, with the bed made, a little table, a little chair. In the middle, inside a glass case, was an ancient, rusting typewriter, an Underwood Golden Touch. Yes, said the maid, it had belonged to Hemingway.

'He had a Royal as well,' she said. 'He lived here from 1932 to 1939 and wrote *For Whom the Bell Tolls*, *The Green Hills of Africa* and other stories.'

She then opened the shutters with a flourish, to let me see the view, over towards the cathedral. She showed me a replica of a boat Hemingway once owned, the *Pilar*. The floor tiles were original, from the 1930s, as were the lamps in the room. It was not used as a bedroom these days, just for visitors to look at.

'We get a lot of people, about ten to sixteen a day, from every country. Look here, at the visitors book – Tunisia, Sheffield, Iceland, New York.'

She seemed very smart, for a maid. What am I saying? Why should maids not be smart, or have good English? But I had seen her maiding, and presumed that was her job. She was just being helpful, opening up the room for me. She said her name was Esperanca and she really was a maid. Showing people the room was only her part-time job.

'That will be two US dollars,' she said. I was a bit surprised. It has all appeared so casual, so laid-back and I'd been thinking I must give her a little tip for being so helpful. She gave me a proper ticket.

Old Havana's so-called main street is Calle Obispo, rather narrow for a main street, a bit scruffy, with a lot of roadworks going on, but with some nice old buildings, and even older-looking shops. What they were selling was mostly pathetic, like those I'd seen in 1980s Russia, with empty shelves and little to buy. I went into Johnson's Druggeria which was wonderfully Victorian, with dark wooden rails, cubby-holes and home-made-looking bottles of potions and powders. It looked totally false, a mock-up for a period film set.

While walking round Old Havana, I was asked several times if I was interested in buying cigars, which I declined. They only asked once, quickly, taking no for an answer, without any hassling. Most of them, apparently, are stolen cigars, or phoney cigars made out of rubbish. I was also asked if I wanted a taxi. Each time I was surprised, not at the question, but at being recognised as a tourist, a foreigner. I like to think I dress well, pretty boringly, and I wasn't carrying a camera or map.

How was I going to fulfil my self-created task of finding either expats or returnees in Cuba? With difficulty, in a country where no one has been allowed in or out those forty years. But that evening I had dinner with a British freelance journalist, Pascal

Fletcher. He lives in Havana, working mainly for the *Financial Times*.

We went to one of the *paladares*, private restaurants recently allowed by the state, one of their first examples of private enterprise. They are usually in people's own homes, with a maximum of twelve seats. Hard to find, as of course they can't advertise or have any proper signs outside. He couldn't locate the one he was looking for, a new one which someone had told him about, despite driving round for about fifteen minutes, so we went to one he had been to before. It was called the Gringo Viejo, and was in the basement of a private house, family-run, with the staff very willing to please. It could easily have been a restaurant in Camden Town.

Pascal, despite his christian name, which comes from a European grandfather, was born and brought up in England. He went to a minor public school in Berkshire, then Cambridge where he studied languages. He did an MA in Latin-American studies in London and joined Reuters in 1977. In 1989 they moved him to Cuba where he met and married his wife, Isis, a Cuban who had been married to a Palestinian surgeon.

He was then moved to Brazil, promoted to bureau chief, in charge of over thirty staff. 'The theory in Reuters is that once you reach the age of thirty-five, you are expected to move up the hierarchy. So I had done well, but I missed being a hack, missed getting out and about interviewing people. It had become screen-based slavery, stuck in an office all day. The job was exciting enough, as São Paulo is a huge financial centre, a big power base. But I grew very unhappy. So I gave it up. I didn't have another job to go to. I decided to come back to Cuba.'

For the sake of your wife?

'Not really. She wasn't all that keen to come back. But I had been happy here. I like the combination of a laid-back Caribbean lifestyle mixed up with an introverted Latin-American form of socialism. There is a certain paranoia here, and betrayal does happen. "There's always an eye watching you." That's a Cuban song, and it is true, though you might not see it as a visitor. But I like it. I like the life. I like the people.

'I took a huge financial loss to come back. My retainer from the *Financial Times* is very small, though I do some work for Reuters as well. I have no savings, nothing in the bank, yet I am forty next birthday with a wife and two children to support. You couldn't say I have done well financially in life. I suppose I earn about £12,000 – and spend it all, just living.'

Pascal's car is a Lada, bought cheaply when the Russians left, who sold off hundreds of their cars at bargain prices. 'I paid only $3,000 for it. You can now buy Japanese cars here, which in theory are much better than Ladas, but Cuban mechanics have all been trained on Ladas. All they can do with a Jap car is kick it. They don't know how they work.'

His wife has a sixteen-year-old daughter, Ismail, whom he has legally adopted, and they have a five-year-old son, Geoffrey, both at local schools. Primary education is good, he said, but secondary and university is beginning to suffer as many teachers try to get out of teaching and into tourism.

This is the result of the two economies I had already noticed: one in pesos, one in dollars. The pesos shops, for locals, have nothing to sell, but in the dollar shops, for tourists or Cubans with access to dollars, you can buy anything. Dollar means US dollar, not Trinidad and Tobago. Cubans are not daft. They might hate Americans, but they do love Uncle Sam's dollar.

It's now reached the stage where someone cleaning cars for foreigners is better off than a surgeon – because he will be paid in dollars and the surgeon won't.

Everyone is of course government-employed, as there is no private enterprise – apart from the little private restaurants, and even they were being reduced. The average wage was 200 pesos a month, roughly equivalent to $10. Professional people, like teachers and doctors, got 300 pesos a month, with a head of department getting 500. Minuscule wages, compared with the West. The Cuban government will of course point out that everyone gets free education, free health, cheap rent. Most people live in government-owned blocks of flats.

The chaos and corruption in Russia since the fall of the Soviet empire has convinced the Cuban authorities they are right, that communism is best for the people. On the other hand, the recent changes brought about by tourism, which Cuba needs, as it is no longer subsidised by the Russians, has exposed ordinary Cubans to a different way of life, different values, different goods, if of course you have the dollars. In Russia, when I was there, ordinary

Russians were not allowed even to enter foreign currency shops. In Cuba you can, if you can get your hands on the dollars.

After the meal, out in the street, a young Cuban stopped me and asked if I'd like a taxi. I said no thanks. I told Pascal that it had been happening all day, being taken for a foreigner, and I couldn't see why.

'Well, it's obvious,' he said. 'You're wearing shorts. No Cuban wears shorts...'

I did have a drink with Pete, my Beatles friend, and met Ernesto who was running the Beatles conference. In fact quite a few drinks, during which I apparently agreed to come and give a little talk at the conference in a week's time.

Next morning I thought, oh no, what have I done? I was going off to explore elsewhere in Cuba, and hadn't planned to return to Havana; now I'd have to, somehow, if I could change my transport arrangements, if only I could get anyone to answer the telephone at the bloody travel agent. So my headache got worse.

Luckily I had discovered a swimming pool, hidden away on a roof on the second floor, so I spent my last morning there. The pool itself was attractive enough, but the surrounds were nasty concrete, and wherever you were, in the water, sitting by the side, you could hear and smell every car and lorry in the street below. Traffic in Havana is light, for a city of 2 million, but the noise, the pollution and the fumes are overpowering. The vehicles are ancient, so they puff and pant, creak and crank, giving out clouds of smoke like steam engines. Sunbathing by the pool was like sunbathing on a traffic island.

At the poolside bar, I could hear a North American accent. A young man of about thirty, flabby, pasty-faced, was tucking into a plate of burger and chips. I thought at first he must be Canadian, as Canadians are Cuba's number one tourists. In 1998, 164,000 came from Canada, followed by Italy, 140,000; Spain, 103,000; Germany, 101,000; France, 72,000 and Britain, 64,000.

Britain is still way behind, for the moment, despite the increases of the last few years. I had not heard one English voice while walking round Havana, which was nice. One likes to feel one is in a foreign country, while in a foreign country.

I went to the bar for a beer and asked him where he was from. 'Colorado,' he said, slightly lowering his voice. On holiday? 'Kind of.' He was in real estate, he said. Just thought he'd come over for a few days and look at the investment possibilities. No chance, I said. You can't buy or sell any houses in Cuba.

'You're kidding.'

I explained that the government owned everything. And at the moment, they were not selling.

He had arrived via Cancún in Mexico, as American citizens were supposed to have nothing to do with Cuba. Cuba doesn't mind Americans coming into Cuba. It's the USA who objects.

'You're not supposed to come here, unless you have special visa, doing humanitarian work. I could get fined $25,000 if they find out. Luckily, they didn't stamp my passport on the way in, so I should get back into the States okay.' He obviously felt quite brave, quite adventurous, daring to come to Cuba.

'Everyone in the States thinks Cuba is a real scary place, with spies and secret police everywhere. When I rang home last night, to say I'd arrived safely, my wife says, "And how is it, er . . . down there?" She was worried about saying "Cuba" in case the phones were all bugged.

'But it all seems pretty normal to me, don't you think so?'

Very like America, really, I said, in this hotel. I stayed at a similar one in Austin, Texas where the traffic fumes round the pool were equally noxious.

He had found the Cubans very friendly, not at all anti-American, and was pleased things were so cheap. Best of all, was being able to pay for everything, everywhere, in US dollars.

He'd had a walk on the seafront this morning, along the Malecon, and had come to some graffiti on the sea wall which had amused him. 'It said, "We're not scared of you, Yankees," with a finger pointing towards the US. I thought that was neat. I didn't take a photo, just in case I was being watched.'

He hadn't travelled much, apart from Mexico, and had never been to Europe. 'I've heard a lot about England,' he said.

That's nice, I replied.

'Yeah, and I'm told Noocastle is a neat place.'

You're up to date, I said.

'Noocastle's good for horseback riding,' he said. 'And you can stay in people's homes!' Wow. I said, great research.

'There's only one problem with England,' he said.

Oh yeah, what's that?

'The language. I'm told in some places they're hard to understand.'

Very true, I said.

He'd finished his burger and chips and called for the bill, getting out his American Express card. The waiter said sorry, they can't take it. My friend looked mystified. I told him I'd paid with a Visa card, no problems; had he got one of those? He got it out, gave it to the waiter who went over to talk to someone at the till. He returned to say they couldn't accept that either. His Visa card was on an American bank. 'If we accept it,' said the waiter, 'they won't send us any money from America.'

He'd forgotten his room card, and had no cash on him, so I said I'd lend him $20. He could pay me back later. He was very grateful.

He still owes me, now I think about it. I'd forgotten I was booking out of the Havana Libre that afternoon, off to explore elsewhere in Cuba.

CHAPTER ELEVEN

Cuba: Varadero

I waited in the hotel reception for a coach to Varadero, Cuba's main tourist resort, some ninety-five miles down the coast from Havana. I'd paid for it in London through Cubana, and been given a voucher, but no other details. It eventually appeared, an hour late, with a totally different name on the side. Then it trailed round several other Havana hotels, picking up other people, all furious and exhausted, before they'd even begun their trip.

I had forgotten what it's like travelling package-style. For the last twelve years I've travelled independently, or at least got my travel firm to make individual arrangements for me.

When our children were young, we always went on package holidays or package flights, and my idea of hell was Gatwick in August. The hours, the days we got stuck there with no escape. It was so wonderful when it all ended, never being packaged again.

The coach at least was quite comfortable, with a WC, and the road was in good condition, better than I had feared. Once we left the outskirts of Havana, there was not much traffic and the driver was soon speeding along. Until, wham, he pulled up suddenly for an emergency stop. A car ahead, one of the ancient 1950s American limos, had disintegrated, just yards in front of us. There was no crash, no collision, it just gave up the ghost, no longer wishing to live, and died, right there in front of us.

Our coach was doing about forty miles an hour at the time and I'd noticed this old car ahead, lumbering along, wondering how the owner could possibly get any spares, when almost in slow motion it began to buckle, the wheels splayed out, and it sank to a halt on its belly. Our driver had done brilliantly to brake so quickly, without any sign of panic or fury, not even pumping his horn. Perhaps it happens all the time. Out of the dead car climbed an elderly black couple, apparently unharmed, who stood there, staring at the wreckage. Our driver pulled over and round it, and went on, without a flicker.

Once into the country, it turned out we had a tour leader, a woman of about fifty in a blazer, who kept up a running commentary in Spanish, telling us about the scenery and the joys of Cuba. I did walk down the aisles, and heard a couple speaking French, but I was the only Brit. Everyone else was Spanish-speaking, from either Spain or Latin America.

We followed the coast, all the way, most of it low volcanic rocks, with the occasional little beach, and the occasional river gorge with a high viaduct. I could see low hills in the distance, but not much sign of the wonderful intensive, co-operative farming which our guide was boasting about.

It was hard to accustom my eyes and mind to the size of Cuba, after all the titchy Caribbean islands I had visited, where distances deceive and you begin to think ten miles is a long way and twenty miles must be the end of the world.

Cuba is by far the largest island in the Caribbean, some 780 miles long, about the length of Britain from Land's End to John o'Groats. No wonder Columbus couldn't find the end of it. It's mainly gently rolling, with nothing higher than 6,500 feet, easy to get around.

Some strange red and green windmill-looking things began to appear along the coast. I wished our guide would explain them, instead of extolling the virtues of the revolution. I then realised they were not windmills but little oil derricks, pumping away. Then we came to an oil refinery, and could clearly smell it. There's currently a lot of oil exploration in Cuba, on and off the coast. Our Man in Havana was about to go on a tour of some of the sites, so he'd told me, with a view to some British petroleum firms getting involved.

It would be interesting to see what would happen if Cuba struck lucky in oil, and became a Caribbean Gulf state. Instead of the sheiks becoming billionaires, would every Cuban get rich? Whatever the moans about Castro, and I had begun to hear quite a few, I'd heard no suggestion that he was lining his own pockets. Cubans believe he genuinely leads a simple life.

I was heading for Varadero, a thin pencil of land sticking out into the Caribbean, some twenty miles long, supposedly one vast white sandy beach, so I had read in the guides. In the 1920s the fabulously wealthy Franco-American Du Pont family had built themselves a fantasy holiday home there which they had called Xanadu. Other wealthy folks had followed. Come the revolution, all these homes were taken over by the state. Come the 1990s and the arrival of tourism, new hotels were being added almost every month.

The best hotels, and the most unspoiled part of the beach, are towards the middle and far end of the peninsula. Alas, I found myself dumped at the very beginning, in the little town of Varadero itself. It happened so quickly that I wasn't properly concentrating, so busy looking out for the lovely unspoiled beach. The driver had my case out on the pavement and was back on the coach before I realised this was my hotel. I was the only one dropped off. As he roared away, people were staring out of the coach thinking, poor sod, glad I'm not staying there.

It was a hideously cheap and nasty concrete block, right on a busy road. I dragged my case along the pavement till I found the entrance and got out my voucher. I had paid, in London, in advance for the next six days. My Havana hotel had turned out perfectly adequate and had cost only £45 a night, a bargain by London prices, or West Indian prices. For this one, I had paid only £16 a night. Which I'd thought was amazingly cheap. Now I knew why. It was a dump.

Even worse, my room wasn't even in the hotel but in an even uglier apartment block further along the busy street. So I had to hump my case back along the pavement. I was on the eighth floor, reached by a very shaky dark lift. The room was hideous, with broken plastic furniture and torn curtains as if they'd had squatters. There was air-conditioning but the noise was horrendous and water was leaking all over the floor. I switched it off. And the heat was unbearable, so I switched it on again. At least its noise drowned some of the outside traffic.

I went down again, along the street, and asked at reception if I could have another room, anywhere, I'd pay anything. The hotel was full, she said. I'd got the last room, and was lucky to get it because it wasn't a room normally used. I could see why.

I asked if she could recommend another hotel, but she said the whole of Varadero was full. People were ringing her all the time.

I'd been told all this in London, but I still couldn't believe it. There are now over 30,000 beds in Varadero. There must be one spare. Anything must be better than mine.

I set off down the busy street, and was soon in a lather with the heat and my bad temper. The town is on a grid system, with the streets in blocks, named by numbers, from Avenue One to Avenue Sixty-Nine. I tried a few hotels, most of them little better than mine, some of them much noisier, but they were full.

An old man in jeans stopped me and pointed to a hole in one of his knees, quite an artistic little hole, as if he'd done it himself. I expected him to ask for money but all he wanted was me to give him some shampoo from my hotel. My hotel! It's a bloody dump. It hasn't even got soap or lavatory paper.

After walking for about an hour, I came across a sign for the state travel agent who had arranged my hotel. It was in an upstairs office, just one room. I opened the door and inside were two girls sitting watching television, while the telephone blared away. The younger one was painting her toenails. The older girl eventually got up and sat behind a desk and glared at me, not pleased to have been interrupted. I said I was unhappy with the room they had booked me and wanted to change hotels.

'Is full. Varadero is full.'

Yes, but could you just try a few hotels? I'm on my own, so the simplest single room would do, any price. I'm awfully sorry. But please, just try.

Reluctantly she rang a number then hung up, saying no rooms, is full. 'Anyway I can't book you. It must be done through the computer in Havana. And they are now closed for the weekend. Come back on Monday.

She then sat down again in front of the television, while the phone started ringing.

I went out, walked down the street a couple of blocks, then came back.

'What about private homes? You know, like the *paladares*. Isn't it possible to get a room in a private house?'

'Is not possible,' she said. 'Is not allowed.'

But haven't you got, er, any friends, who might be grateful for a few dollars?

She thought for a while, then picked up the phone and spoke

to someone. When she hung up, she said yes, there was a room.

'But she say no women,' she said.

Seemed a strange condition, a male-only room, but I said that's all right, it's just me, on my own.

'She means you can't bring a woman back to the room.'

Bloody cheek. But I suppose a single man, in want of a room, might be in want of other services. Of course not, I said, as primly as possible.

She got some paper and a pen and drew a map, gave me the name of a café, and also a photograph of a friend of hers, whose mother had a room spare. If I went now, I could see it.

So off I hurried, almost running the next twenty blocks. When I got to the café, I showed the photograph to a woman behind the bar and she said no, she had never seen that girl. There must be some mistake. What was I after anyway? She looked at me suspiciously. These decadent Western men, come over here with their dollars, trying to corrupt our people. I didn't want to go into details about the room to let, presuming it was illegal.

As I was standing there, the girl in the photograph arrived and was greeted warmly by the woman behind the bar. The girl then took me to her mother's house, a low concrete bungalow, rather jerry-built, but it was on the beach side of the road. Her mother opened the door and took me through a kitchen, filled with plastic flowers and garish ornaments, into a little room with a single bed. It was clean enough, neat enough, but very small and claustrophobic. There was a fan, which she switched on, to let me see that it worked.

Could I really spend the next six nights in this tiny room? Stuck here from six o'clock every evening when it gets dark, with nothing to do? On the other hand, I would get to know a real Cuban family. The girl did seem rather friendly and cheerful.

'I don't live here,' she said. 'It's just my mother and father. So there will be no noise.'

Her mother, who didn't speak any English, looked worried about having an absolute stranger staying in her house. I asked how much, not that it really mattered. The girl spoke with the mother then said it would be $25. I said I'd just have a walk on the beach and think about it. On the beach were a couple of low-class hotels, very like mine, but they seemed to be filled with German yobs with tattooes all over their arms, walking around carrying boogie boxes. I went back and told the woman no thanks. She seemed quite relieved.

That night I found a nearby bar where I had four *mojitos*, my new best favourite rum drink, and fell into bed at eight o'clock, half drunk, and went straight to sleep in my horrible hotel.

Next morning, I decided to walk even further, right to the end of Varadero, hoping I might come to a better and bigger class of hotel, who might have a vacancy. I got right to the end, which took for ever, by which time the beach had become splendid, much broader, much whiter, much more dramatic.

I saw a notice saying Museum, right on the beach, and went inside. It appeared to have been a private villa at one time, perhaps one of those owned by some rich American. The girl who gave me a ticket, price $2, was wearing a swimsuit. In the background, I could hear a baby crying. I was totally alone, going round the museum, but from time to time the girl came out, still in her bathing costume, holding the baby, taking a quick look at me, in case I might run off with any of the treasures.

One room contained a lot of old bones, very dusty, labelled 'half early'. In another room was a medal from the Paris Exposition of 1900 which had been awarded to Varadero for the quality of its salt. The best displays were about Irene Du Pont, who had built the famous holiday mansion at Varadero. I admired her binoculars and other personal bits. Then I examined the photos again and realised Irene was a man.

On the way back through the town, I decided that I couldn't possibly spend another night in my fleapit hotel room. All the other hotels in Varadero were obviously full, so I might as well pack up and go home early. Then I realised I couldn't. I'd promised to speak at the Beatles thing in Havana – in five days' time. What a mistake.

I then noticed a tourist office I hadn't seen before. I went in and asked them about hotels. Same story. Varadero is full, all is full. The girl did seem more interested in my problem than the other girl, and said come back in an hour, she just might have something. I went on the beach, had a swim, and came back.

By an amazing stroke of luck, there was a room vacant at the

Melia Varadero, the best hotel in town. Someone who had booked
had not turned up. Brilliant, I said. How much? Eighty-five dollars
a night, with breakfast. A lot more than my dump at $16, but
reasonable for a good hotel. Can I pay by Visa?

'Oh no. You must pay me in dollars. In advance. That will be
$425.'

I haven't got that sort of cash, I explained.

Get it from the bank, she said. You just need a Visa card and
passport. But it's Sunday. The banks will be closed. She picked up
the phone, rang a bank and said no, they're open. I got the dollars
in seconds, far easier than in a British High Street.

I went back to my hotel and triumphantly checked out, feeling
very pleased with myself, even though I was leaving a hotel for
which I had paid for the next five days. No refunds. Certainly not.
I wondered if the person who hadn't turned up for the new hotel
had also paid in advance. Presumably. That was the system. Most
hotels are pre-packaged, which was why, on my own, just turning
up, I had failed to find a room. But was it some sort of fiddle?
Presumably. Why else would she want it all in cash? Where was
the money going? Who knows, who cares, as long as I get somewhere half-decent for the next five days...

The Melia Varadero is part of a three-hotel complex, owned and
run by the same people, a joint Spanish-Cuban venture, covering
about two miles of beautiful beach, with an adjoining eighteen-
hole golf course. Architect-designed, as opposed to the usual
Soviet-style blocks, and quite artistic, classy in the modern international style, i.e. glass lifts, masses of comfy sofas, bamboo chairs
in spacious reception areas, mirrors and gilt ornaments and drapes,
long corridors leading nowhere, streams full of fish flowing
through the main reception, amusing bridges, real live turtles,
birds in cages, a variety of different eating experiences and of
course the inevitable glassy row of shops selling glitzy, ridiculously
priced designer leisure tat. It could be anywhere in today's tourist-
resort world, but for Cuba, after what I had seen, it was quite
remarkable.

Such a shame it was chaos in reception. I had arrived at two
o'clock, the earliest checking-in time, clutching my little voucher,
fearing it might all be a con. I didn't even have proof that I'd paid

$425 cash. The girl had assured me the voucher was my receipt.

Masses of package tours, in monster coaches, had arrived at the same time. I observed an airline crew ahead of me, from Monarch by the look of their uniforms, who were waving their vouchers, insisting they had fourteen bedrooms, booked and paid for, for their fourteen members. They were being told sorry, we have no rooms. We are full. After lots of arguing and shouting, they were given two rooms – between the fourteen of them.

When at long last it was my turn, I expected the worst, but no, they had my room. I was given a key and a bellhop was told to take me to my room. He led me to the fourth floor, unlocked my room for me with a flourish, beckoned me to go in – and there was a man and woman in bed.

Down to reception, again, where the queues seemed longer and noisier and even the bell-boy had trouble pushing through. This time I was led to a room on the second floor which was empty, with a fridge and TV. I switched on and there was some old man rambling on in Spanish, the camera glued to his face. In foreign countries it's always amusing to see posters or adverts for their TV stars who are household names and faces to them, but just old blokes to us. As of course Terry Wogan or Desmond Lynham would be to them. Then I realised it was Castro.

He seemed to be alone, at a desk, using his hands a lot, as if talking to one person, perhaps even at his own fireside, grandad grinding on to his grandchildren, telling his same old, hammed-up stories. It was only after twenty minutes, listening to his monologue while I unpacked, that the camera moved slowly back and revealed that he was in a massive hall, with about 2,000 people, all sitting there in total silence. Castro was on a stage, flanked by various dignitaries. From time to time there were close-ups of their faces, all trying hard not to look bored. I wondered if people all over Cuba were taking bets on which officials would fall asleep.

I went to explore the hotel and then the beach, where I had a swim. The sea was turquoise, translucent, with just the gentlest of refreshing waves. After about an hour, I returned to my room to find Castro still grinding on. I went downstairs to look at the eating experiences, which ranged from Chinese to Italian, all with sparkling table cloths and flunkeys, mostly in full evening dress –

and all empty. Eating on one's own in a crowded place can be amusing. Alone, on one's own, is just sad.

So I went back to my room again and ordered a pizza and a beer from room service and watched Castro, still chuntering away. After another hour, I thought, no, the joke's over, I'm too tired, so I switched him off. From the next room, I could hear voices raised, a couple having some sort of row, but I couldn't make out the language. Oh well, back to Castro. More soporific than people arguing.

When I eventually fell asleep, Castro was still going strong. I reckoned he must have been speaking for almost seven hours, without a pause, without going to the lavatory. By the look of the 2,000 in the hall, some were getting desperate, crossing their legs, their faces contorted. One thing about Western democracy and a free mass media is that while inane political soundbites may be aimed at the lowest common denominator, thank God they don't last long.

Next morning I had a swim before breakfast, which was wonderful, and the breakfast was very good as well, buffet-style, rather lavish, which made it easy to pocket some ham and cheese and bread which I took to my room and put in the fridge.

I spent the day on the beach, swimming and exploring, walking as far as the famous Xanadu, where the Du Ponts had once lived, now a restaurant. An impressive house, but it didn't look Caribbean or Latin-American. With its black painted wooden balconies it reminded me of a skiing hotel in the Austrian Alps.

There were all the usual beach facilities, umbrellas and chairs, boats and volleyball pitches, beach photographers. I couldn't hear one British accent, while walking the length, although quite a few I took to be Canadians.

Later, inside the hotel, I found the area used by the holiday reps, sitting at little tables, in their little blazers and friendly smiles, repping away. I walked up and down till I heard an English accent. A young man with a shiny face and a yellow blazer was trying to look serious and concerned as a middle-aged, hatchet-faced couple with Birmingham accents were haranguing him. Something to do with their stay at the Nacional in Havana. 'It was crap,' said the woman, ''scuse my language. And it was your fault.'

'Actually we don't have a rep in Havana.'

'But our brochure says you do.'

'Yes, but we use a rep from a Cuban company. We are not allowed to work in Havana. We have to use their reps.'

'But we couldn't find them.'

'Yes, I'm very sorry. It's not our company's fault. We are forced to use them.'

'Well, what are you going to do about it?' said the woman.

'How do you mean?' said the rep.

'Well, we lost two days of our holiday. We've saved all year for this, you know. So what are you going to do?'

'Well, I'll report it,' said the rep, brightly, 'that's for sure, don't you worry.'

'And then what?'

'Well, I'll report it to head office. I'll let them know.'

'Then what?'

'Well, it's up to them what happens. All I can say is sorry. Now, have you seen about all the tours you can do? I can highly recommend the trip to Trinidad, that's excellent, and the Bay of Pigs is good, or what about a nightclub; we have some triffic ones. Now be careful about making phone calls from your room, it'll cost $8 a minute, and postcards will take eight to twelve weeks to get to England, so look upon them as next year's Christmas cards, ha ha ha...'

It did the trick. The Brummie couple were calmed down. They slowly got out of their seats and let the next one in the queue have his go. It was a stocky, cocky-looking man of about forty-five with close-cropped hair and a strong Essex accent.

'I ain't actually one of your customers,' he said.

'Thank Gawd for that,' said the rep, quick as a flash.

'I heard English being spoken, and thought you might help...'

He said he was in property, spending a year abroad for tax reasons, and wanted to know the chances of buying something in Cuba. The rep said no chance. Well, there's also another question, said the man, a personal question I'd like to ask.

I'd been listening all the time, while sitting on a couch, pretending to read the brochures. The man suddenly became aware of my presence. He put his arm round the young rep's shoulders, gently eased him out of his seat, and made him walk a few yards through the lounge, while he asked his personal question. I didn't hear a word, curses.

When it was my turn, I said I wasn't one of his customers either. In fact I wasn't even on holiday. I was doing a book. Did he have time for a drink or a meal? He said that sounded good. But he'd have to ask June. She was the boss. He'd leave a message in my room, later on.

As I was going back to my room, I met the Essex man, the property buyer, who rushed up to me. He said he was called Ken and he was fed up with this hotel, full of bleedin' foreigners, did I know a hotel with more Brits in it. I said he hadn't a chance of getting any hotel, and I told him my problems.

He said come and have a quick drink at the bar. He seemed very friendly, cheerful, desperate to talk. He'd made a packet, he said, starting with a discount store, then converting derelict warehouses in the East End for yuppies.

'Just bought a place last week in Key West, Florida. Know it? Lovely place, only half a million dollars. There's three important things when you invest in property – location, location, location. I'll spend two weeks a year there and let it out the rest. I'll make $50,000 clear a year – that's 10 per cent. You can't get that in Blighty. Tell you something, if you've got any money, get out of sterling. You mark my words...'

I asked if he was on his own, as he'd seemed so desperate for company, and he said no, his girlfriend was with him. He had been married, two lovely kids, but that was years ago. She couldn't keep up with him when he started moving up the social scale. His girlfriend was only twenty-three, a country girl from Suffolk, who had taken a room in one of his cheaper properties.

'Come and have a meal with us this evening. It'll be on me.'

No thanks, I said. I'm having dinner with someone.

Having thought I'd be stuck for five days with no Brits to talk to, I'd now made contact with two lots.

Darren, the holiday rep, suggested we met at a steak restaurant in a modern block further down the coast. He arrived with June, who turned out not just to be his boss but his girlfriend. She was

Welsh, blonde and attractive, aged thirty. She had done French, German and Spanish at school but decided not to go to university because she wanted to travel. She got a job as a rep with Thomson Holidays, worked in Corfu and Ibiza, which was where she met Darren. She was a manager by then, in charge of eighteen other reps. Darren, the newcomer, was seven years younger.

'It was a good career move,' said Darren, 'getting to sleep with the boss.'

Darren doesn't have a word of Spanish, but didn't consider it a handicap, as his job was looking after Brits all day. But June used her Spanish for her admin work, which mostly seemed to be having rows with the airlines and the hotels about overbooking.

'Cubana is the worst. It is quite common for people with tickets to get turned away. I shout at them and say we have a legal contract, you have made a deal with us, and they just say, "We are full." There's nothing you can do. The holidaymakers then shout at us. Yes, it can be very stressful.

'All hotels and airlines oversell. That's normal practice. You have 100 rooms, say, in your hotel, or 100 seats on your plane, but you'll do deals for 110 to the package firms for the season. You know the chances are that all won't be sold at the same time, so this helps you not to run with empty seats or empty rooms. At popular times it can happen – everything gets sold. But hotels usually also have rooms spare, for individual people. Not here in Cuba. This market is totally a packaged market. They don't cater for people coming off the street. So at a popular time, which it now is all the time, it's bloody chaos.'

'They're funny, the Brits,' said Darren. 'They come all this way, then moan there are no other Brits to talk to. It's the question I get asked most. That and any night life.

'I could make a million if I could open a John Bull pub in Varadero. I'd put in Sky for the football, a bit of disco. I'd clean up. But they won't let you of course.'

June had lots of stories about the financial fiddles to get seats on planes. 'If you flash a few hundred US dollars, you can get on almost any Cuban plane, even when it's supposedly full. In ten years of repping, I've never known that happen before.'

'Another fiddle,' said Darren, 'is in restaurants when they say their Visa machine is not working, just so you are forced to pay in dollars.'

Their basic pay was small, paid in England, so low they didn't get taxed, but most of their income came from a cut of the trips which guests go on. Each was making in all £20,000 a year. Not huge, but their spending was minimal, with their accommodation and meals free, and nowhere to go in the evenings. In the last year they had saved £30,000 and were hoping to buy a flat in England somewhere, to secure their future.

They were still enjoying repping, but would like a place with a bit of action in the evening, such as Ibiza. That was really something. Before I left, I asked Darren what it was my Essex friend had wanted to know.

'Oh, that's the third most common thing I get asked. Where are the women?'

On the beach, I met a young man who looked like John Travolta, handsome and smiley, carrying a camera and a garish T-shirt, followed by an overweight scruffy girl, dragging herself along behind him. He offered to take my photo, saying that in two hours I could have a T-shirt like this, with my photograph on the front. On the front of the one he was carrying was a couple who looked liked *Baywatch* stars. How much? Only $13, he said, all smiles.

His name was José and he'd trained for seven years as an engineer, but his pay in pesos was so small he couldn't live on it. Now his life was so much better. Most days he averaged twelve T-shirts.

'But today, I have not sold one. If only I had the contract to go inside the hotels, I could make a lot more. Most people just sit by their hotel pool all day. My boss, he can't get the contract to go inside the hotels. It is a shame.'

But he'd spotted a likely German family and rushed off, followed slowly by his dumpy assistant. Her job, presumably, was to rush off, or slope off, with the film once he'd taken someone.

Coming back through the grounds of the hotel, I was stopped by a security guard, a young, bright-looking black man. All he wanted to do was admire my sandals, ask where I'd got them.

I don't think he was after my sandals, just making conversation.

He took me inside his little guardhouse and showed me two books he was reading. One was an English textbook and the other a nineteenth-century Spanish novel.

'I used to be a helicopter pilot. The Russians trained me, which took a long time. When the Russians left, they took their helicopters. I lost my job. It's taken a year to get this job. It's not much, but I hope it will lead to something better.'

I got a taxi down the coast, to the far end, and the taxi driver turned out to be another Russian-trained pilot – this time on MIG fighter planes. He had actually been trained in Russia and lived there for four years, flying MIGs in the Soviet air force.

'When the Soviet Union collapsed, I was sent back to Cuba. I'd saved a bit of money, which I spent on drink and women. I then had nothing, no job, nothing. I was so stupid. I was rock bottom. Then I met my wife, the woman who is now my wife. She saved me. A man is not a man without a woman. She got me organised again, and I got this job. It's good. You don't make the money people think you do. Look, it's all on the meter. I can't put it off. But with the tips, well, then you can do quite well.'

Walking down my corridor one morning, on the way to my room, I ran straight into Ken, my property friend. He was coming out of the room next door to me. I had never realised he was there. I knew from Darren there were only nine Brits in the hotel, out of 450 rooms. What a coincidence we had been put next door.

He introduced me to his girlfriend, Karen, who was blonde and attractive and rather smart, not at all country girl-looking. So why was he looking for women? Once again, he suggested a meal, then perhaps we could all go to a nightclub he'd eventually discovered, further down the coast.

'Not for me,' I said. 'I go to bed at ten o'clock, latest.'

'Oh, Ken never goes to bed till about four. He can stay up all night drinking, and be as fit as anything in the morning. I need my beauty sleep.'

They went off arm-in-arm, lovey-dovey. I must have been mistaken about hearing them arguing in their room. But I carefully walked on, past my own room, just in case they might think I might be prying on them.

It was the manager's cocktail party that evening. I was there well in time, not wanting to miss a free drink and goodies. Only fifty turned up and we got only one little drink each, no nibbles, but there was a string quartet playing, which was nice.

It also gave me a chance to grab the manager, Mr Hernandez. He was black, about six foot five and looked more like a baseball player than a hotel manager. I asked if I could come and see him in his office, just for a chat.

His first name turned out to be Nelson, so I said he must be rather proud of it, since Nelson Mandela.

'It is part of our history. First in Cuba, after the Indians, came the Spaniards, so I am Hernandez. Then the English came for a time, and I am Nelson.'

He was born in the nearby town of Matanzas, where he still lives, and went to university in Havana to study veterinary surgery. He was a basketball player, playing for Cuba, but as an amateur, as there are no professional teams. For six years he worked as a vet on a big farm, out in the country, then for eight years in the government's economics department.

In 1990, when the first hotel was being built at Varadero, he decided to change career and find a job in hotels. For the dollars? 'No, it wasn't just the money. I was thinking what can I do with my life. It was more a development for me. And also the country. Tourism is now the front line of our economy.'

He started in the hotel in Human Resources, and after three years became an assistant to the manager. Three years later, he was made hotel manager. There was a general manager, a Spaniard, who was on leave at that time, so technically he was just second-in-command. All the same, quite a meteoric rise, I said. 'Yes, I went up like a Nasa rocket.'

Since going into hotel management, he has regularly been abroad for courses or conferences – Canada, Spain, Argentina, Brazil. He had just come back from Canada where he'd been on a two-month intensive English course. He got down from the wall his certificate from the National School of Learning in Nova Scotia which had awarded him a Diploma in Advanced English and Communication. The citation was in pompous old-fashioned legal English, granting him 'all the honors, rights and privileges there-unto appertaining to this diploma as evidence thereof'. I read it twice and still couldn't follow it. But he beamed, proud of its very obscurity.

The three Spanish-Cuban Melia hotels were the only example so far of foreigners getting any sort of ownership in Cuba. There were some other hotels in Varadero which had German, Jamaican and Mexican involvement, but they were still Cuban-owned.

In his hotel there were only four foreign workers: two Spaniards, a German and a Mexican. All other 416 were Cubans. Was it a problem, getting suitably trained staff locally?

'Not now. You forget all Cubans are very well educated and can easily adapt. But we now have our own hotel school, so if I want someone, they send along four or five for me to interview.'

One day soon he hoped the American blockade would be over and Americans would be back as tourists. When?

'I don't know. Perhaps two years?'

I told him about all the highly educated people I'd met doing relatively unskilled jobs. On his reception desk, I'd talked to a woman in her forties who'd been a university lecturer. Surely this was going to drain good people away from the professions?

'Oh no. We have many doctors and teachers. We have so many we can send them abroad to help others. Fifty of our doctors have been in Honduras helping with the hurricane damage. We have enough to go round. Since the revolution, everyone has been able to study in Cuba.'

It reminded me of Russia, this loyalty to the regime in front of foreigners. He also boasted of the good health generally of the Cubans. 'We have good medicine, and we look after ourselves.'

Then what about all the smoking? In the famous photos of Castro and Che, they are smoking cigars.

'Castro has not smoked since 1974. But you are right. Cubans do smoke too much – and also drink too much black coffee. But apart from that, we are very healthy.'

I asked what his salary was, a question not worth asking hotel managers in most parts of the world, as they wouldn't tell you.

'I get 800 pesos a month.'

I said that must be about the most any Cuban can earn. He said yes, probably. A doctor only gets about 450. All the same, 800 pesos was only about $40. Not much you can buy with that. Ah, but he did get a share of tips.

He doesn't have a house of his own but lives in his father's house, along with his wife and four sons. I asked if he'd called any of them Nelson, to keep the tradition going. 'Just half of one,' he said.

You what? I thought I'd misheard, or his advanced English was not as brilliant as the certificate said.

'Our oldest son is called Rodnel. The Rod part is from my father's name, Rodolfo. Nel is from Nelson.'

I mentioned the overbooking, which Darren and June told me about, and I'd seen in action.

'Yes, we have had lots of complaints. This last month has been crazy. But we are working on it and hope to get a better system soon.'

I've heard that one before, from managers all over the planet.

I was packing on my last morning in Varadero. I had quite enjoyed it in the end, because of the beach, the swimming and having a chance to speak to working Cubans. Or Koobans, as I should call them. Cubans refer to their country as Kooba.

From the next room, I could hear screaming. It was Ken's girl-friend, at the top of her voice, sounding absolutely petrified.

'*Stop it. Stop it. Stop it. No don't, Ken. Ken, not that.*'

My stomach felt cold. I listened, but couldn't hear his voice at all. Just the girl shouting. Then came the sound of glass or some ornament being smashed.

'*No don't. Not that.*'

I couldn't tell from her screams if she was being physically abused or if Ken was doing something to her possessions, tearing up clothes, breaking jewellery. But her screams were terrifying and must have been heard all down the corridor.

I opened my outer door, looked down the corridor, but there was no one around. Should I bang on their door, tell him to stop? In which case he'd probably thump me. He did look a pretty tough bloke.

I got my bag and went to pay the bill and check out. While I was at reception, I told one of the receptionists about the screams from the next-door room.

I suggested she sent a security man down the corridor. When he next heard the screams, he should enter and ask if someone needed help. No need to say that I have reported anything, if you don't mind. I don't want to be followed back to Blighty.

Then I got in my taxi back to Havana.

CHAPTER TWELVE

Cuba: Havana Again

I got back to Havana, taking a taxi all the way; oh, spare no expense. I did have a voucher for a coach, but that was going straight to the airport, and much later in the day. I could have got a plane, but I'd seen some of them flying overhead, khaki-coloured, circa 1940s by the look of them. So I did a deal with a taxi driver, agreed a price of $100. He looked trustworthy, and his car was quite new, so we arranged a time and rendezvous. Not at the normal rank, as of course he was doing this without his bosses knowing. Some hope. They were obviously all in it. The taxi that turned up was about twenty years older, very beat-up, as was the taxi driver, a different man, much older and unshaven. But we got there okay. I like to think in those ten days I contributed well to the Cuban economy, paying for hotels I didn't use, coaches I didn't ride. And now agreeing to speak at their conference.

I went to have a drink with Ernesto, organiser of the Beatles conference, at the Inglaterra Hotel, where Pete and Janice, my Beatles friends from London, were staying.

The Beatles were banned in Cuba, so Ernesto said, on radio or television, from 1964 to 1966. 'As I was a baby at the time, I wasn't quite aware of it.' Ernesto was about thirty-six, rather dark hooded eyes and receding hair and excellent English. He could even do a passable Liverpool accent.

Banned because they were seen as examples of decadent Western music?

'That wasn't quite the reason. The Cuban revolution was still young and they wanted to preserve our own cultural values. Elvis was also banned. I can understand the ban, but culture should have no boundaries.'

His two older brothers were Beatles fans and managed somehow to get copies of their records, which Ernesto loved listening to. 'At school, all my friends were Beatles fans. We always celebrated John Lennon's birthday on 8 October. I suppose because they had been banned, we wanted to know more about them. It was hard, because we could not buy Beatles records in Cuba. Friends abroad would send them, and we'd pass them round. Now you can buy them – if you have the money.'

He read English at university and then went on to become a university lecturer in English, where he met his wife Anna, also a university lecturer. In 1996, along with some friends, he helped organise the first International Beatles Conference in Cuba. It lasted three days and the speakers, mainly Cubans, gave very learned lectures on their Beatles researches. Ernesto produced a book about the conference: *Los Beatles en Cuba*. Bit of a liberty, the title, as they never went there, but correct in an abstract sense. The Beatles are now everywhere.

Ernesto gave up his university job a year ago to become a freelance translator. 'As a university lecturer, I was getting 300 pesos a month – about $15. You can live on that, just. In Mexico, you die if you are poor. In Cuba, you will not die.'

He'd had one good translating job so far: helping Michael Palin who'd been over making a TV series about Hemingway. 'I earned enough in those two weeks to be able to survive for about six months. It means I've been able to spend my time writing and researching the Beatles.'

How many Beatles fans are there in Cuba? 'We don't have a fan club, as such. But everyone in Cuba is a Beatles fan.' At that moment the hotel pianist started playing 'Hey Jude', as if on cue.

We were then joined by a friend of his, also a Beatles fan, who asked if I'd like to hear a Castro joke. It was the first such offer I'd had. In Russia, once the booze was out, and we were on the beach, everyone started telling Gorby jokes.

Castro goes on an official visit to India where a maharajah gives him a present of a baby elephant. Castro asks how old it is and is told it's just a few months old. He then asks how long elephants live for and he's told they can live to 120 years old. At this, Castro starts crying. The maharajah asks him why. 'Because I don't want to see the elephant die,' Castro replies.

A fairly affectionate joke. Cubans make remarks all the time about Castro thinking he'll live for ever.

He told another story about Castro, this time with the Pope, who was recently on a visit to Cuba. Castro and the Pope go for a walk together, each boasting about their miraculous powers, when they come to the sea. The Pope keeps walking, because he can walk on water. Castro, not to be outdone, also walks on the water. This is seen as the most amazing modern miracle and gets enormous coverage round the world – except in the USA. They print a small story with the headline: 'Fidel can't swim'.

I did laugh at that one. Which encouraged him to tell a third story. Castro is giving one of his interminable speeches and at the end he says he has some good news. 'We are going to change our clothes in Cuba,' he announces to cheers. 'You will change your clothes with him over there, and she will change her clothes with her...'

I only smiled at that one, but no doubt it has Cubans clutching their sides, having to put up with their lack of choice in clothes. Ernesto said it was a struggle getting clothes for his two children, but luckily he had bought lots in London. This surprised me. I thought Cubans couldn't go abroad.

'I had to prove I had been invited, that I needed to go to London for research, at the British Museum and other places, and that I had somewhere to stay. Luckily Pete put me up.'

So what was the research?

'I am writing a book about Cuban and English music, going back to the 1930s. The big 1950s bands like Ted Heath's Band usually did a Cuban Latin-American number. Then there was Edmundo Ros, King of the Mambo.'

How had he found London?

'Very capitalist, but I suppose that wasn't so surprising. I've only ever lived in a place which is socialist. It was very busy, very commercial, very money-orientated. In Cuba we still do things from the heart. In Cuba we still respect each other. In London people hurry past and don't look at you. There are beggars in the street, people in sleeping bags. They asked me for money of course and I had to say I had no money. Which I hadn't. In London, I lost the sense of being a human being.

'I got my air ticket paid, thanks to sponsorship from Castrol and Havanatours and other firms. I could never have afforded it otherwise. But it meant when I got there, I had no money to spend.

'People were friendlier outside London. I went up to Liverpool for my researches, and also went to a Beatles convention in Liverpool. I was very disappointed by it. It was purely commercial – people there to make money, selling bootleg records and other stuff.

'In Cuba our Beatles convention is nostalgic, not commercial. We have to sell tickets, but that is purely to cover costs, not to make a profit. We do it for love of the Beatles, not for love of money. As you will see . . .'

The conference was being held in Havana's International Press Center. There were around twenty different events, from lectures, film shows, videos and discussions to live music. The sponsors included Castrol, the British Council and the British Embassy.

I arrived in time to hear one of the live groups, three Cubans on stage with guitars, singing Beatles songs. They were brilliant. Their accents, intonations, music, as good as any Western Beatles cover group, and there are many today. I also watched a rather blurry video of the Beatles' first appearance on the *Ed Sullivan Show* from 1964.

The theatre was full for my talk, around 150, and I felt a bit embarrassed, as they were not to know I was here by chance, and had not prepared anything. I started with a little quiz, partly to fill in time and to test their knowledge.

I asked five simple questions: which town in England were they from? Who brought up John? Who was their manager? What is Ringo's real name? Who was Martha?

I thought the questions might be too hard, especially the last two. I gave out scraps of paper which Ernesto marked, as I did my talk. I nattered on about how I came to do the Beatles biography, how I went to Hamburg, what it was like being in Abbey Road when they were doing *Sergeant Pepper*.

As I spoke, in English of course, my every word was translated into Spanish by two young translators. Each of the 150 in the audience had their own headphone, so could hear in Spanish what I was saying. At the end, when they were invited to ask questions, I put on a headphone and their questions were translated into English for me. The technology, and their translation skills, were incredible. I was most impressed.

Even more so when it turned out that over 100 out of the 150 had got every one of my five questions correct. Full marks to Cuban education, I say.

Also at the conference, to my total surprise, were the Quarrymen, the five original members of the group that grew into the Beatles. They are referred to in all the books about the Beatles, but I had never known what happened to them, after John and the Beatles went on into history and they remained a mere footnote.

They call themselves John Lennon's Original Quarrymen and their leader is Rod Davis. I'd never met him, back in the sixties, but I had met Pete Shotton, who was John's best friend at Quarry Bank High School in Liverpool.

In the late 1950s they were an ad hoc skiffle group, as in so many schools around Britain at the time. Most of them couldn't play a proper instrument, or had much musical talent. It was just the thing to do, friends mucking around together. Pete Shotton was on washboard, Colin Hanton on drums, Len Garry on tea chest, Eric Griffiths on guitar and Rod Davis on banjo. Plus John Lennon. Members came and went, got bored, gave up.

In July 1957 they gave a performance at Woolton Parish Church fête, a vital day in the history of the Beatles as it was the day Paul McCartney met John for the first time. He joined the group, then George Harrison, and later Ringo, by which time the original members had all long gone.

In 1997, to celebrate forty years since the foundation of the Cavern Club in Liverpool, they were each tracked down and invited to a party.

'I had not been in touch with the others for forty years,' said Rod. 'We hadn't been invited to play. I just went along for the free drink, but I put an old tea chest and washboard in the boot of my car, just in case. In the event we did play together, for the first time in forty years. Then later that year we were invited to the fortieth anniversary of the Woolton Parish fête. This time we played to about 3,500 – compared with a couple of hundred back in 1957.'

Rod was the only one of the five who had kept up an interest in playing music during the forty years, playing his banjo as an amateur, for fun, mainly American bluegrass music.

After Quarry Bank, Rod had gone on to Trinity College, Cambridge where he read languages. He lived abroad for some years teaching, then came back and became a tour guide in London. He then got a job as a lecturer in tourism at a polytechnic in Uxbridge. From which he has now retired.

Pete Shotton spent most of his working life in shops and restaurants, his friend John Lennon having helped him to buy his first supermarket. Rather a nice present. But he did make it work for him and recently sold a chain of some fifty Fatty Arbuckle restaurants in a multi-million pound deal. He is now retired and living in Southampton. His first wife died of cancer when she was thirty-five. He has since been married twice.

Len Garry and Colin Hanton both still live in Liverpool: Len is a teacher and Colin is an upholsterer. Eric Griffiths lives in Edinburgh and has a small chain of dry-cleaning shops.

'Because of the fortieth anniversary reunions,' said Rod, 'we got invited to various Beatles conventions, such as Utrecht. We also did a small tour in the USA. We're going to Las Vegas next and then to Vancouver.'

They were in Cuba for five days, each with their wife or partner. They didn't get a fee, but they did get free flights and a free holiday.

I asked Rod if he'd wished this had all happened earlier.

'I have not gone through life crying for fifteen minutes every morning because I could have been a Beatle. I've got no regrets about the life I've led.

'I now know it's harder work than I thought it would be. I do all the draggy stuff like getting our work permits and visas when we go abroad to play. It's also very very tedious being on the road, especially at our age. But it's fun. That's really why we're doing it, to amuse ourselves.'

Pete Shotton, after forty years in shops and restaurants, said he was loving it. 'I never had a musical gene in my body. I was in the Quarrymen just because I was John's best friend. I didn't like it much at the time, as I was so shy and easily embarrassed. I didn't care for standing up in front of people. Now I'm no longer shy – in fact they can't keep me down.'

What about groupies? After all, that was and is one of the major attractions for anyone going into rock 'n' roll. In Cuba, with their passion for the Beatles, they must have quite a range of very intelligent, well-educated Beatles groupies.

'Oh yes, we get them,' said Pete. 'The trouble is they're also in their late fifties. But at our age, you can't be choosy . . .'

It took me some time, some heavy hinting, but before I left Havana, I managed to invite myself to Ernesto's home. This can be hard to achieve in a country like Cuba at this moment in its history. And it's understandable. Who wants some flash Westerner poking around their modest living quarters?

He lives about six miles out of town, under the tunnel, in an area called Guiteras. The taxi driver got lost. All the streets and all the buildings looked the same, row after row of depressingly similar five-storey concrete blocks built in the 1970s, quite spaciously laid out, with trees in the streets and little gardens, but all in desperate need of repair and redecoration. And yet there were no signs of vandalism or graffiti which you would expect on similar run-down estates in Britain. In Carlisle, where I was brought up, there is one council estate, Raffles, which has become a no-go area, where houses are boarded up, people are afraid to live. Ernesto's estate might look depressing but it didn't seem scary.

And it also didn't seem Caribbean. Communism has seen to that, building vast communal housing blocks, the sort you see nowhere else in the West Indies. It could have been a Moscow suburb, but for the palm trees. The poor and less well off in the Caribbean are normally reduced to crumbling wooden shacks which can look quite attractive outside, if they are of the chattel-house, gingerbread-boarded variety, and get snapped by tourists, but are not so attractive to live in. In the deprived Caribbean countries, with real poor and no government support of any sort, such as Haiti, they are left to rot in the streets, sleeping in the open gutters. By comparison, life in a Cuban council block is luxury living.

When we eventually found Ernesto's block I could see that each flat had its own little concrete balcony. Most of them were draped with washing, giving it a Mediterranean feeling. Some had been enclosed, made into an extra living space.

Ernesto lives on the fourth floor in a flat which has three bedrooms, living room, kitchen and bathroom. He and his wife and two children share it with his parents. His father used to be a fisherman then became a construction worker, helping to build this block of flats.

It is his father's flat, which will eventually become Ernesto's, though he can never sell it, only pass it on to his own children. Swaps can take place, are allowed, and are quite common. If someone thinks they are swapping a better or bigger place for a smaller or worse place, some money might also change hands. That is unofficial, but happens. It's unofficial because of course any sort of trading in houses or flats is illegal.

Ernesto opened the front door to his flat and led me into their little living room, more an entrance hall really, sparsely furnished, with a black painted couch and a couple of chairs. On the main wall was a large poster of the Beatles. Which naturally I admired. I noticed a broken window, and wondered if I'd got it wrong about the lack of vandalism. He said that had been a strong wind some weeks ago, part of Hurricane Mitch. They had been lucky. It had only touched the coast of Cuba on its way to wreak havoc in Honduras.

Inside the flat, the two families try to live independent, separate lives as much as possible. Ernesto and his wife Anna spend most of their time in their own bedroom while his mother and father live mostly in their bedroom. Each has a fridge and their own television. Ernesto and Anna's bedroom has their double bed, clothes and possessions, TV and fridge – and also their baby, two-year-old son Dhani. I thought it was Danny at first, but once he spelled it out, I knew the connection. Named after George Harrison's son.

Dhani was still asleep in his cot, so we crept out and went into the other bedroom which is where their daughter Zuilma sleeps. She is aged six and was at school that morning. This bedroom also doubles as Ernesto's study and half of it was crammed with records, books, computer and music systems.

Ernesto doesn't have a phone, a car, nor of course his own house, but I had to admit his Beatles collection was one of the best I'd ever seen. He even had my biography, in Spanish, very worn and tatty, as it had been round hundreds of hands. I looked through his Beatles records, and his Beatles videos, and he had everything I had, plus a few South American versions I'd never seen before.

I also noted a whole set of the *Monty Python* tapes. And copies of all Michael Palin's travel films. I then realised where they had come from – sent by Michael Palin as a present, after Ernesto had worked for him. Michael Palin lives a couple of streets away from me in London. I said I'd tell him his presents had arrived safely. (Postage of any sort to ordinary Cubans is hell. When I later sent some Beatles stuff to Ernesto, I sent it via a friend at the British Embassy, but still never heard for months if it had arrived or not.)

Ernesto works from this half room as a freelance translator and writer. Fortunately, Anna has a job, in a hotel, on a computer, so can support their family. Ernesto makes very little in the way of financial return from his writings.

But what about the book you told me about, Ernesto? The one about the first Beatles convention. Yes, he edited it, compiled and wrote several of the chapters, but received only 500 pesos – around £15. I thought authorship in the UK was paid badly, which it is for about 80 per cent of UK authors, but not quite that badly.

'It's a government-owned publisher, of course, and payments are all standard. It works out at 10 pesos per page for all the contributors.'

He presented me with a copy, which was kind, as it was one of his last ones. All 2,000 printed quickly sold out. I saw his full name, Ernesto Juan Castellanos, on the cover, a stiff paperback, 230 pages, priced at 15 pesos. That works out about 50p. Little wonder it sold out.

'The publisher can't reprint, as they have run out of paper. They have to buy the raw material in dollars and the books are sold in pesos. They are looking for sponsorship to be able to print and publish my next book.'

Next book?

'I am actually working on three books at the moment. There's the book about the second conference, all finished, waiting to be published. There's *The Long and Winding Road* which is a history and analysis of Beatles albums. Then the book I went to London to research. I'm calling that *And I Love Her*. It's about the influence of Cuban music on British music, especially on the Beatles.'

Come on, Ernesto. You are not really saying the Beatles took stuff from Cuban music?

'Of course. I have analysed every song they ever wrote and I have counted twenty-eight songs which include maracas, twelve songs which include bongos, ten with cow bells and one with a guiro – that's a bit like a washboard.'

I can see a vague influence when it comes to instruments, but they were often chosen and used after the music had been written and created. I wouldn't say their actual music was much influenced by Cuban music. However, I didn't want to argue. He is the expert.

I noticed a guitar, propped up in a corner, and asked whose it was. He said it was his. He plays in a Beatles-style group. 'We've got a rehearsal later today.'

Not here?

'No. At someone else's place. These flats have very thin walls. You can hear everything, laughing, crying, anything, especially when the windows are open.'

Which of course they are, most of the day, in a tropical climate. There is no air-conditioning in the flats, but Ernesto did have a ceiling fan in his and Anna's bedroom.

We could hear Dhani waking up, so Ernesto went to investigate. He got him up, washed him all over, put on a clean nappy, then got him dressed. Rather snazzily, in denim dungarees, blue polo shirt and baseball cap.

'All bought in London.'

I thought you had no spending money? Those sorts of kids' clothes cost a fortune, even for Brits.

'Ah, but I went to car boot sales. Those dungarees cost 25p. The only things I bought in England were for the children. And I bought them all at car boot sales.'

I sympathised with him about getting any sorts of clothes in Cuba, judging by the shops I'd seen.

Clothes are not rationed, but almost everything else is, for Cubans with no access to dollars. Food rations, for old or young, included one bread roll per day, six eggs per person per month, three pounds of potatoes and three pounds of beans per month.

These allowances, bought with ration coupons, are relatively cheap, so in theory no one should starve. There are also street markets, in which people sell vegetables and pork they have produced themselves, for pesos, but they are much more expensive.

I asked if Ernesto did the shopping, as well as looking after Dhani. If so, that must be hell. From my experience of Russia, people seemed to spend half of each day in massive queues.

'No. A boy does it. I pay him 30 pesos a month and he does the queueing for me. He keeps our ration books. Each day he brings our bread roll ration. He looks after about twelve other people, so that's his job, which gives him an average wage.'

What if he cheated you, gave you rubbish food, or pinched some of your rations?

'I don't think he would, but I wouldn't care.'

Rum is cheap to buy, on sale in pesos, but beer and wine can only be bought in dollars. Normal Cubans can't afford either.

'The worst thing at the moment is cooking oil. That's shot up in price, yet everyone needs it for their cooking. It now costs the equivalent of about $2\frac{1}{2}$, which is a fortune for all Cubans. That's the biggest moan you hear at present.'

A lot of Cubans, said Ernesto, add to their food resources by keeping some animals of their own. Country folks, I presumed, people with a bit of space.

'No, here. In these blocks. People keep animals. The man above me kept a pig on his balcony, up on the fifth floor. You could smell it every day. It was appalling. Luckily he killed it last Christmas.

'My father till recently kept three chickens and a rooster in a pen on our balcony. The cockerel's crowing kept Dhani awake all the time, so my father killed them.'

Apart from noisome animals, you can also get noisome neighbours, in any block of communal flats, anywhere. Was that a problem? From time to time, he said. They had had an alcoholic neighbour who neglected himself and his flat and water overflowed, bringing down other people's ceilings.

However, they have never been burgled, or had their walls or flats vandalised, thanks to their own security system.

'Each block has what's called a Committee for the Defence of the Revolution. Through this we organise our own security, with each person taking turns at guard duty at night. There are twenty flats in this block, with an average of five people per flat. So that's 100 people in our block. It works out around one night per month. We usually do it in pairs. You just sit at the entrance and talk to each other all night. It's not a hardship.'

He doesn't miss being a university lecturer, despite the lack of money and insecurity of his present life. He was worried, though, unlike the hotel manager in Varadero, about the effects of so many people leaving the professions for tourism.

'It is understandable why they leave, when you get only 300 pesos a month after five years of studying. The worry is that people of eighteen will decide not to go to university at all and go straight from school into working in a bar or a hotel. Any bartender in a hotel lives better than a surgeon or architect because he gets dollars from tips.'

My taxi driver had returned to pick me up, take me to Havana and my plane back to London. Ernesto said he would come into town with me, save him getting the bus. First he had to take Dhani to his babysitter. I went with him as he handed him over to an elderly woman in the next block.

As we got into the taxi, Ernesto remembered something he had forgotten.

'My lens,' he said. 'For my eye.'

He then dashed upstairs again to his flat while I sat waiting for him in the taxi, thinking, what is the plural of lens? Surely he should have said 'lenses'? As a former English lecturer, he'll probably know better than me.

When he came back, I asked him why he'd said he'd gone for his lens not lenses.

'Because I have only one lens, for one eye. I did get a pair two years ago, which greatly helped my eyesight, but I lost one of them some months ago. I can't get another one. The factory that makes them has closed because of lack of the raw materials which are imported. I did look at lenses when I was in London, but they were too expensive. So I am just managing with one lens in one eye. No, it's not a hardship, not really.'

But it was presumably the reason why on first meeting him I had noticed his very worn and strained eyes for a relatively young man.

In the taxi, Ernesto fell a bit silent. He was worried that in our conversation he might have appeared to criticise the government or the system. I said he hadn't done so. Everyone knew about the two economies, the pluses and the minuses. The government itself must be weighing them all up, working out how to achieve a balance in the future.

I could see he was proud of his country, its health and education systems, music, culture, full employment. And I said I hoped to come back and see him and Cuba again some time. Cuba, it seemed to me, was probably the most interesting country to visit at the moment, in all the Caribbean. He seemed pleased by that.

End Word

On my West Indian wanderings I had given myself the task of meeting and talking to expatriots and returnees – and ended up on an island where there are none. Sorry about that. Rather ruins the shape. But I'm sure there will be in the future. Once Cuba and the USA are chumming again, thousands if not millions of Cuban exiles will return from Miami and elsewhere. That will be fascinating, to see how they get on, if they can settle in a country so different from the USA, if they can mix and live with the people who never left.

All returnees have those re-entry problems, whether they are returning after a short spell away or are returning to a country they have never actually been to before, which they know about only through their parents or their family legends.

Elsewhere in the Caribbean, where movement is relatively free and easy and returning is now common, most returnees do find it hard. They have to button their lip, as many observed, and not boast, even indirectly, of the place they left behind, where things were bigger, better, more efficient. They must not appear to criticise or act superior to those who stayed behind. They have to cope with petty jealousies and envy, often for little reason, for imagined slights. They must not be flash, even if they have come back with a better car and build themselves a bigger house than anyone else. They can end up in a no-man's land, having cut themselves off from the adopted country they have now left, yet find they have more in common with it than their supposed homeland. It was noticeable how often the returnees, the JCBs as they call themselves in Grenada, tended to stick together.

As for expats, there could well be a flood of them to Cuba, once the present restrictions cease. People didn't exactly flock to Russia once communism collapsed, but they might well do so with Cuba.

The weather for a start is pretty good, the people vibrant and welcoming, the towns and buildings, cars and countryside still caught in a time warp and the *mojitos* are excellent, much nicer than vodka.

If you are going to be an expat in the Caribbean, going out there to work, not just enjoy yourself, you have to be prepared to work hard. All my expats said that. And be willing to take any job that comes along, not necessarily the one you have been trained for. You have to adapt to delays, shortages, slownesses, inefficiencies, the laid-back attitude to life.

The hardest jobs of all, or so it seemed to me, are in the area which most people think will be easy, will be fun: opening a beach bar, restaurant or similar, mine host, standing around, posing while getting a tan. Those two ex-gas-fitters in Tobago, whom I have seen again since that chapter, are doing even better with their restaurant, and now have bought a hotel – but they look even more exhausted.

It is best to arrive with some sort of specialist skill or experience, which can be carried or adapted and used anywhere. And from which you can knock off at five o'clock, in time to benefit from the supposed paradise you have come to enjoy.

I was surprised to find that ex-Scotland Yard boss in Mustique – yet I later found another, doing a similar job, in Antigua at Jumby Bay, though I didn't write about him, as his story was much the same. Until I met them I hadn't actually imagined ex-cops finding nice jobs in the West Indies. In theory, almost any job in this modern world can be transported, or adapted, if you think it out, search for where and how it might be needed.

On the booming tourist islands, like St Martin, everyone said that good carpenters, electricians, plumbers would always get work. But I suppose they always will. In the same way that computer skills are in demand all over the globe. Work permits and associated restrictions put on foreigners have to be coped with in all the West Indian islands now, which means it's best to find a job first, or at least arrive with enough capital to keep going for some time.

Those Europeans and North Americans who do decide to go and live and work in the West Indies are not of course primarily driven by the need to find a job but by a fantasy in their heads.

They feel unsettled, disjointed, unhappy, unfulfilled where they are, a dangerous feeling, which can cover a multitude of failures or weaknesses, many of them not always apparent. As that American on the beach in St Martin said, people who screw up in one place usually screw up in the next place.

A sinking relationship or faltering marriage is often at the heart of this desire to move on, which usually results in the cracks opening even more, once you are thrown together full time, seeing all the fault lines close up. What people are often escaping from is themselves. But you knew all that.

Having decided, after all, that you are going to the West Indies, either for good or for a holiday, where should you go? And what sort of background information might you need? Read on...

Appendices

Christopher Columbus and the West Indies

It's useful for every Caribbean traveller to have a working knowledge of Columbus, the man who got there 'first'. But don't say that, or you'll get into arguments. Just say that he was a very important European explorer, part of the history of the Caribbean, and of the world, about whom everyone should know.

You will come across him all the time because most islands claim some connection with him, even if he never landed and only sighted their island in the distance, while going the other way. Possibly, might be. The more active, imaginative tourist boards manage a few direct quotes, in which of course he says their particular island was the fairest/nicest/greatest for snorkelling/best for rum punches he had ever seen.

He did in fact visit or view at least a hundred West Indian islands, zipping around some of them quickly, very like a modern Western tourist on a package holiday or on a Caribbean cruise. If it's Wednesday, it's Puerto Rico. He didn't send postcards, but he did write letters and a journal for the Queen and King, telling them what a good time he was having, what amazing sights he had seen. And he brought back souvenirs, as tourists still do, though some of his are not allowed today. It's illegal in most countries, for example, to take in foreign plants and fruits and bringing back slaves is definitely frowned upon.

By giving a potted biography separately, now, it's saved me from mentioning him too much in the individual chapters.

Columbus was born in Genoa in 1451. There was for several centuries some mystery about his place and date of birth, but that has now been agreed. So he was Italian, known in Italy today as Cristoforo Colombo. In Spanish-speaking countries he is known as Cristobal Colon. Look out for places named after him.

He was the oldest of five children, son of a weaver, fair-haired and blue-eyed – unusual but not uncommon in Italy today. He attended a local guild school till about the age of ten when he began working for his father. Later on, he said he had gone to the University of Pavia. This was a fib, trying to improve his CV.

He went to sea from about the age of fourteen, as a sort of commercial traveller at first, working for various merchants, up and down the Mediterranean, but along the way he picked up the basics of seamanship, such as they were.

At the age of twenty-five he was shipwrecked off the Algarve coast in Portugal, made his way to Lisbon and for the next ten years was a resident of Portugal. He married a Portuguese woman and had a son. During this period he dreamed up what he called his Grand Design – to sail West in order to reach the East.

Educated opinion had accepted that the world was round since the Greeks. Even ordinary sailors knew the world was not flat. They just had to look at the horizon. From a distance, you see the top of the mast of another ship first, before its hull. When approaching land, you see mountains, before you see the beaches – ergo, there must be a curve in the sea, even though it looks flat. But no one had ever demonstrated the world was a globe by sailing all the way round it.

Columbus saw himself making his fortune if he could do it. Portugal was the leading naval and colonial power, but the Portuguese were having trouble getting to the East, from whence came spices and silks and perfumes and other middle-class essentials of the fifteenth century. The rise of the Moors, in northern Africa and the Middle East, had cut off the traditional trade routes. Columbus saw a new way of getting to the East: by going the other way.

He managed to get an audience with the King of Portugal, and put up his brilliant idea. By going into the unknown, he would not just establish new routes but discover some brand-new countries for Portugal. The King thought about it and said go away, what a stupid idea.

Columbus then moved to Spain. He spent most of the next eight years hanging around the Spanish court, fathering another son by a woman not his wife, trying to get his plan accepted. Queen Isabella and King Ferdinand had other things to worry about. They were at war, fighting to get the Moors chucked out of mainland Spain. The Moors were eventually expelled in January 1492, and it was for this reason, in the euphoria of victory, that Columbus was allowed go off and 'discover' the New World.

He set off from Palos in southern Spain on 3 August 1492, with three little boats and ninety men. His flagship was the *Santa Maria*, seventy feet long, no bigger than a tennis court. They had a compass, an hour-glass, an astrolobe which could measure latitude, but no proper way of measuring speed or distance, and of course no maps.

They sailed south first, to the Canaries, leaving from the little island of Gomera, heading across the southern Atlantic. Columbus estimated from his previous voyages that there were trade winds which would blow him across.

Landfall was on a small island in the Bahamas on 12 October – thirty-six days after having left the Canaries. Columbus called it San Salvador, in honour of their safe arrival, the name by which it is known today. He sailed round various islands of the Bahamas, hoping for gold or anything worth taking home, then came to Cuba, which by its size he thought might be the mainland.

He had noticed that the native peoples he had met so far were not black, like Africans, but more like Asians. He called them Indians, thinking he was in the West Indies, as opposed to the East Indies. Hazy maps of the East did exist, so he decided that Cuba could be Japan, if it wasn't mainland China. No European knew that a whole continent was out there, blocking the way.

In Cuba, he noticed some local Indians smoking dried leaves which they called tobacco. The world's first sighting. He didn't try it himself and didn't see much future for this weird habit.

Columbus then sailed the fifty miles or so across the Windward Passage and came to another big island which he called Hispaniola. It was green and attractive, with the sort of mountains and even fish which reminded him of Spain. Today, Hispaniola is two countries: Haiti and the Dominican Republic.

He landed in the north of what is now Haiti, made friends with the local Indians; in fact had a jolly good time with the local chief and his women, drinking and eating, leaving the *Santa Maria* with only a cabin boy on board. In the night, a storm blew up and the *Santa Maria* was wrecked. Out of the salvaged timbers, Columbus built a little fort which he called Navidad, as the accident had happened on Christmas Eve. Navidad was the first Western settlement in the New World.

He left a small garrison behind in Navidad, then headed back for Spain with the two remaining boats, the *Nina* and the *Pinta*, much smaller than the *Santa Maria*. They arrived home safely, after many storms and dramas, to a triumphal reception.

Columbus was lavished with honours by the Queen and King. Spain was now able to compete with its deadly rival Portugal in carving up the world between them. The Pope was called in to arbitrate, deciding which areas of influence would be Spain's and which would be Portugal's.

Columbus's second voyage in 1493 was a stupendous affair. He set off with 1,200 men, 117 ships, plus animals and supplies to establish proper settlements in the New World. They landed first in Dominica, on a Sunday, hence its name, sailed on to Guadeloupe and then the Virgin Islands, so named because they reminded him of the medieval legend of the 11,000 virgins. He went on to 'discover' Puerto Rico before finally arriving back in Hispaniola. Amazing to think he took a new route, all round the houses, yet ended up exactly where he had planned. Arriving in Navidad he found his whole garrison had been murdered. Probably their own fault, ill-treating or taking advantage of local Indian girls.

He went to Cuba again, but still couldn't get round it, so sailed to Jamaica and landed near what is now St Ann's Bay. He returned to Cuba, spent four weeks sailing along the coast, convinced it must be a peninsula, part of mainland China. He called a halt, just before he reached the end. If he had sailed for another day, he would have seen Cuba was an island – and would then have discovered Florida.

On his third voyage, in 1498, he crossed the Atlantic much further south, avoiding most of the West Indian islands he had already discovered, and landed on Trinidad – naming it either after three peaks he'd spotted on the horizon or in honour of the Holy Trinity. Columbus was a sincere Catholic, believing he was doing all this for God and Isabella, the Holy Catholic Queen.

He moved on to what we now call Venezuela and it was there, on 5 August 1498, that he set foot for the first time on the new continent of America. He didn't realise it at the time, thinking he had reached yet another island.

He then returned to Hispaniola, where the main Spanish settlement had been established in Santo Domingo, in what is now the Dominican Republic. Trouble broke out amongst the Spaniards, and with the local Indians, which Columbus, as governor, failed to settle and only made worse. He had always been much more interested in exploring than governing, though he loved the titles. It not only ended in tears – but chains. Columbus was clamped in them and dragged back to Spain to be tried for his failures. Such ignominy. After all those wild celebrations on his first return.

He managed to explain it was not his fault, and the Queen pardoned him, but he lost possessions and titles and never had the same stature again.

In 1502 he managed to organise a fourth and final voyage, more modest this time, landing in Martinique after just twenty days' sailing from the Canaries. He went to Hispaniola again, then spent a long time exploring the coast of Central America, in Nicaragua and Honduras, desperate to find a way through or across and somehow reach the Pacific and make it to the East, as he had always planned. But his ships were worm-eaten by then as was Columbus himself, showing signs of going a bit potty. On the way back they got stuck in Jamaica and nearly died.

He did get back to Spain. Two years later, on 20 May 1506, he died in Valladolid. In poverty by then, so he said, cheated out of all the titles he had been promised and the honours he deserved. He didn't even achieve the posthumous satisfaction of having America, the continent he had 'discovered', named after him. That happened by chance in 1507 when a German mapmaker, Martin Waldseemüller, was about to publish some new material and was wondering what name to stick on the New World bit. He had just been reading an account of some travels by Amerigo Vespucci and so decided to call it America. Not Amerigo. All the continents so far had female names – Europa, Africa, Asia – so he had to give the new one a feminine ending.

While I was working on a biography of Columbus for the 500th anniversary celebrations of the 'discovery' of America in 1992, Columbus was still a hero, revered by every schoolchild in the Americas. Many do think he not only got to the USA, which he didn't, but stayed on and became an all-American guy himself. By the time of publication, he was no longer a hero. Those who were ethnically and ecologically aware had decided that Columbus was the ultimate bastard, responsible for centuries of colonial oppression and destruction. While I was in Haiti, his statue was thrown into the sea.

Was he a baddie? In the context of the times in which he lived, he was not thought so. Great explorer, if a lousy administrator. He can't personally be blamed for what subsequent Spaniards did, or the actions of the British, Dutch and French who fought amongst themselves over the next few centuries about who owned which island. But it is true he was the first known European who returned and told his story, the one who started it all.

He did not of course 'discover' the New World. It was always there. So were the people. There were Arawaks who were peaceful, and Caribs who were warlike, fighting amongst themselves. Where had they come from? Like the Europeans, they had sailed there, from the mainland of Central and South America. And before that? It's thought they had originally migrated down through North America, at a pre-Ice Age time when the land mass was connected to Asia. So in one sense, they were Asians. Which was what Columbus believed.

Columbus did like the people of the West Indies, the landscape, the flora and fauna, and recorded all his impressions. He loved moving on, seeing places, new islands. To be safe then, don't call him the Great Discoverer. Think upon him as the First Tourist, setting trails which we all follow to this day.

Tourist Numbers in the Caribbean

Some 15 million tourists have a holiday in the Caribbean each year – and that's not counting people on cruise ships, who are of course having their holiday on board, not on shore.

Half of them come from North America, a quarter from Europe, and the rest from elsewhere in the world. In 1998, Puerto Rico attracted most tourists, 3.4 million, followed by the Dominican Republic, 2.3 million; the Bahamas, 1.5 million; Cuba, 1.4 million; and Jamaica, 1.2 million.

Note: in this book, by West Indies or Caribbean I mean islands or countries in the Caribbean Ocean. It does not include any mainland countries, such as Belize, which are sometimes classed as being part of the Caribbean.

DESTINATION	TOURISTS (*thousands*) 1998	DESTINATION	TOURISTS (*thousands*) 1998
Anguilla	44	Guadeloupe	693
Antigua and Barbuda	234	Haiti	146
Aruba	647	Jamaica	1225
Bahamas	1540	Martinique	548
Barbados	512	Puerto Rico	3461
Bonaire	62	St Kitts and Nevis	93
Cayman Islands	404	St Lucia	252
Cuba	1416	St Maarten	458
Curaçao	198	St Vincent and Grenadines	67
Dominican Republic	2309	Trinidad and Tobago	347
Dominica	65	Turks and Caicos Islands	106
Grenada	115	US Virgin Islands	418
Total			**15,340**

UK Tourists in the Caribbean

Traditionally, the most popular destinations for Brits were the ex-British colonies where they spoke English, drank Guinness, knew how to make a decent cup of tea, such as Barbados and Jamaica. These figures for 1998 show that Barbados has been overtaken by the Dominican Republic, if only just. Jamaica was third with 116,000. The Dominican Republic is of course Spanish-speaking, though you might not think it in the new purpose-built holiday complexes aimed at the European package-holiday market. That is where the main growth is in the tourist market, along with Cuba. Cuba has only taken off for British visitors in the last two years, but it's likely to be competing with Barbados for British visitors in the next few years.

COUNTRY	1998	COUNTRY	1998
Anguilla	2,738	Guadeloupe	269
Antigua and Barbuda	57,500	Jamaica	116,552
Aruba	3,008	Martinique	3,691
Bahamas	50,300	Montserrat	1,403
Barbados	186,690	Puerto Rico	8,440
Bonaire	883	Saba	428
British Virgin Islands	13,018	St Kitts and Nevis	12,847
Cayman Islands	23,895	St Lucia	63,160
Cuba	64,272	St Vincent and Grenadines	11,984
Curaçao	2,162	Trinidad and Tobago	47,760
Dominica	5,577	Turks and Caicos Islands	2,175
Dominican Republic	188,184	US Virgin Islands	3,308
Grenada	23,311		
Total			**891,655**

Opinions

It's ridiculous trying to say which is the Best Island, the Best Beach, though I have said it to myself, many times, as Columbus did, only to wander on, explore further, and then say, oh no, this is now my favourite, this must be my number one. It all depends, on what it all depends on. But here goes.

Best island for beginners: BARBADOS
In the sense that for Brits it's easy to get to, easy to adjust to, especially for first-time visitors. Things work, people are friendly, still pretty safe, lots of facilities, great beaches, excellent hotels. A great introduction to the Caribbean. Though don't expect the rest of the islands to be as efficient as Barbados.

Prettiest islands: TOBAGO, ST LUCIA, DOMINICA, GRENADA
In that they have a combination of all the best tropical features: white beaches (except Dominica), rainforests, hills and valleys, lush vegetation, yet are still not overdeveloped.

Quiet islands: BEQUIA, DOMINICA
Empty ones of course are quietest of all, or the near-empty titchy ones like Mayreau, which is beautifully quiet, but takes for ever to get to. Bequia combines reasonable accessibility, a good harbour, excellent restaurants, with a leisurely pace of life. Dominica is bigger – but still unspoiled.

Busy islands: PUERTO RICO, MARTINIQUE, GUADELOUPE, US VIRGINS, TRINIDAD
Meaning busy with traffic, people, action, developments, which might be just what you are looking for. They do, though, have bits where you can get away from it all.

Chic islands: ST BARTS
Few arguments there. They think it's the Côte d'Azur.

Cheap islands: DOMINICAN REPUBLIC, CUBA
Nowhere in the Caribbean is cheap. Just think of the transport and labour costs getting stuff out there. But the Dominican Republic, because of its mass-market package holidays, has some very cheap offers, and in Cuba, still a communist country, prices generally are still pretty low.

Exciting islands: JAMAICA, TRINIDAD
Can be too exciting, if you are daft enough to walk in the dodgier parts of Kingston or Port of Spain, but both islands have a cultural and musical tradition which the smaller islands lack. Especially at Carnival times, or similar.

Most fascinating island: CUBA
Has to be. It's only recently opened up, so there is so much to see which most Westerners have never seen. Havana has old architecture and old US automobiles. In the middle and south are smaller towns, like Trinidad, which are unspoiled examples of the Spanish colonial days. People are friendly, it's all pretty safe. Cuba is not just a holiday destination. It's a slice of the social, political and economic history of our times.

Best cities: HAVANA, CUBA; SANTO DOMINGO, DOMINICAN REPUBLIC; SAN JUAN, PUERTO RICO
Okay, so you don't go to the Caribbean for the cities, but these three are architecturally fascinating, giving hints of the Spanish Empire at its height. In the case of Santo Domingo and San Juan, their old city bits and buildings have been well preserved. In Havana, alas, no one seems to care, but decay does lend a certain majesty to its old quarters.

Nicest towns: ST GEORGE'S, GRENADA; PORT ELIZABETH, BEQUIA
Pretty places, small, bijou, but with a bit of life and no nasty overdevelopment.

Best for sailing: VIRGIN ISLANDS, GRENADINES

Not that I know much. But I have sailed, in both places, and there was a lot of other sailors pottering round, with masses of little harbours and facilities. They must know something.

Best for snorkelling: VIRGIN ISLANDS AND CAYMAN ISLANDS

So I'm told.

Best for golf: BARBADOS, PUERTO RICO, JAMAICA, DOMINICAN REPUBLIC, NEVIS, TOBAGO

All now have major golf courses, designed by jolly famous designers of golf courses.

Best place for honeymoons: VIRGIN ISLANDS, ST LUCIA, ANTIGUA, JAMAICA, NEVIS, BARBADOS

Obviously you know best what exactly you want on a honeymoon, but these islands have hotels, such as Sandals, which specialise in honeymooners. Could be a reason not to go there.

Best whole-island resorts: MUSTIQUE; JUMBY BAY, ANTIGUA; PETIT ST VINCENT, GRENADINES; PETER ISLAND, GRENADINES; NECKER, BRITISH VIRGIN ISLANDS; PARROT CAY; TURKS AND CAICOS

Meaning islands which are wholly given over to being a tourist resort, usually a very small island with one hotel and some villas, as on Jumby Bay. Mustique is a bit bigger than the others, and has its own little village, but is still essentially a private island. Necker, Richard Branson's seventy-four-acre island, is private, in that you just can't land there, but is available to rent.

Best beaches: WEST COAST, BARBADOS; GRAND ANSE, GRENADA; VARADERO, CUBA; SEVEN MILE BEACH, GRAND CAYMAN; NEGRIL, JAMAICA

These are all Big Beaches, miles long, so good for walking along and exploring, with all sorts of facilities. As a generalisation, the flatter islands, like the Bahamas, Anguilla, Caymans, have lots of big beaches but lack vegetation.

As for small beaches, hidden away and undeveloped, two of

my favourites are Englishman's Bay, Tobago, and Colombier in St Barts though it's recently lost a lot of its sand.

Best hotels
Barbados has a clutch of the best, poshest, most luxurious, notably Sandy Lane (expected to re-open in 2000, they hope), Cobblers Cove, Coral Reef, Sandpiper, Glitter Bay, Royal Pavilion.

Equally posh and luxurious are: Jumby Bay, Antigua; La Samanna, St Martin; Cotton House, Mustique; Petit St Vincent; Biras Creek, British Virgin Islands; The K Club, Barbuda; Cap Juluca, Anguilla; Round Hill, Jamaica; Parrot Cay, Turks and Caicos.

Best time to go
For Brits and Europeans, our winter is best, in order to get away from our winter, but it means the prices are then the highest, especially over Christmas and the New Year. For popular places at this time you have to book a year ahead.

November and December are quite cheap, up to Christmas, and mean you can still get a winter break and top up your tan. April to November is cheapest of all.

Hurricanes are possible from June to November, but these days there are plenty of early warnings. Temperature all round the year is around 80 degrees. It gets dark at six o'clock in the winter (our winter) and six-thirty in the summer.

Best travel companies
Who specialise in the Caribbean, know what they are talking about, have staff you can talk to who have been to the places you are twittering on about. I mostly always use Elegant Resorts who have never let me down: The Old Palace, Chester CH1 1RB; tel for Caribbean dept and brochures: 0870 33 33 390.

Guide to the Islands

Listed alphabetically, except in the case of the Dutch West Indies which have been listed as a group.

Where a country consists of several islands, the smaller islands come after the main island, though sometimes an important 'smaller' island, which is a holiday destination in itself, such as Nevis, is listed on its own, alphabetically.

#: indicates that there is a whole chapter on this island in the book itself.

Star Ratings: purely an indication of my personal preference – nothing to do with size or importance.

★★★ Islands I can't wait to go back to. Because they are just so lovely, people so nice, beaches so yummy, hotels excellent, oh just everything, really.

★★ Places that I enjoyed, glad to have visited, which had some good features to recommend, to which I might go back.

★ Interesting – but I don't plan to return.

★ ANGUILLA

Population: 10,000

Name: comes from *anguila*, Spanish for eel, because of its shape, supposedly first given to it by Columbus.

Geography: sixteen miles long by three miles across; very flat – biggest bump is only 213 feet high; dry, scrubby, pretty boring scenery, but lots of nice sandy beaches. Shoal Beach most popular.

History: British, don't you know, since 1650, one of our last remaining bits of red on the world map (along with the Cayman Islands, British Virgin Islands, Turks and Caicos, and Montserrat). In 1999 it became one of Britain's Overseas Territories, which means they are British citizens, able to move to the UK if they want to. Alas, native Brits don't have the same reciprocal rights.

Capital: The Valley is the administrative centre, but has a population of only 800, if you can find them.

Language: English, of course.

Currency: East Caribbean dollar.

Hotels: Cap Juluca, very attractive Moorish design, on excellent beach, expensive – recently voted no. 1 Caribbean hotel by readers of Condé Nast's *Traveller*; Malliouhana also quite classy.

Best Things: the white sandy beaches, some forty of them; friendly, relaxed locals.

Poor Things: interior is dry and featureless.

Fascinating Facts: more Anguillans live elsewhere in the Caribbean than live on Anguilla. National bird is the turtle dove.

★★ ANTIGUA

Population: 65,000

Name: Columbus called it Santa Maria de la Antigua after a statue of the Virgin Mary in Seville Cathedral.

Geography: sixteen miles by fifteen, sort of amoeba shape, squashed at edges, hence lots of bays. Supposedly 365 beaches, one for every day of the year, as every tourist is told, on the hour.

History: British from 1632, important military and naval base. Lots of battles and blood to keep French and Spanish at bay. Independent since 1981.

Capital: St John's, population 30,000, run-down in parts, not a lot worth seeing.

Language: English.

Currency: EC dollars.

Hotels: Jumby Bay, whole-island resort off north coast, on map sometimes known as Long Island; Curtain Bluff.

Best Things: English Harbour with restored Nelson's Dockyard, some very good historic buildings, well preserved, despite a lot of tourist tat; Shirley Heights – not a woman but a hill over-looking English Harbour (name comes from General Shirley, governor of Leeward Islands in 1781). Good for yachties; lots of fine beaches, tourist facilities, shops.

Poor Things: dodgy politics, financial haven for some funny money, but safe enough for tourists.

Fascinating Facts: Nelson served for three years in Antigua as a young captain; Viv Richards's cricket bat, with which he scored fastest century, on show in Museum of Antigua in St John's.

Barbuda: Part of Antigua. Flat, scrubby island, thirty miles to the north, some eight miles across. Population 1,500, most of whom live in Codrington, named after Christopher Codrington. He rented the whole island as a private estate in the seventeenth century, paying rent to the Crown of 'one fat sheep, if demanded'. Featureless, rather dreary, backward island, little to recommend it, except the K Club, luxury hotel, Italian-designed, with excellent beach, visited by Princess of Wales.

ARUBA: see Dutch West Indies

★ BAHAMAS

Population: 300,000

Name: from Spanish *baja-mar* meaning shallow sea.

Geography: an archipelago of some 700 islands, all very flat – never getting above 200 feet high – stretching over an area of 600 miles from near the coast of Florida to Haiti. Only fifteen have been developed. The best known, and most populous, is one of the middling-sized islands, New Providence Island on which is sited the main town, Nassau.

New Providence has 65 per cent of the population. Grand Bahama, with its chief town Freeport, has 16 per cent, and still growing. Other islands of interest are Abaco, Eleuthera, San Salvador.

History: site of Columbus's first landfall in the New World on 12 October 1492, on the island of Guanahani, as it was known by the Arawaks, renamed by Columbus as San Salvador. He soon moved on, as no gold in sight, or anything of interest. The islands were virtually uninhabited for the next 150 years, till some seventy ex-Brit Puritans arrived from Bermuda, plus twenty-eight slaves, wanting religious freedom, and settled on Eleuthera (named after the Greek for freedom). Next two centuries dominated by pirates such as Blackbeard, and slave traders, dodging in and out the islands. Can be similarly dodgy today, only the trade is more likely to be drug running. Independent country inside the Commonwealth since 1973.

Proximity to Florida, just fifty miles away, has meant economy, culture and life generally are dominated by the USA. Still nothing much of interest in the Bahamas in the way of natural resources or landscape – apart from fab beaches. Economy is based on financial services, casinos, tourism, especially cruise liners.

Capital: Nassau, population 120,000, on New Providence Island, connected by bridge to Paradise Island. US-style holiday tourists, streets crowded with gaping cruise-ship passengers. Still a few attractive, pink-washed old colonial buildings. Newest attraction is Sol Kerzner's Atlantis Resort development.

Language: English – of the American English variety.

Currency: Bahamian dollar, on par with US dollar.

Hotels: lots of glitzy hotels on Paradise Island, such as the monster Atlantis Resort or the more sedate Ocean Club. Harbour Island, off Eleuthera, is also posh, but quiet.

Best Things: for night life, action and casinos, Nassau is waiting for you. Hurry, hurry. To get away from all that excitement, head for the Family Islands, such as Abaco; very good for diving.

Poor Things: boring interior landscape, mostly scrub; very expensive; underworld of drugs and crime, though tourists generally safe.

Fascinating Facts: despite all the Americanisation, the police still look like stage British police. Note the cute white helmets. And cars still drive on the left – even though many have left-hand drives. Bahamas gets 3 million tourists a year – ten times the number of its inhabitants.

★★★ BARBADOS #

Population: 260,000

Name: from *Os Barbados*, bearded fig trees found on the beach by early Portuguese explorers. They didn't stay, but left some pigs.

Geography: twenty-one miles long by fourteen wide, wild beaches on Atlantic side, calm on the Caribbean, middle is rural, with sugar cane fields, rolling countryside, few rivers, no real hills or rainforest.

History: first British settlers arrived in 1627, and stayed on, thanks to all that wild pig to eat. Remained British, with no nasty Spanish, French or Dutch invasions. Independent since 1966, but still seen as 'Little England' by rest of Caribbean because of Brit-style churches, place names, traditions, parliamentary system, cricket-playing. There's even a Trafalgar Square.

Capital: Bridgetown, busy, sprawling, with not a lot to see, despite all that history. Careenage and Garrison most interesting areas.

Language: English, of course.

Currency: Barbados dollars.

Hotels: some of the best, most luxurious hotels in the Caribbean, mostly on the west coast. Sandy Lane is the poshest, most expensive, stiffest, followed by Coral Reef, Royal Pavilion, Glitter Bay, Treasure Beach, Royal Westmoreland. Smaller, more relaxed but equally luxurious are Cobblers Cove and Sandpiper.

Best Things: that west coast, some ten miles of white sand and pretty bays; east coast is dramatic, especially Bathsheba Bay; lots of interesting old plantation houses and gardens out in the country; good bus service, roads; phones and public services all work; locals friendly, all pretty safe, but expensive.

Poor Things: Caribbean experts and know-alls now consider it too overdeveloped, too British, with too many flash newcomers.

Fascinating Facts: higher literacy rate, 97.4 per cent, than the UK.

BARBUDA: see Antigua

BONAIRE: see Dutch West Indies

★★ BRITISH VIRGIN ISLANDS

Population: 19,000

Name: the myriad of islands reminded Columbus of the legend of the 11,000 virgins, massacred on a medieval pilgrimage.

Geography: sixty islands, some very small, hardly more than lumps of rock or sandy islets (known as cays), only sixteen of which are inhabited. Two main ones are Tortola, about ten miles long, which has 80 per cent of the population, and Virgin Gorda.

History: although discovered by Spaniards, British since 1666 – one of the five British Overseas Territories in the Caribbean.

Capital: Road Town on Tortola – not very attractive. On Virgin Gorda, Spanish Town is the main centre, but it's not Spanish and hardly a town, being little more than one street, a row of shops and a marina.

Language: English, natch.

Currency: not English but US dollars.

Hotels: Biras Creek and Little Dix Bay, both on Virgin Gorda; Peter Island.

Best Things: loved by yachties, who can sail easily in and around the islands, or pose and booze in the yacht harbours. Some great beaches. Some nice, quiet little islands. On Virgin Gorda, best thing is the Baths – enormous, smooth rocks with caves and pools.

Poor Things: islands mainly flat, featureless, tourist-dominated. If you don't like beaches or the sea, norralot on offer.

Fascinating Facts: Virgin boss Richard Branson owns his own Virgin island – Necker Island, available to rent, at a price.

CARRIACOU: see Grenada

CAYMAN ISLANDS

Population: 37,000

Name: from Carib word *caymanas* meaning crocodile.

Geography: three fairly flat islands – Grand Cayman, Cayman Brac and Little Cayman. Grand Cayman is the largest, twenty-two miles long by four wide, half of which is mangrove swamp. Has 90 per cent of the population. The other two are relatively undeveloped, especially Little Cayman which only has 100 people.

History: spotted by Columbus, who moved on, after he and his sailors had stuffed themselves on the turtles. Sir Francis Drake arrived 100 years later, also looking for turtles. Been British since 1670. Run for a time as a dependency of Jamaica. When Jamaica became independent, the Caymans stayed Brit and since 1999 have been an Overseas Territory.

Now a major offshore financial centre. Has 592 licensed banks, many of them little more than a plaque on the wall.

Capital: Georgetown on Grand Cayman, population 15,000. Prosperous little business town with lots of modern blocks. Well, those banks do need walls.

Language: English.

Currency: yes, lots of it. Officially Cayman Islands dollar, but US ones accepted everywhere.

Hotels: mostly of the chain variety, i.e. Hyatt, Marriott.

Best Things: for those who live there, the economic prosperity, created by all that offshore banking; for tourists, good diving, hassle-free, little crime, fine beaches. Best is Seven Mile Beach, outside Georgetown.

Poor Things: very Americanised, boring landscape.

Fascinating Facts: crocodiles long gone, but still turtles to be seen, mostly in the Cayman Turtle Farm, which has 12,000 green turtles, bred for local consumption, as meat or in soup, the only commercial turtle farm in the world.

★★★ CUBA

Population: 11 million

Name: from Arawak word *cubanacan* meaning central. Cubans pronounce Cuba as 'Koo-ba'.

Geography: largest Caribbean island, almost 1,000 miles long by 150 wide; three chunks of mountainous areas running down the spine – highest is Pico Turquino, 6,000 feet high. Sandy beaches mainly on the north coast. Lots of gentle, hilly landscape with rich soil, ideal for sugar cane.

History: Columbus didn't realise it was an island. Thought it might be Japan or China. But he did notice the natives were smoking tobacco and also had canoes – both Arawak words, now part of every language. Spaniards later came back, African slaves imported, sugar cane grown, plus tobacco. Usual colonial story.

Movement for independence at the end of nineteenth century led to civil war which brought in the Americans, wanting to protect their investments. They occupied Cuba for four years.

Republic of Cuba established in 1902. Lots of nasty dictators, corruption, military coups till Fidel Castro took over in 1959, turning it into a communist state. Americans not best pleased. Still in a huff and not speaking.

But Cuba is now open for tourism, panting for it, throwing up new hotels at a frantic pace, mainly at Varadero, a beach resort some 100 miles from Havana.

Capital: Havana, population 2.2 million, biggest city in Caribbean.

Language: Spanish.

Currency: Cuban pesos, but US dollars not just accepted, gobbled up everywhere. So don't change into pesos.

Hotels: in Havana, Santa Isabel and Nacional Hotel are best. Inglaterra and Ambos Mundos a bit cheaper, with great atmosphere. Habana Libre, formerly Hilton, huge but functional. In Varadero, Melia Varadero.

Best Things: Havana, definitely, which has amazing buildings, even if many are decaying; excellent for spotting monster 1950s US motors, many held together with string; friendly people, ungrasping, unthreatening; the music; quiet roads with few cars.

Poor Things: the food; public transport; the infrastructure.

Fascinating Facts: Ernest Hemingway lived in Cuba from 1939 to 1960, and is still as famous there as Castro; Bacardi rum came from Cuba but the firm left when communists took over – replaced today by state-run Havana Club. Cubans have excellent national health and education systems: life expectancy for men is seventy-four and women seventy-eight, higher even than Barbados.

CURAÇAO: see Dutch West Indies

★★ DOMINICA

Population: 74,000

Name: pronounced Dom-in-eeca, and not to be confused with the Dominican Republic. First spotted by Columbus on a Sunday, hence the name.

Geography: twenty-nine by sixteen miles, but so hilly, roads so poor, takes so long to get anywhere, that it feels about four times bigger. The interior is mostly rainforest, now a national park, rising to a height of 4,747 feet, with lakes and rivers. Possibly the most 'natural' of the Caribbean islands. Because of the terrain, there were no big plantations and still hardly developed. Poor beaches, but good snorkelling and diving.

History: a stronghold of the Caribs. Today about 2,000 Dominicans are said to be descended from Caribs (elsewhere they were wiped out or died of European diseases). Spaniards moved quickly on, leaving French to settle the island, then fight over it with the Brits. French influence strong, as Dominica is sandwiched between two French islands, Guadeloupe and Martinique. Britain gained control in mid eighteenth century, then mainly neglected it. Independent republic within the Commonwealth since 1978.

Capital: Roseau, pronounced Rose-oh, fairly tatty, but being cleaned up.

Language: English, though many towns and places still have French names. Creole French is still spoken.

Currency: EC dollars.

Hotels: very few, and none in the luxury class. Fort Young Hotel in Roseau is about the best. Of the smaller places, Petit Coulibri Guest Cottages, 1,000 feet high, right amongst the rainforest, is one of the best in all the Caribbean.

Best Things: all that nature, a paradise for lovers of fauna and flora; Trafalgar waterfalls, very popular tourist attraction; Boiling Lake, equally attractive, but harder to get to as it means a six-mile trek.

Poor Things: lack of beaches, abundance of clouds, no luxury hotels, poor transport, but, come on, you can't have everything, especially if you want your nature natural.

Fascinating Facts: home of Rose's lime juice, first established to provide a lime drink for thirsty British sailors. Had a woman Prime Minister, the redoubtable Dame Eugenia Charles, from 1980 to 1995 – longer than the UK had one. Jean Rhys, author of *Wide Sargasso Sea*, came from Dominica.

★ DOMINICAN REPUBLIC

Population: 7.7 million

Name: from its capital, Santo Domingo, which got its name from Columbus's father, Domingo.

Geography: shares with Haiti the island of Hispaniola, the second-largest island (after Cuba) in the Caribbean. The Dominican Republic has about two-thirds of it, stretching some 200 miles long by 100 across, about the same size as Scotland. Contains the highest mountain in the Caribbean, Pico Duarte, 10,417 feet high. Lots of fertile plains, but also desert-like arid regions.

History: original HQ of the Spanish Empire in the Americas. They never found the gold they hoped for, but by eighteenth century sugar cane had made it the richest colony in the Indies. Civil wars and emancipation of the slaves led to Dominican Republic getting its independence in 1844. Then a sequence of nasty dictators and/or quasi-American rule. Politically still volatile at election time. A Latino, mixed-raced country rather than a black Caribbean island. Racial harmony – except they don't like Haitians. Mass-market tourist boom in last ten years, mainly on the northern coast around Puerta Plata.

Capital: Santo Domingo, oldest city in the New World. Oldest surviving buildings date back to 1503, easily beating anything in the USA. So there.

Language: Spanish. Very little English spoken, outside the tourist centres.

Currency: Dominican peso.

Hotels: lots of mass-market, chain-type, big international hotels, which might be anywhere.

Best Things: Santo Domingo, especially the old city around the Calle de Las Damas and the cathedral. Lots of excellent beaches.

Poor Things: constant hustling in tourist areas, dodgy traders, power cuts, prostitutes, officious police, overdevelopment on some beaches.

Fascinating Facts: raided by well-known pirate and notorious baddie Sir Francis Drake in 1586 – or well-loved hero and goodie, if you happen to be a Brit. The Dominican Republic went bust in 1907, then got occupied by the USA who stayed for eight years.

DUTCH WEST INDIES

Geography: consists of two lots of three islands, commonly known by their initials as the three Ss and the ABC islands.

The three Ss are Sint Maarten, Sint Eustatius and Saba, sometimes known as the Dutch Windward Islands, situated between Antigua and the Virgin Islands. Then about 500 miles away, near the coast of South America, are the ABC islands: Aruba, Bonaire and Curaçao.

History: the Dutch didn't get into the Caribbean till the seventeenth century, then they did what the other European colonial powers did – bit of this and that, trading, pirating, fighting each other. The Dutch wanted strategic ports to help their Dutch West Indian Company, rather than amassing land and colonial glory. St Eustatius changed hands twenty-two times till 1816, when it and the other five islands became Dutch.

Apart from Aruba, they are all still part of the Dutch Commonwealth, but politically they are run from Curaçao, rather than Holland. For many centuries, all six were referred to as Curaçao. Today they hardly appear Dutch, apart from road signs and the odd gabled building in Curaçao.

Capital: Curaçao, seat of the Dutch West Indian government (except for Aruba) though each island also has its own governor.

Language: officially Dutch, but no one speaks it as a mother tongue. They either speak Papiamento – a sort of Dutch–Spanish creole – or English.

Currency: again officially Dutch Antilles guilders, but US dollars more acceptable. Aruba has its own Aruba florins.

★ Sint Maarten #: only half an island – the other half is French, St Martin. Smallest island in the world to be shared by two nations. Takes its name from the fact that Columbus discovered it on St Martin's Day. Total population is 80,000, roughly shared between Dutch and French halves. Capital of the Dutch side is Philipsburg, busy with cruise liners, but rather run-down (not as chic as Marigot, capital of the French side). Very developed, lots of hotels, villas and apartments, feels American rather than Dutch. (See also St Martin.)

★ Sint Eustatius: generally known as Statia. Very small, just five miles by two, population 2,000, yet in the eighteenth century it was crowded and rich, known as the Golden Rock. The Dutch kept all their trading warehouses here, filled with sugar, tobacco, rum; the island changed hands many times as greedy rivals tried to grab it. Very quiet, poor beaches with black sand, but good for escapists. Capital and only settlement is Oranjestad.

★ Saba: pronounced sabre, as in the sword. Even smaller, just two miles across. Population 1,500. One big volcanic rock, rising to 2,900 feet, Mount Scenery. Attractive slopes, with tropical rain-forest on top. No beaches or even any flat bits, very little to do apart from walking and climbing. Most visitors are day-trippers from St Martin. English spoken everywhere as the island is 60 per cent European stock, descendants of Scottish fishermen and English missionaries, who repelled boarders by chucking rocks at them. Very clean and tidy. Almost every roof is painted red. Capital is The Bottom. Guess why. No, not because it's at the bottom of the mountain – because it's at the bottom of a hollow, some 850 feet up.

Curaçao: Long and thin, thirty-eight miles by nine, the largest and most populated of the Dutch West Indian islands. Population 140,000.

Traditionally the heart of the Dutch West Indies; named after the Portuguese word for heart, *coracao*. Its power built up by Peter Stuyvesant, now known for a packet of cigs, but in 1638 he was governor of Curaçao then director-general of the Dutch West Indies. Centre of the slave trade in the eighteenth century: about two-thirds of the slaves taken to the Americas went through Curaçao. In the early twentieth century became industrialised when oil found in Venezuela and Royal Dutch Shell built oil refineries on Curaçao. Economy became depressed when oil prices fell. Now trying to attract tourists. Capital is Willemstad.

★ Aruba: also long and fairly thin, twenty miles by six wide, population 90,000. Like Curaçao, it prospered with the arrival of the oil industry. Now heavily into tourism, with some good beaches, lots of rather flashy, mass-market hotels going up. In 1986 Aruba went independent, mainly because they didn't like being bossed around by Curaçao, but remains within the Dutch kingdom.

★ Bonaire: during Curaçao's colonial glory, Bonaire and Aruba were kept as farms, feeding the colonial classes. Also long and thin, twenty-four miles by five, population 12,000. Quiet and undeveloped, compared with Curaçao and Aruba. Some reasonable beaches. Good for bird-watching, diving. Capital Kralendijk.

★★ GRENADA

Population: 100,000 (includes Carriacou and Petit Martinique)

Name: Spaniards named it after Granada in Spain. (The Grenadines refer to a string of smaller islands, very popular with yachties, shared between Grenada and St Vincent.)

Geography: pear shape, like quite a few West Indian islands; twenty-one miles long by twelve across; southern bit fairly flat, then rises to the north and interior with lush tropical vegetation; highest bit 2,757 feet. Known as the Spice Island and still produces a third of the world's nutmeg, plus cloves, cinnamon.

History: was mainly French till 1783, then British – thus the mixture of French and British place names. Independent since 1974. Internal power struggles in 1979 led to communist government, backed by Cuba, which in turn brought in the Americans in 1983. Democracy restored.

Capital: St George's – probably the most beautiful of any Caribbean capital, great curved open harbour, with no nasty warehouses and dirty docks cluttering it up, quite hilly at one end, with green hills behind.

Language: English.

Currency: EC dollar.

Hotels: Calabash and Spice Island.

Best Things: St George's; friendly laid-back people; island still not overdeveloped; tropical rainforest area, now a national park; Grand Anse beach, two miles long.

Poor Things: roads still ropey.

Fascinating Facts: nutmeg was introduced in 1843. Someone, as a surprise at a plantation party, sprinkled a bit on a rum punch, and bingo, been used ever since. Look out for about the only remains of US invasion, a burned-out plane on an old airport near Pearls on the east coast.

Associated Islands

★ Carriacou: twenty miles north-east of Grenada, green hilly island, but not as mountainous or as lush as Grenada; eight miles long by four across; known for its boat-builders; population 5,000; capital Hillsborough; beginning to be developed for tourism; some good beaches.

Petit Martinique: small offshore island of Carriacou, population 800.

★★ GUADELOUPE

Guadeloupe, as a French department, is responsible for St Martin and St Barts, some 140 miles away, but they are very different islands and are listed separately.

Population: 410,000

Name: Columbus named it after Our Lady of Gaudelupe de Extremadura, thanking her for protection during a storm.

Geography: shaped like the wings of a butterfly, about 100 miles across. Technically two islands, separated by a very narrow channel, crossed by a bridge. The right-hand wing, Grande Terre, is flat, with sugar plantations, some good beaches on its south coast, busy, developed. The left-hand wing, Basse Terre, is mountainous, dominated by volcanic Soufrière, 4,812 feet high, less developed, fewer beaches, but prettier island.

History: after Columbus, Spaniards tried to settle, but the Caribs fought them off. First permanent European settlers were the French in 1635. Big bloody battles in eighteenth century with Brits who occupied it for four years, then gave it up in 1763, in exchange for all French rights in Canada. When slavery abolished in 1848, Indian workers were brought in – hence Guadeloupe today has a very mixed population – but the culture is predominantly French. So things work, roads, health and social services all good, but cost of living expensive. Agriculture still very important, mainly bananas and sugar, but tourism expanding.

Officially a department of France since 1946, same status as departments in metropolitan France.

Capital: Basse Terre, population 53,000, sleepy, colonial, administrative capital; biggest town is Pointe-à-Pitre on Grande Terre, population 140,000, very noisy, busy.

Language: French, plus Creole. Not much English spoken.

Currency: French franc.

Hotels: mostly on south coast of Grande Terre. La Cocoteraie is swishest.

Best Things: lots of good restaurants, colourful markets, well-ordered island, interesting boat trips to offshore islands.

Poor Things: roads brilliant – but hellish busy. Beaches also busy. No direct flights from the UK, only from France.

Fascinating Facts: cock-fighting and bullock cart-racing still popular; underwater park developed by Jacques Cousteau; *les vendeuses de la plage* – ladies who strip off on the better-class beaches, purely to model and sell beachwear, of course.

Offshore Islands (popular with day trippers from Guadeloupe)

Marie Galante: a smaller, rounder version of Grand Terre, about fifteen miles across, flat, good beaches, population 13,000.

Les Saintes: very pretty little islands, 3,000 population.

Désirade: isolated, more barren, undeveloped, population 1,600.

★ HAITI

Population: 6.6 million

Name: from the Arawak Indian name for the whole island, Quis-queya, meaning high land.

Geography: the western third of the island of Hispaniola. Along with the Dominican Republic it is the Caribbean's most mountainous country, rugged ranges in the interior rising up to 8,000 feet. But there are fertile plains – once rich, now poor in soil, through neglect and deforestation. Wood is the only fuel for cooking for most people, so in many parts they have stripped the land bare.

History: Columbus visited Haiti's north coast on his first voyage, and it ended in disaster when the *Santa Maria* went aground. Out of the wreckage a fort was established – the first known European settlement in the New World. The Spaniards later settled in the south of the island, making Santo Domingo (in the Dominican Republic) their new HQ. Haiti became a French colony in the seventeenth century, creating some of the richest sugar plantations in the Caribbean.

In 1804, inspired by the French Revolution, the slaves revolted and Haiti became an independent republic. Most of the twentieth century saw a sequence of bloody coups and violent dictators, not helped by US commercial intervention, culminating in the reign of the dreaded Papa Doc Duvalier who became President in 1957. Now in theory democratic, but still unstable and violent.

Tourism, usually the best hope for the economy of any Caribbean country, all but ceased under the Duvalier regime and hotels closed. Haiti is the poorest country in the Western hemisphere. Very overpopulated, in relation to its lack of natural resources, with low productivity. Most of the population are rural. Voodoo religions still thrive. Life expectation is forty-seven for men, fifty-one for women. Adult literacy is 45 per cent. Haiti's history is the most tragic in the Caribbean.

Capital: Port-au-Prince, population 1.4 million, mostly one big slum, vibrant, noisy, pretty scary.

Language: French, officially, but 85 per cent of the population speak only Haitian Creole.

Currency: Haitian gourde, divided into centimes. But best to stick to US dollars or French francs.

Hotels: the Oloffson in down-town Port-au-Prince, the setting for Graham Greene's *The Comedians*. Montana, in suburb of Pétionville, for more peace and quiet and views. Mont-Joli in Cap-Haïtien.

Best Things: despite all the tragedies and poverty, the Haitian soul shines through in its art and music. Haiti native art is the best and cheapest in the Caribbean. Even the most run-down 'tap tap' bus is beautifully hand-painted: some fascinating historic forts and palaces, mostly ruined and hard to get to. Cap-Haïtien, in the north, once the colonial capital and tourist resort, has a good atmosphere and is relatively safe, by Haitian standards.

Poor Things: poverty, violence during times of political unrest. Tourists not generally targeted, but Port-au-Prince was the only place in the West Indies where I was truly, truly scared. Communications lousy, transport poor, water dodgy.

Fascinating Facts: Haiti is the oldest black republic in the world, founded 1804.

★★ JAMAICA

Population: 3 million

Name: from Arawak 'Xaymaca' meaning land of wood and water.

Geography: third-largest Caribbean island, stretching some 150 miles long by fifty wide. Mountains to the east, rising to 7,400 feet. Best beaches are on north coast. Rivers, falls, rainforest, flora and fauna – Jamaica has the full tropical range.

History: Columbus, as ever, woz there, but Spanish settlements soon died out and Brits easily took over in 1655. Remained British from then on. Sugar plantations established, keeping Britain sweet and the plantocracy rich. Independence in 1962, but still part of the Commonwealth. Can be, let's say, lively at election times, i.e. a few deaths. Strong in tourism, now agriculture less lucrative. Some important industries, such as bauxite, aluminium.

Capital: Kingston, population 750,000. Great harbour, some fine buildings, but street life dodgy in some areas.

Language: English, man.

Currency: Jamaican dollar.

Hotels: most of the big international chains have a hotel in Kingston; elsewhere, posh places are Half Moon Club or Round Hill at Montego Bay, Jamaica Inn at Ocho Rios, Strawberry Hill in Blue Mountains.

Best Things: strong cultural life, music and literature; home of dreadlocked Rastafarians; birthplace of reggae and Bob Marley, the Caribbean's greatest musician; Negril, seven miles of sand; vitality and basic friendliness of most Jamaicans; their football team, getting to the 1998 World Cup.

Poor Things: reputation for crime is now being overstated, but best beware at election time or in rougher parts of Kingston. It was the only place in the West Indies I got mugged, but all my own fault as I'd got lost. Montego Bay not the glamour destination it used to be. Hustlers on most public beaches.

Fascinating Facts: Noël Coward and Ian Fleming had homes in Jamaica, though not together. Coward's Firefly now open to the public.

★ MARTINIQUE

Population: 400,000

Name: said to have been named by Columbus after St Martin, though the Caribs had called it something similar, Madinina, meaning island of flowers. Take your pick.

Geography: fifty miles long by twenty-five wide. (Guadeloupe is about a third bigger.) Mountainous in the north, up to 5,000 feet, with tropical rainforest. Cliffs and black sands on the north and east (Atlantic) coasts. Whiter beaches on the south, Caribbean coast. Bananas and pineapples on hill slopes, sugar cane in the plains. Main tourist areas are Pointe du Bout, across bay from Fort-de-France, and Ste Anne on southern peninsula.

History: similar to Guadeloupe. French settled it in 1635, Brits pinched it, then swapped it, along with Guadeloupe, for Canada. A department of France since 1946 and a region since 1974. Still strongly agricultural, with some industry, such as oil-refining, but tourism becoming mainstay of the economy. Most tourists, 72 per cent, are from France, except those on cruise liners who are mostly from the USA.

As Barbados became the richest Brit island, Martinique was the flagship for French culture in the Caribbean. Still considers itself more chic, literary, sophisticated, developed and just, well, more French than Guadeloupe.

Capital: Fort-de-France, population 100,000, situated on a large bay, popular with cruise liners. Crowded, bustling, very French.

Language: French, plus French Creole. Not much English.

Currency: French franc.

Hotels: wide range, but nothing really stunning, mostly big French hotel chains. Recommendations welcomed.

Best Things: lots of good restaurants, lively markets; tropical rainforest round Mount Pelée; excellent hospitals, said to be the best in the Caribbean.

Poor Things: tourist areas very busy, crowded, expensive.

Fascinating Facts: the biguine, a dance, as in 'begin the biguine', originated in Martinique; Mount Pelée is volcanic, but hasn't erupted since 1902 when 30,000 died and whole town ruined; Empress Josephine, wife of Napoleon, was born in Martinique in 1763.

★ MONTSERRAT

Population: 12,000 pre-1997 volcano, then down to 4,500

Name: yet another of Columbus's inspirations – named after an abbey in Spain where Ignatius Loyola saw a vision.

Geography: pear-shaped, about eleven miles long by seven wide, poor beaches, mostly black. Soufrière mountain, in the south, not all that high, just 3,000 feet, but boy, has it caused trouble. A steaming volcano, which erupted in 1997, killed twenty who had decided to stay in the exclusion zone. It led to evacuation of most of the island. Not exactly a tourist destination at present, but we all hope it will be again.

History: first settled by Brits from St Kitts in seventeenth century, then the Irish, who established only Irish-Catholic colony in the Caribbean; over 1,000 Irish families arrived. Later attacked by French, with some help from resident Irish. British since Treaty of Versailles in 1783. British Overseas Territory since 1999.

Capital: Plymouth – totally evacuated in 1997.

Language: English.

Currency: EC dollars.

Hotels: Even pre-volcano, not a lot, except for Vue Pointe Hotel, simple, friendly, family-run.

Best Things: the charm and friendliness of the people.

Poor Things: has to be the volcano.

Fascinating Facts: despite lack of beaches and tourist hotels, Montserrat had 400 luxury private villas pre-volcano, owned by wealthy Brits and North Americans, wanting to avoid tourists. Sir George Martin, of Beatles fame, had his AIR studio on Montserrat, where Paul McCartney, Elton John, Sting, etc. recorded. Ruined by Hurricane Hugo in 1989.

The Irish connection continues: Montserrat celebrates St Patrick's Day, the national emblem shows a shamrock, the Irish harp appears on their stamps. While in Montserrat in 1996 I spent one evening reading the telephone book, not having much else to do, and found it packed with Ryans, Farrells, Dalys.

MUSTIQUE: see St Vincent

★★★ NEVIS

Population: 9,000. Still politically part of St Kitts – just two miles away – but likes to consider itself separate. Could be one day.

Name: pronounced Nee-vis, not as in Ben Nevis. Spaniards thought the mist and clouds hovering over the island looked like snow, so they called it Nuestra Señora de las Nieves – Our Lady of the Snows.

Geography: small, round island, eight miles by six, with its mountain, Nevis Peak, neatly in the middle, 3,232 feet high.

History: in 1623, St Kitts and Nevis were the first West Indian islands to be settled by the British. Both grew very wealthy on sugar cane, especially Nevis which had a population of 45,000 in the eighteenth century with some grand estate houses and elegant ladies. St Kitts and Nevis became an independent country in 1983, still within the Commonwealth. Nevis has its own Prime Minister and active movement for total independence.

Capital: Charlestown; some nice historic buildings, quiet and sleepy.

Language: English.

Currency: EC dollar.

Hotels: Four Seasons, big and American; Montpelier Plantation and Nisbet Plantation, smaller and awfully English.

Best Things: some good white beaches, if a bit windy; interesting inns and plantation houses; quiet and peaceful, some excellent walking.

Poor Things: few decent restaurants, apart from hotels. That wind, if you're unlucky.

Fascinating Facts: Nelson married wealthy local widow Fanny Nisbet in Nevis. Alexander Hamilton, one of the creators of the American constitution, was born in Nevis in 1757 of a Nevisian mother and Scottish father. Got killed in a duel, but his face lives on, appearing on US $10 bills.

★ PUERTO RICO

Population: 3.8 million (another 2 million live in the USA)

Name: Spanish for 'Rich Port'. Still very apt.

Geography: just slightly smaller than Jamaica, about 100 miles across by forty wide, similar shape, but much bigger population. Mountainous in the interior, with coastal plains. Only small part of the rainforest is left, but now a national park.

History: Columbus landed in 1493, and this time the Spaniards stayed on, using the island as a handy base for their Central American conquests, and for fighting off subsequent British, French and Dutch attacks. Looked like they would get their full independence from Spain in 1897, till, bad luck, the Spanish–American war broke out. Spain handed over Puerto Rico to the US. US citizens since 1917, though with own government.

Puerto Ricans look and sound Americanised Latin-Americans, very fond of baseball. Quite industrial, compared with most Carib countries – textiles, chemicals, electricals. Agriculture still important, mainly tobacco and coffee. Tourism·dominated by cruise ships, mainly from the US.

Capital: San Juan, population 1 million. Totally American at first sight, with six-lane highways and skyscrapers, but historic Spanish buildings in old San Juan, founded 1510.

Language: Spanish and English, both official languages, but majority of people speak Spanish as their first language.

Currency: US dollar.

Hotels: lots of US chain hotels in San Juan, mostly with beach frontage – fine sandy beach, but busy.

Best Things: old San Juan, well-preserved buildings and palaces inside the old walled city; good flight connections with USA and elsewhere in Caribbean; the local coffee.

Poor Things: hardly seems Caribbean, might as well be in Miami, till you get out into the countryside.

Fascinating Facts: San Juan has the biggest shopping mall in the Caribbean – Plaza Las Americas. Exciting, huh. The word 'hurricane' comes from the Indian god Juracan said to have lived on the highest peak on Puerto Rico and controlled the weather.

SABA, St EUSTATIUS, SINT MAARTEN: see Dutch West Indies

★★★ ST BARTS

Population: 6,000

Name: after Columbus's brother, Bartholomew. Saint-Barthélemy in French, but generally known as St Barts or St Barth's. Part of the French West Indies, i.e. part of France, controlled from Guadeloupe, but very different from rest of French West Indies.

Geography: small island, just six miles across and three wide, but hilly with some coastal cliffs. Not suitable for plantations, so no black slaves imported. Lots of white sandy beaches and small coves, hidden away.

History: first settled by French in 1645, mainly people from Normandy and Brittany. Ceded to Sweden in 1784, hence the name of its capital, then back to France in 1878. A totally white island. More like the south of France than the Caribbean.

Capital: Gustavia. Handsome harbour with lots of posh yachts and vee chic shops, boasting all the big names from Paris.

Language: French, *naturellement*.

Currency: French franc.

Hotels: Eden Rock, Isle de France, Le Toiny.

Best Things: pretty island – even the little airport is chic – with some very good hotels and restaurants; some good beaches, particularly Colombier which has to be reached on foot.

Poor Things: very expensive; French staff, young and chic, can be a bit superior. No sign of West Indians, or West Indian culture.

Fascinating Facts: still traces of seventeenth-century Breton culture, in peasant bonnets and rural dialects. The Rockefellers, Rothschilds and Fords have all had holiday homes on St Barts – an indication that peasants or bonnets are not all that common today, whatever their tourist people like to maintain.

★ ST KITTS

Population: 33,000 (42,000 including Nevis, which is listed separately)

Name: originally known as St Christopher after the saint, or possibly after Columbus, though he never landed. Shortened to St Kitts from the eighteenth century.

Geography: ten miles long, ending in a straggly bit, four miles across at widest; three lots of volcanic mountains in the interior, rising to 3,792 feet high; small amount of rainforest left; some reasonable beaches, but mainly black sands (Nevis has better beaches).

History: St Kitts was the first island settled by the Brits in 1623 and became important for its sugar plantations. Shared with France for some years, hence the smattering of French place names mixed up with the English. British colony from 1783 onwards. Independent since 1983. St Kitts, Nevis and Anguilla were one state, till Anguilla broke away. Nevis might follow, in the future, as it doesn't like being bossed by St Kitts.

Capital: Basseterre, population 15,000. Damaged by fire and earthquakes over the centuries. Busy and modern, compared with Nevis's sleepy capital Charlestown.

Language: English.

Currency: EC dollars.

Hotels: like Nevis, has some fine plantation house hotels. Nicest is Rawlins Plantation.

Best Things: some historic buildings and old forts. Friendly locals. Good nature and mountain trails in the north.

Poor Things: history of political scandals, usually involving drugs; poor beaches.

Fascinating Facts: St Kitts and Nevis are among the few West Indian islands with monkeys, imported by the French 300 years ago; the main mountain was originally named Mount Misery by the Brits but has now been renamed Mount Liamuiga, from the Carib word for 'fertile land'. Much nicer, don't you think?

★★★ ST LUCIA

Population: 150,000

Name: Pronounced 'Loosha'. Supposedly discovered by Columbus on St Lucy's Day, though he never actually got there.

Geography: one of your pear-shaped islands, twenty-seven miles long by fourteen across at its widest, but seems much bigger. Spectacular old volcanic peaks in the south, the Pitons, 2,619 feet high, used as a symbol of St Lucia, with outstanding tropical scenery. Beaches, capital and main tourist bits are in the flatter, dryer northern third. One of the main banana islands in the British West Indies.

History: Spaniards claimed it, then Brits raided it, French poked their noses in, all the usual blood and gore. By 1814, when St Lucia finally became a British colony, it had changed hands fourteen times. Independent from 1979. Still traces of the French influence, in names and rural patois.

Capital: Castries, 60,000 population, rather dusty, untidy, traffic jams in rush hours.

Language: English.

Currency: EC dollars.

Hotels: Nothing truly stunning. East Winds, Windjammer and Anse Chastanet are the best. Large number of all-inclusive hotels, not liked by some locals as they say tourists don't spend much time or money outside their hotels.

Good Things: the Pitons; some old forts; friendly people.

Poor Things: roads in bad nick, especially in the south.

Fascinating Facts: scenes from *Dr Doolittle* and *Superman Two* were shot in St Lucia; two Nobel prize winners came from St Lucia – Derek Walcott, Literature, 1992, and Sir Arthur Lewis, Economics, 1979 – and both went to the same secondary school in Castries. Beat that, Eton or Manchester Grammar.

★ ST MARTIN # See also Dutch West Indies for Sint Maarten.

Population: 30,000

Name: supposedly named after St Martin by Columbus.

Geography: northern half of little, funny-shaped island, about ten miles across, fairly flat, no rainforests, but some fine beaches.

History: divided equally and happily between Holland and France since 1648. St Martin is part of France, administered from Guadeloupe. Very different from white St Barts, being mainly a black island, and from Guadeloupe, in that it has developed into a booming tourist resort, with lots of hotels and villas, popular with Americans.

Capital: Marigot – charming harbour, nicer, neater, chicer than the capital of the Dutch side.

Language: French officially, but most speak a bit of English.

Currency: French franc, but US dollars accepted everywhere.

Hotels: lots of them, plus villas to rent, but the most stunning is La Samanna, one of the best in the Caribbean.

Best Things: Marigot; La Samanna hotel; the beaches, with lots of St Tropez topless-type beach life.

Poor Things: over-Americanised, too much traffic. Language, laws, currency and public services are entirely different on each side of the island, though doesn't normally affect tourists.

Fascinating Facts: according to legend, the island was divided by a Frenchman and Dutchman in 1648 who set off in different directions to walk round the island. The French got slightly more of the island as the Frenchman walked faster, drinking only wine, compared with the Dutchman, who was on the gin.

★ ST VINCENT AND THE GRENADINES

Population: St Vincent has 100,000. The thirty islands, not all of them inhabited, have another 10,000.

Name: after St Vincent, supposedly.

Geography: the main island is another of the pear shapes, eighteen miles across and eleven wide. Mountains in interior, lushly forested, both north and south, rising to 4,000-foot-high La Soufrière, a volcano which erupted in 1902 and killed 2,000 people. Erupted again in 1979, but no one was killed.

History: Columbus and co. came, saw, but didn't conquer as the Caribs were too fierce and kept out Europeans till the eighteenth century. Then the Brits and French fought over it till it became British in 1783. Independent since 1979. The main export has traditionally been bananas, followed by arrowroot. No mass tourism development, as yet. Big centre for yachties and also flags of convenience.

Capital: Kingstown, population 18,000, busy port, but ugly docks ruin the view.

Language: English.

Currency: EC dollar.

Hotels: little to rave about on St Vincent itself, but Young Island, 200 yards offshore, is attractive if a bit claustrophobic.

Best Things: some good nature trails and waterfalls on St Vincent;

the Botanical Gardens; excellent sailing round the Grenadines; handy for Mustique and Bequia.

Poor Things: most beaches on St Vincent have black sand; Kingstown a fairly boring capital; frequent tales of drug running and money-laundering.

Fascinating Facts: the Botanical Gardens in Kingstown, established 1765, the oldest in the Western hemisphere, display a descendant of the original breadfruit tree bought from Tahiti by Captain Bligh of the *Bounty*.

GRENADINES

★★★ **Bequia#**: pronounced Beck-wee. Biggest of St Vincent's Grenadines, some five miles long by two across, population 5,000. Hilly interior, some good sandy beaches, very pretty main town, Port Elizabeth, situated on a stunning harbour. Lots of good restaurants. Adored by yachties.

★★★ **Mustique#**: three miles by two, private island, owned by the Mustique Company, but open to tourists. Most of the posh villas are to rent, at a price. Several fine beaches. Everything terribly pretty and kempt. Excellent hotel, the Cotton House.

Union Island: three miles by one mile, with two little peaks. Little airport and busy harbour for yachties. Place to change planes or boats, rather than stay long.

★ **Canouan**: two miles long. Now being developed.

★★ **Mayreau**: hard to get to, as no airstrip. Only one little hotel, but loved by those who like to get off the beaten track.

★★★ **Petit St Vincent**: small whole-island resort, 113 acres, run as a hotel. Off the beaten track – but luxurious.

★ **Palm Island**: another whole-island resort.

TRINIDAD AND TOBAGO

★ TRINIDAD

Population: 1.25 million (not counting Tobago)
Name: either geographical, because Columbus spotted three

mountains, or religious, because it was Holy Trinity Day.

Geography: sort of squarish, but hammer-shaped either end. Fairly big, as Caribbean islands go, some sixty by fifty miles. Most southerly of Caribbean islands, just seven miles from Venezuela. Three ranges of hills, but only up to 3,000 feet, none volcanic. Lots of flatlands, especially in centre where sugar cane is grown. Large areas of swampy coast.

History: Spaniards didn't manage many settlements, because of warlike Caribs in parts of the island, then Sir Walter Raleigh didn't help by destroying the Spaniards' main town in 1595. British rule proper began from 1797, though for a while it went back to Spain. Massive sugar plantations, using African slaves.

Slavery abolished in 1834, so massive import of labour from India, plus subsequent immigration from many other parts of the world. Result is that Trinidad is the most cosmopolitan Caribbean country: 40 per cent are of black African descent, 40 per cent Indian, the rest Chinese, white, mixed. Joined politically with Tobago since 1898 as one country. Independent since 1962; a republic since 1976.

Trinidad is one of the most industrial Caribbean islands, mainly based on oil, most of which comes from marine fields. Tourism in Trinidad, unlike Tobago, still only of minor importance.

Capital: Port of Spain, population 350,000, bustling, exciting atmosphere; down-town can be dangerous. Queen's Park Savannah, their huge open park, is very attractive.

Language: English.

Currency: Trinidad and Tobago dollars.

Hotels: not many of the luxury or exclusive tourist variety, though there is a new Hilton in Port of Spain.

Best Things: Carnival, held two days before Ash Wednesday, better and safer than Rio's – hotels need to be booked a year ahead; Trinidadian literature, notably V. S. Naipaul; some interesting rainforests and swamp lands.

Poor Things: lack of decent hotels and beaches.

Fascinating Facts: calypso originated in Trinidad in the eighteenth century, still very big, with an annual competition for the Calypso Monarch held each year before Carnival. Brian Lara, the cricketer, has a pedestrian area in Port of Spain named after him, the Lara Promenade. Don't ask the score if the West Indies are doing badly. Trinidad is the home of one of the three main campuses of the University of the West Indies, the others being Barbados and Jamaica.

★★★ TOBAGO

Population: 50,000

Name: from the same Carib word as tobacco.

Geography: lies twenty-two miles north of Trinidad, and is completely different, small – just twenty-one miles by nine – pretty, with good beaches, non-industrial, a relaxed holiday island compared with its bustling, cosmopolitan and sometimes more violent big brother. (Trinidadians think Tobagonians are all hicks: Tobagonians think Trinidadians are tricksters.)

The southern end, where most hotels are, is the least pretty, flat and dusty, apart from Pigeon Point. North of Scarborough is the rainforest, now a national park, with good beaches up the Caribbean coast.

History: claimed by Dutch in 1628, then twenty-nine different changes of occupation or ownership, including Latvian, till 1802 when Brits finally took over. Joined with Trinidad, not all that willingly, in 1898. Independent in 1962 and a republic since 1976.

Capital: Scarborough, population 10,000. Unusual to be situated on the rougher Atlantic coast, perhaps that's why it's a bit tatty.

Language: English.

Currency: Trinidad and Tobago dollars.

Hotels: more hotel beds in Tobago than in Trinidad, despite being only one-twentieth the size. Poshest is Coco Reef.

Best Things: nice beaches, especially Englishman's Bay; good selection of hotels, guest houses, villas, restaurants; some interesting forts and historic sites; the rainforest; laid-back, pleasant locals.

Poor Things: Scarborough disappointing; main hotel area not very attractive.

Fascinating Facts: no electricity till the 1950s. Dwight Yorke comes from Tobago, so feel free to talk about football, as long as you say he's brilliant.

★ TURKS AND CAICOS

Population: 20,000

Name: Turks comes from Turk's Head cactus, shaped like a fez, which was found on the islands. Caicos is either from the Lucayan Indian words *caya hico*, meaning string of islands, or Spanish *cayos* meaning cays.

Geography: situated near the Bahamas, two groups of forty rather flat, dry, scrub-covered islands, cays and sandbanks, only eight of which are inhabited. Main two of the Turks group are Grand Turk and Salt Cay. Both small islands. The Caicos are bigger islands, but have more scattered population. Most populated and developed island is Providenciales, population 10,000.

History: usual fighting between Spanish, French, Dutch and British for control, not that there was much to control, except the salt trade. British from about 1766; first linked with Bahamas, then for many years with Jamaica. Since 1999 a British Overseas Territory, though US influence is very strong. Salt trade finished, but offshore finance still booming – 14,000 companies in 1997. Tourism important since Club Med opened in 1984, and immediately doubled the number of visitors.

Capital: Cockburn Town on Grand Turk, population 2,000. Not much action on Grand Turk, apart from diving.

Language: English.

Currency: US dollar.

Hotels: Parrot Cay and Pine Cay, two small but luxurious whole-island resorts.

Best Things: lots of bird and animal sanctuaries – and even more financial sanctuaries; good diving; lots of white beaches, plenty of empty space.

Poor Things: not a lot of shade. History of drug-smuggling.

Fascinating Facts: local tourist people like to maintain that Columbus's first landing was on Grand Turk, not San Salvador in the rival Bahamas. Don't believe it.

★ US VIRGIN ISLANDS

Population: 100,000

Name: Columbus named them after the legend of St Ursula and the 11,000 virgins.

Geography: much bigger, more populated, more developed than the British Virgin Islands. There are sixty-eight of them, though not all are inhabited. The main ones are:

St Thomas: thirteen miles by three, population 51,000; forty-four beaches, some very pretty but crowded.

St Croix (pronounced St Croy, as in toy): largest island, twenty miles by six, population 55,000, main town Christansted.

★★ St John: five miles by three, population 3,500; least spoiled, mostly a national park.

History: not settled by Europeans till the seventeenth century, then usual changes of ownership as British, French, Dutch and Danes fought over them – with Denmark winning. Now that was unusual. For two centuries there was a thriving Danish West Indies, till they flogged them to the USA in 1917 for $25 million. The USA wanted them as a naval base. Since 1932, US Virgin Islands citizens have been US citizens. Main activity is tourism, almost all of it from the USA, the majority on cruise liners. Highest standard of living in the Caribbean, and about the highest cost of living.

Capital: Charlotte Amalie, population 12,000, on St Thomas. Magnificent harbour, but busy, congested, with only a few pretty Danish buildings left.

Language: English.

Currency: US dollar.

Hotels: Caneel Bay on St John, Ritz-Carlton on St Thomas.

Best Things: lots of shopping opportunities. Good sailing. St John island, which is now almost all a national park.

Poor Things: too many shopping opportunities. Overdeveloped, over-Americanised, especially St Thomas.

Fascinating Facts: Charlotte Amalie is named after a Danish Queen, but is usually just called St Thomas. In the 1950s Laurence Rockefeller bought half of the island of St John as a holiday home; later handed it over to become a national park.

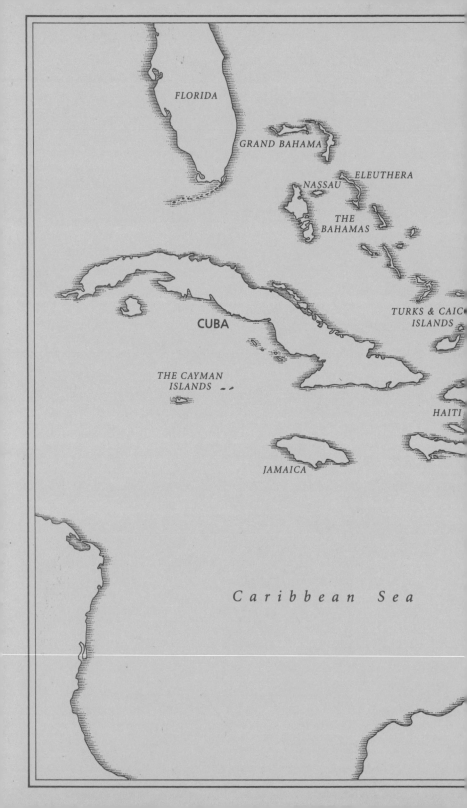